From Birdland to Broadway

From
Birdland
to
Broadway

Scenes from a jazz life

BILL CROW

OXFORD UNIVERSITY PRESS
New York   Oxford

Oxford University Press

Oxford   New York   Toronto
Delhi   Bombay   Calcutta   Madras   Karachi
Kuala Lumpur   Singapore   Hong Kong   Tokyo
Nairobi   Dar es Salaam   Cape Town
Melbourne   Auckland   Madrid

and associated companies in
Berlin   Ibadan

First published in 1992 by Oxford University Press, Inc.,
200 Madison Avenue, New York, New York 10016

First issued as an Oxford University Press paperback, 1993

Oxford is a registered trademark of Oxford University Press

Library of Congress Cataloging-in-Publication Data
Crow, Bill.
From Birdland to Broadway : scenes from a jazz life /
Bill Crow.
p. cm. Includes bibliographical references and index.
ISBN 0-19-506988-9
ISBN 0-19-508550-7 (PBK.)
1. Jazz—Anecdotes. I. Title.
ML3506.C75 1992   781.65—dc20   92-2837

10 9 8 7 6 5 4 3 2 1
Printed in the United States of America

For Mom, and for Dan

While assembling my first book, *Jazz Anecdotes*, I decided that, since I had more than enough material from other musicians to fill that book, I would save my own personal stories for this volume. Although most of this book is new, some of it has appeared in slightly different form in Gene Lees's *Jazzletter* and in my column "The Band Room" in *Allegro*, the monthly newspaper of New York's Local 802, American Federation of Musicians.

New City, New York   B.C.
March 1992

Contents

From Birdland to Broadway

chapter 1

Birdland

Birdland was my alma mater. I studied for a little while at another institute of higher learning, the University of Washington in Seattle, but when I dropped out and moved to New York, Birdland became my college of modern jazz. The illustrious professors there, who taught by example, were some of the world's finest jazz musicians. The dean of them all was Charlie Parker, "Bird," for whom the club was named.

I studied hard and learned my lessons well at Birdland. But if anyone had told me when I first arrived that just two years later I would be playing on that hallowed bandstand myself, I would have scoffed. And had that prophet declared that the instrument I'd be playing at my Birdland graduation would be the string bass, I'd have laughed out loud. I was a brass player, not a bass player.

When I took a Greyhound bus from Seattle to New York in January 1950, I carried a valve trombone with me. In the Army I had switched to that instrument from the baritone horn, which I had been playing since grade school. The baritone horn has a beautiful sound, but it wasn't considered to be a jazz instrument, and I wanted to play jazz.

I'd already made a good start. As a schoolboy in Kirkland, Washington, I had collected and memorized every jazz record I could get my hands on, and I had been jamming with friends in the Army and around Seattle. But at Birdland my education moved up to a new level. At that midtown New York nightclub, I heard modern jazz played nightly by the masters.

Birdland was billed as "The Jazz Corner of the World," even though its entrance was in the middle of the block on Broadway between Fifty-second and Fifty-third Streets. Morris Levy, the owner of the place, had announced its opening in August 1949, but he ran into some difficulty in securing the required licenses. Birdland finally opened on December 15, just three weeks before I arrived in town. To this twenty-two-year-old fresh from the hinterlands, it was a perfectly wonderful place.

I found it hard to wait each day until eight P.M., the hour that Birdland opened its doors. Then I would hurry inside and down the carpeted stairway. After a stop at the ticket window to pay the seventy-five-cent admission charge, I would descend the last half dozen steps into the club itself, where I would be greeted by either Drayton, the headwaiter, or Pee Wee Marquette, the midget master of ceremonies.

Patrons could choose from three sections at Birdland, depending on how much money they wanted to spend. On the right side of the club were booths along the wall and tables directly in front of the bandstand. Along the left wall was the bar. Between the bar and the left side of the bandstand, cordoned off by low wooden railings, was a section we called "the bleachers," with a long wooden bench at the rear and two or three rows of chairs in front of it. There was a cover charge and a food and drink menu in the table section, and if you stood at the bar you were expected to buy a drink. But in the bleachers, once having paid your admission, you were entitled to occupy a seat without further obligation. I sat there every night until they closed at four A.M.

Behind the bar were live birds in cages. The walls were covered with photo murals by Herman Leonard, done in the dramatic high-contrast style that was characteristic of his photography. Against jet black backgrounds, life-size action shots of Charlie Parker, Dizzy Gillespie, Lennie Tristano, and other modern jazzmen stood in sharp focus. The murals created an atmosphere that seemed just right for the home of modern jazz. A sign near the door said that the maximum legal occupancy was 273 people, but on weekends the place was often so crowded that I could barely squeeze into it.

Though Birdland was near Fifty-second Street, it wasn't one of the Fifty-second Street jazz clubs. Those "Swing Street" clubs had been farther east, crowded along both sides of the block between Fifth and Sixth avenues, with a few more in the next block toward Seventh. By the time I moved to New York, none of them were presenting jazz any more; they had all become Chinese restaurants or strip joints except the Hickory House, which still served great steaks, but had replaced its live musicians with a disc-jockey. Fortunately for my future livelihood, that famous old restaurant went back to live music the following year.

In 1948, during a three-day pass from the Army, I had visited the Royal Roost near Duffy Square, where Dizzy Gillespie's big band opened my ears to the revolution that was going on in jazz, but when I returned in 1950 I found that the Roost had closed. Bop City, its successor a little farther up Broadway, was still operating, but it only lasted until the autumn of that year.

There were a few other midtown jazz clubs. A place on Eighth Avenue called Le Downbeat (not to be confused with the original Downbeat Club on Fifty-second Street) opened around that time, where the Barbara Carroll trio, with Joe Shulman on bass and Herb Wasserman on drums, appeared nightly opposite groups like the Billy Taylor Trio and the Oscar Pettiford Quartet. And a club called Snookie's on West Forty-fifth Street presented jazz for a few years. There were also jazz clubs uptown and in Greenwich Village, but it was Birdland, with its live radio broadcasts and its sponsorship of Symphony Sid's nightly programs featuring modern jazz records, that indeed became the "jazz corner of the world" in the 1950s. There, in the bleachers, I was able to literally sit at the feet of the masters of modern jazz.

When I first arrived at Birdland, Charlie Parker was leading a quintet there. It included pianist Bud Powell, drummer Roy Haynes, bassist Tommy Potter, and trumpeter Red Rodney. The house band that played opposite Bird's group had Max Roach on drums, Curly Russell on bass, and Al Haig on piano. It was hard to tell who the regular horn players were in that band because there was so much sitting in. I heard J. J. Johnson, Fats Navarro, Kenny Dorham, Miles Davis, Dizzy Gillespie, Lucky Thompson, Milt Jackson, Sonny Stitt, and dozens of others. It seemed that every musician in modern jazz was playing at Birdland during my first few months in town.

The club was always full of musicians who came to listen. I recognized many famous ones from their pictures in *Down Beat* and *Metronome* magazines, and had others pointed out to me by jazz fans in the bleachers. Being among all those musicians and hearing all that wonderful music every night kept me in a constant state of bliss.

One evening while Bird's quintet was playing, a buzz of recognition preceded Art Tatum as he and a friend slipped into chairs right under the piano in the bleachers. Tatum had been the reigning master of the jazz piano for so long that some critics had begun to take his amazing ability for granted, declaring that Bud Powell was the new king of the keyboard.

Tatum wanted to hear what Bud was playing with Bird. He listened carefully and was complimentary when he was asked what he thought of Bud's playing. As Parker's band left the stand, they all came over to say hello to Tatum, and the musicians in the house band invited him to sit in. He felt his way up to the piano, and those of us who were sitting behind him could see that, as Art slid onto the piano bench, he sat down on his left hand. He did it as if by accident, but he kept that hand tucked under his ample rear end throughout the entire set. Art comped for the other players and took several brilliant solos using just his right hand.

Tatum may have been commenting on the sparse use Powell made of his left hand. Or he could have just been reminding himself that his own two-handed piano style was not currently in fashion at Birdland. Whatever his reasons, Art Tatum let the kids in the bleachers see that he could still play better with one hand than most pianists could play with two.

chapter 2

The Big Town

I had two brief flirtations with New York City before I moved east to stay. There was that three-day pass from the Army in 1948, and an earlier visit in 1945, after my youthful love of the theater brought me to Massachusetts at the end of my senior year in high school. I won a summer scholarship to the Priscilla Beach Theater in Plymouth, and my parents scraped together the money for my train fare from Seattle. I lived all summer in an old Victorian house at Priscilla Beach with seventy-five or eighty other young actors and actresses from all over the country. We studied theater crafts during the day and put on plays at night in a barn theater. Our training was supervised and our plays were directed by two impressive New York thespians, Dr. A. Franklin Trask and his wife, Allison Hawley.

My brother Bob, four years my senior, had been in the Navy since 1942, serving as a fire controlman on the destroyer *Mackenzie* throughout the North African and Italian campaigns of World War II. A deck gun on his ship misfired during the Normandy invasion, blowing off all his clothes and knocking him unconscious. When he recovered, he was transferred to the submarine service, and he was stationed at the sub base in New London, Connecticut, while I was at Priscilla Beach.

Bob came to visit me one weekend at the end of that summer. The war in the Pacific had just ended, and he was looking forward to being discharged from the Navy. When I told him that I was about ready to go home to Kirkland, he said,"You can't leave without seeing New York. It's the greatest place in the world."

"But how would I get there? I'm broke. All I have is my ticket home."

"Is it a Pullman ticket?"

"Yes."

"Then it's easy. Cash it in and buy a coach ticket from New York to Seattle. It won't kill you to sleep sitting up for a few nights. You'll have enough money left over to go down to New York and see the sights before you go home."

It was a great idea. As soon as my summer as an actor was over, I took a bus from Boston to New York, carrying in my pocket a railroad coach ticket to Seattle and about twenty-five dollars in cash.

My only knowledge of the big city came from Hollywood movies and stories by Damon Runyon. I knew a few place names like Times Square and Coney Island, but I didn't know uptown from downtown and had no idea how to find the music I wanted to hear. The information I needed was probably in *Down Beat* magazine, but I hadn't heard of that publication yet.

Bob had told me there were dime lockers at Pennsylvania Station where I could park my suitcase. I walked from the old West Side bus station on Forty-second Street to the IND subway and, for a nickel, took a train (the A Train!) to Pennsylvania Station, one stop away, where I locked up my suitcase. Then I found another train to Times Square.

In those days, that neighborhood, where Broadway cuts across the intersection of Seventh Avenue and Forty-second Street, was a carnival of entertainment. The brightly lit marquees of the giant movie theaters north of Times Square announced their programs with lighted signs and banners that rose several stories high. I was amazed to discover that there were name bands on stage at most of them! I hadn't known that live music would be so available to a seventeen-year-old. I spent nearly a whole dollar to get into the Strand, where I sat through a dull movie twice in order to hear two shows by the Charlie Barnet band, with Al Killian playing lead trumpet and Peanuts Holland taking the jazz solos.

Afterwards, I reeled happily over to the Nedick's on the corner and had an exotic supper of hot dogs and papaya juice. Then I went back to Thirty-fourth Street to the Sloane House YMCA, where Bob had told me I could find cheap lodging. For twenty-five cents, Sloane House gave me a cot with clean sheets and a locker for my clothes. Though I was shy about undressing in a dormitory full of strangers, I slept soundly and awoke early, eager to see everything.

After spending the morning exploring the city by subway, I took advantage of the reduced daytime prices at the movie palaces and heard every band that was playing. I saw Tommy Dorsey at the Paramount with Dick Haymes, Paul Whiteman at the Capitol, Johnny "Scat" Davis's band at Loew's State, and the Condos Brothers and Connee Boswell at the Roxy. I even went to hear Henry Busse's band at the RKO Keith's. I thought his hit record of "Hot Lips" was corny, but it was a chance to see and hear another live band. They surprised me. Busse had modern arrangements and a band full of young musicians who were blowing like mad. Only "Hot Lips" was played with the wa-wa mute and shuffle-rhythm beat that was his trademark.

In the evenings I checked out the jazz in the bars around Times Square: the Circus Bar in the Piccadilly Hotel; the Metropole, which was then on the corner of Forty-eighth Street and Seventh Avenue; and the Aquarium on Forty-seventh Street. I was afraid to go into the Zanzibar, on Broadway, where Duke Ellington's band and Nat Cole were playing. The prices weren't posted outside, and I feared financial embarrassment. For the same reason, I skipped the 400 Club, where Dorsey's band was playing at night.

I had heard something about jazz on Fifty-second Street, but when I walked up Broadway to Fifty-second one afternoon, I only found a ballroom and some auto dealerships. I looked up the block in both directions, but saw no nightclubs. The Hickory House just looked like a restaurant; there was no sign outside to indicate that they had music. It never occurred to me to look farther east. Surely all the nightlife would be near Broadway, the "main stem." I decided that the Fifty-second Street clubs must have belonged to an earlier era, and abandoned my search. By doing so, I missed all the jazz that was being played two blocks farther east, and also missed the chance to discover Charlie Parker and Dizzy Gillespie two years earlier than I eventually did.

The Commodore Record Shop on Forty-second Street near Grand Central Station was easier to find since the address was on their record label. In those days every record shop had booths where you could listen to the merchandise before buying. After a few hours of happy browsing at the Commodore, I got about a dozen records that weren't available at home at MacDougall's Electric Store in Kirkland: Louis Armstrong, Edmond Hall, Jack Teagarden, Frankie Newton, Bill Coleman, Art Tatum, etc. When I told Milt Gabler, the owner of the Commodore, how far I was taking the fragile ten-inch discs, he packed them for me in a carton with a sheet of corrugated boxboard between each record.

I ventured to Greenwich Village one night and found Nick's and Cafe Society Downtown. I didn't like the taste of beer, but I stood nursing one in Nick's for a while, listening to Miff Mole's band. I was afraid to go into Cafe Society. Art Tatum and Billie Holiday were there, but the club looked expensive, and I was sure I wouldn't have enough money. I stood in the doorway and listened to Tatum for a while, but I left when the maitre d' gave me a dirty look.

When I got back to Sloane House I was told that it was full that night. The fleet was in. But the lady at the desk said, "Don't worry, son. We have other locations that we've inspected and approved."

Their free jitney took me down to the St. Mark's Baths in the East Village. It was a Russian bathhouse on St. Mark's Place near Third Avenue, in what was then a Slavic neighborhood. Twenty-five cents bought me a dormitory bed, a locker for my clothes, a safe deposit box for my valuables, and the use of their steam room and pool. For another fifteen cents I could have had a shave, but I didn't have any whiskers yet.

When I walked outside in the morning I was lost until I saw the Third Avenue El at the corner. I knew it crossed Forty-second Street, so, saving the fare, I walked uptown under the elevated tracks until I was back in familiar territory. I broke my last dollar bill for some breakfast and decided it was time to go home.

chapter 3

Home, School, and the Army

Except for my first two months in the Army, I can't remember a time in my life when I wasn't making music. Though my mom, Lucile, didn't care for jazz, I have her to thank for my ears and my early musical training. She had a lovely soprano voice and sang regularly in our church, in local operettas, and on local radio programs in Seattle. She even got fan mail. I remember one letter, addressed to "Lou Seal Crow," that said, "I just love your voice, Mrs. Crow. It is so nice and shrill."

Mom taught singers and elementary piano students at home. She only charged a dollar or two for a lesson, but it helped us eke out a living during the Depression when my dad, Harry, a carpenter, was having trouble finding work. When I was just a tot, I started singing along. She would play a phrase for a student to repeat, and then she would have to wait until I sang it, too, from my crib in the bedroom.

Mom's big upright Holland piano was our home entertainment center. Brother Bob and I took turns making interesting noises at the keyboard whenever Mom wasn't teaching, and in the evenings we all sang while she played. I learned the popular songs of World War I, all of the Methodist hymnal, some Gilbert and Sullivan, and the songs of Carrie Jacobs Bond. At church socials and public gatherings I was introduced to patriotic music and the songs of Victor Herbert and Irving Berlin.

We owned an old Edison windup phonograph and about a dozen records. I remember a cello rendition of "The Swan," several vaudeville numbers including two songs by Sir Harry Lauder, and arias sung by a tenor. The singers all sounded like they were closed up in a tin box. When we were able to afford a secondhand Atwater Kent table radio, I began to learn, from the musical programs being broadcast, the work of songwriters like Jerome Kern, Cole Porter, Rodgers and Hart, and De Silva, Brown and Henderson, as well as operatic and symphonic music.

Realizing that I had an ear for music, Mom began teaching me songs.

I can remember singing with her as she ironed the weekly wash, when my head wasn't as high as her ironing board. Everyone sang in those days, in church, at American Legion meetings, in school, at parties, and at home. Even Dad sang, though his interest in music was limited to the songs of Stephen Foster and "Home on the Range."

I studied piano with Mom until, in the fourth grade, I heard they were forming a school band and decided I would rather play the trumpet. After some questioning about my willingness to practice, Dad got out the Sears, Roebuck catalog and turned to the musical instrument section. There was a brass trumpet, complete with a mouthpiece and a cardboard case, for $9.95. The depression had hit them hard and there was no cash in the house, but my folks sent away for that trumpet.

Al Bennest, our school music teacher, lived on my block. One day he saw me passing his house and beckoned to me. He said, "I want you to hear something," and led me into his living room, where he took a record out of its paper sleeve and put it on his Victrola. It was the first time I had seen flat records. Our Edison phonograph used cylindrical records that took up a lot of storage space. I considered flat phonograph records a wonder of modern science. When the record began to play, I couldn't believe what I was hearing. It was Louis Armstrong's "West End Blues." His opening cadenza changed my whole conception of what a trumpet should sound like, and made me realize that jazz was something special.

I played the trumpet for another year, trying to sound like Louis, but no matter how hard I practiced, I couldn't play high enough to cut the first parts in the grade school band. My folks got me a better horn, but that didn't help. When I took my problem to Mr. Bennest, he looked in my mouth and said:

"The way your front teeth sit, you may never be able to develop a good trumpet embouchure. But I have an idea. The school owns a baritone horn that no one is playing. It has a beautiful sound and a bigger mouthpiece. It might fit your teeth better. I used to play the baritone myself. The fingering is just like a trumpet, and it has all the most beautiful parts in the concert band. Why don't you take it home and see if you like it?"

I was doubtful. I had never heard of a baritone horn. But if Mr. Bennest had played one, I was willing to try it. When I got used to it, I liked it a lot, and within another year I was playing it pretty well. My dad returned the new trumpet and got his money back.

In junior high school I began to realize that some of our band arrangements had special parts for the baritone while on others I was just doubling the trombone parts. I told Mr. Bennest that I could sometimes hear a better part to play, and he encouraged me to try. At the next rehearsal one of the other kids in the band complained, "Billy isn't playing what's written."

Mr. Bennest said, "For him, it's okay."

That was my introduction to improvisation.

In high school, when I heard that Mr. Bennest was putting together an extracurricular "swing band," I applied at once. I was terribly disappointed when he told me the stock arrangements they were using had no baritone horn parts. I went to the first rehearsal anyway, and saw that they were short a saxophone player. My brother had left an old Buescher alto behind when he joined the Navy right after Pearl Harbor. I went home and figured out the fingerings for a couple of scales on it and took it to the next rehearsal. By the time the night was over I had learned to play simple third alto parts.

I played the saxophone in the swing band for the rest of that year, but then our high school merged with a nearby school district and some really good sax players came into our band. I was out of the running on alto sax, but the trap drummer, Wally Bergeron, had graduated. I went over to the gas station where he worked.

"Wally, show me how to play the hi-hat, and what you do with the wire brushes."

With those two quick bits of instruction and Wally's admonition that the trumpets tended to rush while the saxophones tended to slow down, I began playing the drums at the next rehearsal. No other trap drummers turned up until I graduated, so I had time to learn to play. I scrounged up a drum set of my own and practiced a lot in our basement, straining our good relations with our neighbors.

Kirkland had a very good high school concert and marching band even though we were a small-town school with a tight budget. We wore simple navy-blue uniforms. We told ourselves that their conservative appearance reflected our high musical standards, but I secretly envied the flashy red satin marching uniforms of Bothell High, to the north of us.

When a kid whose family had moved from Bothell to Kirkland asked to join our band, Mr. Bennest said, "Sure, what instrument do you play?"

His answer became an often repeated tag line in our band. The kid said, "I carry the flag."

Mom taught me to read and write before I started school, so they skipped me right to the second grade. Consequently, I graduated from high school when I was seventeen. World War II was just coming to an end, but the draft was still in effect, and I got my "Greetings" letter from Selective Service just as I finished my first semester at the University of Washington. I was classified 1-A at the Army induction center in Seattle, but when I asked when I would be called up, no one had a definite answer. I couldn't stand the suspense.

"What's the shortest enlistment period you have?" I asked.

"Eighteen months."

I decided to get it over with. I signed the enlistment papers and a week later my new home was a barracks at Fort Lewis near Tacoma, Washington.

As a prize-winning high school baritone horn player who doubled on drums, I thought I could surely get into an Army band. There were two bands at Fort Lewis, and they both requested that I be assigned to them when I finished my eight-week basic training. But the Engineers band was moved to California before I was released from basic, and my commanding officer wouldn't let me go to the Second Infantry Band because I was in the Engineers.

Instead, I was assigned to the Headquarters Company at North Fort Lewis as a clerk-typist. I had learned to type in high school. They put me to work in the AWOL office, where we handled the paperwork for all the soldiers who were absent without leave. Two master sergeants showed me my job. We each handled the AWOLs from one of the fort's three engineer regiments. The sergeants were both up for discharge, and when they were mustered out, I was left with the paperwork for all three regiments.

AWOL soldiers created reams of paperwork. Report forms had to be filled out, relatives notified, allotments canceled, military and local police alerted. Though I went back to the office after supper every night and worked until lights out, I couldn't keep up with the workload.

The colonel who ran the office sent me a curt note to get my reports out on time. I sent back a memo explaining that I was doing the work of three men, and asked for some help. A corporal (Technician, fifth grade) fresh from clerk-typists' school was finally assigned to work with me. I taught him the job, and by working hard together we caught up on the backlog. As soon as everything was in order I reported to the colonel:

"We've caught up with our work, sir. The new man is a great help."

"I'm glad to hear that, Private Crow," said the colonel. "I've been concerned ever since he arrived. It's not right for a corporal to be taking orders from a private. . ."

Here comes my promotion, I thought.

". . . so I'm transferring you to the file section. The corporal will take over the AWOL section."

The corporal was just as overworked as I had been before he arrived, but it wasn't my problem any more. I finished my filing by noon every day and spent the afternoon goofing off at the service club. There I met a sergeant named Cherry, who listened sympathetically when I told him about my lack of success in getting a band assignment.

"You want to be in a band?" he said. "I'll put you in a band."

"How can you do that?"

"They're forming a new one on the post. I work in the Classification and Assignment section, and I'm cutting some orders right now, assigning musicians from several different companies on the post to the new band. I'll just add your name. Nobody will know how it got there, and once my colonel signs it, it will be official."

Sure enough, two days later my company commander called me in and handed me my orders. I had been transferred to the new Fifty-first Army Band. I ran over to the C & A office to thank Sergeant Cherry, and then I packed my duffel bag and went back to being a musician.

chapter 4

Tacoma, Baltimore, and Washington

No instruments or equipment had arrived at Fort Lewis for the new Fifty-first Army Band. Eager to be playing again, I went home to Kirkland on a weekend pass and got my baritone horn. I had bought one of my own in high school, a King, paying it off on the installment plan with money I earned on after-school jobs. Some of the other Army musicians also had their own instruments with them. We got together and played every day for our own amusement.

I had the most fun playing with Ray Baram, a cornet player from Brookline, Massachusetts. Ray had a great enthusiasm for jazz and was happy to find a soul mate. Ray had lived in New York for a while before being drafted, and he knew musicians like Frankie Newton, Muggsy Spanier, and Pee Wee Russell, who were only names on record labels to me. A self-professed "moldy fig," Ray taught me all the traditional Dixieland tunes. He thought the baritone horn was a quaint tailgate instrument. We jammed together whenever we could, and kept wishing for a good jazz clarinet player to complete our Dixieland front line, but the Army never provided us with one. We had no rhythm section either; our Army band drummers only played the street drums.

One night on radio station KMO in Tacoma, Ray and I heard a disc jockey named Bob Koons playing some jazz records that we liked. Ray called the station and discovered that Bob did his nightly show from the station's transmitter building on the outskirts of the city while doubling as the night shift engineer. He invited us to visit him, and we drove my Model A Ford out to the transmitter.

Bob, a tall, rotund man, chatted amiably with us while his records were playing. He had a lonely job and seemed to enjoy what became our regular visits. We often took our horns with us and jammed in the empty studio. Bob sometimes would announce that he was going to play a new release by a jazz quintet—he made up some bogus name for it. Then he would put a rhythm section record on the turntable and Ray and I would play along with it on the air.

Station KMO subscribed to the new Capitol Records radio transcription library. It was much hipper than the old Federal library the station also used. Capitol's recording artists included the Nat Cole trio and Stan Kenton's new band. Their country and western section had a cowboy singer named Shug Fisher, who cracked us up. Shug stuttered while he sang and, while stuttering, he kept repeating whatever guitar chord he happened to be playing at the time. This resulted in some very funny song meters.

I later discovered that Paul Weston was active at Capitol during those years. Paul's musical wit became famous when he and Jo Stafford created the Jonathan and Darlene Edwards records, and I suspect that he also had a hand in the invention of Shug Fisher.

The Army moves in mysterious ways. The new Fifty-first Army Band was brought up to playing strength at Fort Lewis with a shipment of instruments, music, and musicians from the East Coast. Then we were transferred, bag and baggage, to Fort Meade, Maryland, and were renamed the Second Army Band. I learned that, instead of travelling on a troop train, I could receive a mileage allowance from the Army and drive my car to Maryland. My brother Bob, just home from the Navy, helped me overhaul the engine on my 1930 Model A Ford coupe, and I laid in a stock of spare parts: inner tubes, tire patches, head gaskets, rubber tubing, electrician's tape, and baling wire.

When the band shipped out for Maryland, I loaded my duffel bag and baritone horn into the Ford and headed south to the Columbia River, where I picked up Route 30, the old Lincoln Highway. It was the best northern east–west route in those days. I drove about sixteen hours a day, only stopping for food, gas, and rest rooms. At night I pulled to the side of the road and slept in the car.

The Model A only had a cruising speed of 45 mph, but it ran like a top. There were no four-lane highways then, with the exception of the Pennsylvania Turnpike, which in those days only ran from Pittsburgh to Harrisburg. Once on it, I had to put my gas pedal to the floor to stay above the posted minimum speed of 40 mph. By the time I reached my turnoff onto the road that headed toward Baltimore, I had pressed the Ford a little too hard. My engine began to miss.

I pulled into a gas station in rural Maryland and consulted the mechanic. He cleaned my carburetor, but the engine still ran poorly. He adjusted my magneto (or whatever it was you adjusted) with similar results. Then he unscrewed the spark plugs and discovered that one of them was clogged with carbon.

"Here's your problem," he said.

He put the plug in a sand-blast machine, flicked the switch, and in a couple of seconds the plug was pristine. He regapped it and replaced it, and the car ran perfectly again.

"Great!" I said. "What do I owe you?"

"Dime."

"Only a dime?"

"That's the charge for cleanin' a plug."

"But what about the other work you did?"

"Cain't charge you for that. That weren't what was wrong."

Many times since then I have wished that I lived near that mechanic.

I had heard Juan Tizol on Duke Ellington's records, but I still thought all trombones had slides. I didn't know there was such a thing as a valve trombone until Ray Baram told me that Brad Gowans played one, and that it fingered just like a baritone horn. When I inquired at a used musical instrument store in Baltimore, the man dug around in his back room and found me an old beat-up silver Conn valve trombone. I paid him thirty dollars for it, polished it up and began playing it at barracks jam sessions.

I also took it along on service club dance jobs, on which I played drums. I was the drummer by default. We still had only street drummers in the Second Army Band. None of them played trap drums. I had brought my own set from Kirkland. I kept the valve trombone on a stand beside my drums, and when I took a chorus on it, Gene Kent, our trumpet player, would grab a stick and play my top cymbal for me. I would continue to tramp on the hi-hat and bass drum pedals while blowing the horn. Later, when a New York drummer, Jack Zini, joined our band, I relinquished the drums to him and concentrated on my valve trombone.

Master Sergeant Warren Schaefer, our arranger, formed an eight-piece dance band to play service club gigs. We were popular at the enlisted men's clubs, but the officers' club was different. Instead of making requests, some officers would order us to play the tunes they wanted. There was never any applause. We were enlisted men.

When the Army changed its policy and allowed soldiers to wear civilian clothes off-duty, Schaefer took us to a Baltimore tailor and we ordered matching gray suits. Schaefer listed us with a Baltimore agent as "The Sophisticates," and we worked civilian club dates on our free time. One night the agent booked us into the same officers' club where we had played in uniform. The officers loved the music, competed with each other for the honor of buying us drinks, and gave us a generous tip when the night was over. That was my first realization that management treats workers better if they don't think they own them.

Since Fort Meade was halfway between Baltimore and Washington, Gene Kent, Jack Zini, and I hunted out the jazz clubs in both of those cities. One evening as we were walking by a Baltimore saloon, we heard the sound of a good saxophone, and inside we found a tenor player named Abie Baitch playing with a rhythm section on a narrow stage behind the bar. They played a few jazz tunes and then went into heavy tom-tom renditions of "Night Train" and "Harlem Nocturne" while three scantily clad ladies came out and writhed provocatively.

When the band took a break, we introduced ourselves. Abie invited us to come back with our horns, which we did on the following evening. He said we could blow on the jazz set if we would stay onstage and help them play the show. I had seen burlesque shows at the Palomar Theater in Seattle, but I'd never been so close to a nearly naked woman before. I lost some of my adolescent illusions about strippers when I realized that these women were supremely bored with their jobs. While they turned their backs toward the audience and gyrated their buttocks, they chatted amiably with the band about mundane subjects like movies and baseball.

In another Baltimore music bar we heard Lester Young's wonderful quintet, with Roy Haynes on drums, Junior Mance on piano, Leroy Jackson on bass, and Jesse Drakes on trumpet. And at the Club Bengazi we discovered Charlie Ventura's "Bop for the People" octet, featuring Jackie Cain and Roy Kral. Charlie's brother Benny, who played baritone sax with him, befriended us and introduced us to the rest of the band: Eddie Shaughnessy on drums, Gus Cole on bass, Bennie Green on trombone, and Normie Faye on trumpet. That was the beginning of my friendship with Shaughnessy and with Jackie and Roy, which I renewed when I moved to New York.

In Washington, there was the new Club Ellington, near the Howard Theater. When it opened, we haunted the place every night. A wide, burgundy-colored carpet ran from the entrance straight across the floor of the huge room to the bandstand, continued up over it and right up the wall behind it to the high ceiling. Duke began most nights with half a band. The star players arrived in the order of their own sense of importance, some getting there just in time for the last number of the first set. But Duke always had something interesting for his band to play, whatever the instrumentation might be at the moment. I was impressed with the tenor playing of Al Sears, who was given a lot of solo space.

At the back of the band on the highest riser, Sonny Greer sat behind a white enamel drum set that included tympani, chimes, and a huge Chinese gong that rose behind him like the sun disc behind a statue of an oriental deity. High on the side wall over Duke's piano was a little wrought-iron balcony with a door through which Kay Davis would step, without a microphone, to sing her vocalise parts with the band. Her voice carried all the way to the back of the room, and blended prettily with the horns.

Duke had announced that he intended to make Club Ellington the band's home base, but it didn't work out that way. As soon as he went back on the road, the club's business fell off, and before the band had a chance to return, its "home" had closed.

The Second Army Band also went on the road. We toured Maryland, West Virginia, Pennsylvania, Ohio, and Indiana with the Second Army Baseball Team. In each town we would play a concert before the team's game with a local ball club. It was supposed to be a recruiting tour, but the few recruits we attracted were either musicians or ballplayers. That tour gave me my first taste of the long bus rides and dingy hotels that are a part of being on the road with a band.

As we checked into our first hotel in Evansville, Indiana, Warren Schaefer told us younger musicians:

"If you leave your door slightly ajar at night, one of the hookers who work the halls will come in to visit you."

We didn't know if he was putting us on, but we were afraid to try it. In the morning, Schaefer said, "I left my door ajar, but all that happened was, when I got up this morning, a pair of my shoes were missing!"

When my eighteen-month enlistment came to an end, the music in the Second Army Band had become so enjoyable that I didn't want to go home. Sergeant Schaefer had formed a stage band with which I was playing valve trombone and singing a few ballads. As the band's company clerk, I had my own private room. Baltimore and Washington were full of good music, and we had frequent jam sessions at Fort Meade. I decided to stay. I extended my enlistment for another eighteen months.

As soon as I did that, things began to go downhill. First we lost our great-sounding rehearsal hall. It had originally been a G.I. church, but had been decommissioned when the barracks around it had been converted to family housing. A conservative colonel passed by one day and was shocked that jazz was being played in the building. Even though it was no longer a church, it still had a steeple, and the colonel thought it sacrilegious to play that kind of music in a church-shaped building. We were ordered to move out.

Then Sergeant Schaefer was shipped out to Korea. The stage band concerts ended, and we spent most of our time playing for drill field marching. My last months in the Army were so boring that I couldn't wait to get out. I sold my Model A Ford to a military policeman, and when I was discharged in January 1949, I shipped my instruments and clothes home and hitchhiked back to the West Coast on an Air Force bomber from Langley Field, Virginia. The Korean War began in June of the following year. I got out of the Army just in time.

chapter 5

Seattle

As a veteran, I was eligible for a free college education on the G.I. Bill of Rights. I re-entered the University of Washington, signing up for courses that would get me a degree in radio broadcasting. Though I was a musician, I had been convinced by parents and teachers that I wouldn't be able to make a living that way. All the professional musicians I knew outside the Army either taught school or worked other day jobs and only played on weekends.

At the U. of W. I took slide trombone lessons with Ken Cloud, the local Tommy Dorsey, and I played drums with his dance band whenever he got some work. I had bought a new Reynolds valve-slide combination trombone, but the slide seemed cumbersome to me. I could move around much better with the valves. When I would practice, I'd labor away for a while as a beginner with the slide and then switch to the valve section to remind myself that I knew how to play.

One day while I was practicing at the university's music building annex I heard a knock at the door of my cubicle. A dark-haired young man popped his head in, his eyes shining eagerly behind a pair of horn-rimmed glasses.

"Hi, my name's Ken Kimball. I'm a piano player. I heard you blowing and wondered if you'd like to come to our jam sessions? Weekday afternoons at five in the rehearsal room at the other end of the building."

That began a wonderful year of music for me in Seattle. Ken introduced me to a lot of other young jazz players from the Seattle area. Not all of them were enrolled at the university, but they gathered there to play. Among them was Dick Nelson, a trumpet player from my high school band.

I had been living at home in Kirkland and driving back and forth to school, but when Dick and two other musicians I met at the annex sessions invited me to share their houseboat on Lake Union near the university, I moved right in. We played all the time, starting every morning while still in our pajamas. Whoever wasn't taking a chorus would make the coffee. After classes we'd invite friends over and play some more, but we had to play softly at night. Sound carried well over the water, and there were complaints from the other houseboats if the music was too loud.

One week when Woody Herman's band was in town, someone found the hotel where Gene Ammons was staying. Gene had joined Woody when Stan Getz left the band. We called from the lobby of his hotel and invited him to come and jam with us. Gene came right downstairs with his horn. Our houseboat quickly filled up with musicians when the word spread that Gene was there. We felt like amateurs beside him, but it was wonderful to hear him play.

Jazz as a vocation began to seem more possible to me after I met Buzzy Bridgford, a drummer from Olympia, Washington, who showed up at an annex session one afternoon. Buzzy had been on a couple of name bands and had spent some time in New York, but a serious auto acci-

dent had brought him back to convalesce at his mother's home in
Olympia. When he recovered, he headed for Seattle to check out the
music scene.

Wayne L. "Buzzy" Bridgford (the nickname was chosen by his father
and appeared on his birth certificate) bore a resemblance to pictures I
have seen of Dave Tough. Delicate-boned but wiry and strong, he seemed
to me the spirit of lightness and surprise. He laughed easily and his
dark blue eyes were alive with interest in everything. Best of all, he
swung irresistibly when he played the drums.

Buzzy thought I had talent, and was intrigued with my naïveté. He
decided to take charge of my education. He showed me where my playing was vague and brought rhythm and swing into focus for me, illus-
trating his points with appropriate jazz records. Along with this practical instruction, he told me all the personal details he knew about famous
jazz musicians. He made the jazz life sound wonderful, and convinced
me that I could find a place in it.

Buzzy was a little overwhelming at times. Though he was usually even-
tempered, he was capable of dramatic expressions of rage. I was shocked
when he got into an argument with a girlfriend in a Chinese restaurant, yelling angrily in public. He ended the argument by hurling a
cup and saucer against the wall. It amazed me that the world didn't
come to an end. The waiter cleaned up the broken crockery, and everyone pretended it hadn't happened.

Buzzy was often manipulative, but he never took unfair advantage
of me. His idea of a perfect manipulation was to get what he wanted
while seeing that the people he was manipulating also got something
they wanted. He often conned me into adjusting my life to his conve-
nience, but he repaid me a hundred-fold with the things he taught me
and helped me discover for myself. He prided himself on his ability to
size people up psychologically, and was interested in the writings of
Freud, Jung, and Wilhelm Reich. The books he loaned me on psychology and philosophy started me thinking about the direction of my own
life.

Buzzy introduced me to Freddy Greenwell, a fine tenor player who
had great ears and a wonderful imagination. Freddy had been with
Claude Thornhill's Navy band during the war. Though there were several good saxophone players around Seattle, I was the most impressed
with Freddy. When I later heard Al Cohn in New York, I thought, "He
sounds a lot like Freddy."

I had heard that Don Lanphere, from Yakima, Washington, was also
a good tenor player. He'd been out in the world making a name for

himself with big bands, but I hadn't heard him play yet. When he passed through Seattle he came to the club where Freddy was working, and there was much excited speculation about a possible cutting contest. I was curious to see how Freddy, a modest man, would respond to the challenge.

When Don was invited to the bandstand they began playing "Indiana" at a bright tempo. Don played several choruses that let us know he was good, all right, but my money was on Freddy. I'd heard him enough times to know what he could do. But when Freddy followed Don, he just played one beautifully phrased chorus of the melody and sat back down. I was delighted to discover that jazz didn't have to be a contest.

There were jazz bands at a couple of Chinese restaurants in Seattle, and Ken Kimball was working in one of them. It was a very low budget operation. When there were no customers, the family who ran the place would stay in the kitchen, turning off the heat and lights in the restaurant. The band would put on their hats and coats and sit on the darkened bandstand, waiting for some action. When customers began to climb the long wooden stairway to the restaurant, their footsteps would alert the staff. The lights and heat would come on, the band would shuck its outerwear and begin to play, and the diners would be greeted at the door by a smiling host and bustling waiters.

Kenny found a better-paying job and got me on it with him, playing drums in a quartet led by trumpeter Ward Cole at the new Cirque Club in downtown Seattle. With piano, drums, trumpet and tenor sax, we played for shows and dancing. Ward eventually left to join Ted Weems's band, and Paul McCrea, our tenor player, took over the quartet.

Paul came to work one night laughing.

"I just asked the girl at the record store downstairs if she had a copy of *Daphnis and Chloe*. She thought a minute, and said, 'We got *Chloe*.' "

The Spike Jones record of that tune was still in stock.

One night a young dancer came by our club after he finished his show at another Seattle nightspot. He was working with his father and his uncle in the Will Mastin Trio; his name was Sammy Davis, Jr. Sammy evidently hadn't used up all his energy on his own job. He sat in with us and did a complete show, dancing, singing, doing impressions, playing the trumpet, taking a drum solo. He was a good singer and a charming entertainer, and he was the best dancer I had ever seen.

When our job ended, I followed Sammy to an after-hours club, where he did another complete performance with the house band. Counting the shows he was being paid for, he must have put in four or five solid hours of dancing that day. There seemed to be no limit to his energy.

The Cirque Club usually presented variety acts, but for a couple of weeks we had the pleasure of accompanying Ivie Anderson. We had just struggled through the previous week accompanying a guy who caught lighted cigarettes in his mouth while blindfolded. I could play enough drums to keep time for the quartet, but I hadn't learned to play a proper long roll. I got complaints every night from the cigarette act, who wanted the drums to roll in a continuous crescendo until the cymbal crashes at the climax of his catches. It was a great relief to discover that Ivie just wanted us to swing for her.

Ivie was semi-retired at that time, but she had been very successful during the 1930s and '40s. She began her career singing with bands and revues in Chicago. Her big break was getting a featured spot with Earl Hines at the Grand Terrace in 1930. Duke Ellington heard her there the following year and hired her. She became nationally known through the recordings she made with Duke, and can still be seen and heard in reruns of the Marx Brothers movie *A Day at the Races,* singing "All God's Chillun Got Rhythm."

Ivie's rich voice and sure rhythmic phrasing fit Duke's band perfectly. Few of her fans knew that she suffered terribly with asthma, since she rarely let it affect her performances. Juan Tizol said in an interview, "She could be feeling bad on the stage and go out there and sing, and you couldn't tell she had asthma. She was terrific."

Ivie left Ellington in 1942 when her health began to get worse. She bought an interest in an apartment house in California, where she lived comfortably. She also owned a restaurant called Ivie's Chicken Shack. When the urge to sing became too strong to resist, she would book a week or two of work on the west coast.

At the Cirque Club, we were lucky that Ken Kimball was a good sight-reader. Ivie came to the rehearsal with a huge stack of sheet music. When she saw our faces fall, she laughed.

"Don't worry about all this! I just want to have the music handy in case I get requests for something we didn't rehearse."

After we ran over her theme song, "Ivy," and a few Ellington tunes that she liked to include in her show, she said, "Okay, whatever else I do will depend on the crowd. Just stay with me."

Ivie would start her show on the bandstand with us, but by the third tune she would be out among the tables, trailing a long microphone cord behind her. She quickly divined her audience, finding the right music for them and calling tunes to us. As Kenny searched through her sheet music she would chat amiably with the crowd, easing into a song as soon as she heard her key note.

One night a table of eight was making a lot of noise during her act. Instead of calling them the rude drunks they were, Ivie concentrated the power of her performance on them. They still ignored her and continued to babble loudly among themselves. Patrons at other tables made angry shushing noises, but Ivie said, "No, don't do that. These people came in here to be entertained, and they don't seem to be enjoying the show. Now, let's go over here and see what's the matter."

She went to their table and talked to them with the tender concern of a nurse ministering to the sick. She got their attention, found a song they liked and sang it for them. They didn't sober up, but they quieted down and paid what attention they could. When the song ended she had the entire audience with her.

Ivie's repertoire was broad, ranging from the Ellington material through folk songs, English art songs, show tunes, and the good stuff from Tin Pan Alley. She phrased everything with a subtle swing that gave each song tremendous power and made it easy for us to accompany her. We happily followed her strong lead, and she never took us anyplace that wasn't musical.

For the last number of each show Ivie always put the microphone aside and walked to the center of the room among the tables. By this time she had established complete silence and attention. She would sing a final ballad, starting softly and increasing her volume very gradually as the song progressed. By the final phrase her tone had broadened to a cellolike richness, and her last high note was thrilling.

She seemed to be riding high every night. None of us had any idea how ill she was. It was a shock when the news came later that year that Ivie had died in California. She was only forty-five. Thanks to the Ellington reissues on compact disc, examples of her sound and her swing are still available. Listening to those tracks recorded so long ago I see her again, a small plain woman with luminous eyes and a voice filled with ecstatic power, filling a roomful of entranced listeners with glorious song. She was terrific.

chapter 6

Coast to Coast

After a rehearsal at the Cirque Club one afternoon, I was in the record store downstairs, browsing through the Charlie Parker bin. The girl behind the counter came over and said, "You must be a jazz musician. Nobody else ever looks at those records."

Her name was Janet Thurlow. (She is now married to trombonist Jimmy Cleveland.) She told me she was a singer, and wondered why she hadn't seen me at a club on Madison Street called the Washington Social and Educational.

"You've got to come down and hear Bumps Blackwell's combo and meet all the guys."

I went there that night after my job, and Janet introduced me to Bumps. When he heard that I played trombone, he invited me to join his rehearsal band. In it I met trumpeter Floyd Standifer, altoists Buddy Catlett and Pony Poindexter, trombonist Major Pigford, and tenor man Gerald Brashear, all very good players. Quincy Jones, Bumps's sixteen-year-old arranger and trumpet player, welcomed me by putting a solo for me into his latest chart.

Janet wanted me to meet every musician she knew. She took me up to Jack McVea's hotel room one morning while he was still in bed, insisting that I come in and say hello to him. She also introduced me to a blind piano player, R.C., who had been scuffling around Seattle trying to get work for his Maxim Trio, modeled after Nat Cole's group. R.C. could sing just like Nat. When his trio was idle, R.C. played piano with Blackwell's combo and would occasionally take a few choruses on alto saxophone. Quincy spent a lot of time at R.C.'s house, learning chords from him.

Though blind, R.C. had worked hard at being independent, and was able to do most things for himself. He didn't have a seeing-eye dog, but he had a phenomenal sense of direction. One night he and Janet and a couple of other friends rode in the old Chevrolet I was driving to an after hours place I hadn't been to before. R.C. was in the back seat, involved in conversation, and I wondered if he remembered that I didn't know the way.

"R.C.? Where do I turn?"

"Just keep on keepin' on. I'll tell you when."

As I drove on down the road, R.C. continued his animated conversation. Suddenly he called out, "Okay, make the next left!"

I don't know what landmark he heard, but he took us right to the place by ear.

I found out what R.C. did best one night at the Washington Social when Janet kept urging, "Come on, R.C., sing the blues!"

When he did, I jumped right out of my chair. I had a lot of Chicago and Kansas City blues records, but I'd never heard anything like the blues R.C. sang and played that night. I asked him later, "R.C., why don't you sing like that all the time?"

"Hell, where I come from *everybody* sings like that. You can't make a nickel singing that way!"

A year or so later, I was sitting in a diner on the way to a gig in Baltimore, looking over the tunes on the jukebox with our piano player.

"Have you heard this Ray Charles record?" he asked.

"That's not my favorite vocal group," I replied, thinking it was a record by the Ray Charles Singers. He grinned and dropped in a dime, and there on the jukebox was R.C. singing the blues! Since then he's made quite a few nickels singing that way.

Betty Christopher, a piano player from Chicago who had studied with Lennie Tristano, came to the Pacific Northwest with an all-girl band and got stranded when some bookings in Canada and Alaska evaporated. The band broke up in Seattle, and there Betty met Buzzy Bridgford. A romance developed between them, and Buzzy figured out a way to keep her in town.

The Washington State liquor laws were just coming out of the dark ages in 1949. Since the repeal of Prohibition, there had been liquor stores where you could buy a bottle, but until the end of the war, the public consumption of liquor had only been legal in "private clubs." Every nightspot would call itself a private club, selling its membership for one night at the door. You brought a bottle and checked it, and the club made its profit serving you high-priced mixers along with your own liquor.

The state had finally legalized liquor by the drink, but only in places that served food. All legal establishments still had to close at midnight, so the illegal after-hours clubs that had always flourished in Seattle remained wide open. A man named Russian John owned several of them. Buzzy knew of one that was hidden in the basement of a Veterans of Foreign Wars clubhouse near the waterfront. Buzzy talked to the guy who managed the VFW club for Russian John:

"This is a rounder's club. All the hipsters and hookers and high rollers are hanging out here, and you're giving them Hawaiian music. Get rid of those guys and let me bring a jazz band in here. Jazz is the kind of music that belongs in a place like this."

The boss decided that Buzzy might be right. He let him bring in a quartet to see how his customers liked it. Buzzy hired Betty on piano, Doug Goss on bass, and Freddy Greenwell on tenor sax. The crowd at the VFW responded favorably, and it became a steady gig for them.

Every night at midnight, when I finished my job at the Cirque Club, I would run down to the VFW with my valve trombone and sit in. In response to the Afro-Cuban influence that Dizzy Gillespie had brought into modern jazz, Buzzy found me a set of Cuban bongos to play on some numbers. Though I played nearly every night, I wasn't on the payroll, but Buzzy sometimes cut me in on a share of the kitty. I was happy just to be allowed to play.

A handsome young pimp named Duke used to come into the club every night escorting two or three gorgeous girls. I was surprised when Buzzy invited him to sit in on the drums. Duke turned out to be one of the hippest drummers I'd heard in Seattle. He played a lot like Max Roach, and really had it together. I couldn't believe that anyone who could play jazz that well wouldn't be doing it if given a choice. I asked him, "Why aren't you playing all the time?"

"I can't afford it. I'd lose too much money."

A gold miner from Alaska came into the VFW club one night and began passing out ten-dollar bills to the waitresses. He was surprised that the band didn't respond when he threw a twenty in the kitty and asked us to play a sentimental pop song. At intermission, Buzzy gave him back his money and explained that we only played jazz. The prospector hung around until closing time and then invited Buzzy and Betty to accompany him to another club that was still open.

When they walked in, everyone stopped what they were doing and catered to the big spender, gathering up the tips he kept handing out. The house trio left the bandstand and played right at his table in order to collect their share of the loot. The prospector kept looking at Buzzy and Betty as if to say, "This is how you're supposed to act."

Betty finally decided it was time for her to return to New York. When she left, Ken Kimball took her place at the VFW. Buzzy decided to follow Betty east, and urged me to come with him, saying, "If you want to be a musician, you've got to go where the music is."

I accepted his logic and his invitation. I had lost interest in the courses I was taking at the university as I became more involved in music. The Cirque Club had just gone bankrupt and closed. At loose ends, I was willing to try New York if Buzzy thought I could play there. We started east together on a Greyhound bus on New Year's Day, 1950.

As we changed buses in Chicago, Buzzy looked at a handsome, dark-haired passenger in the line ahead of us and shouted, "Porky!" It was Woody Herman's lead trumpeter, Al Porcino, on his way back to New York. Al's slow, measured vocal cadence gave a Runyonesque quality to the road band stories with which he kept us entertained for the rest of the trip. I thought the chance meeting with Al was a good omen. I felt like I was already on the New York jazz scene.

As I owned few clothes, I studied Al's with interest. He wore a salt-and-pepper tweed Burberry overcoat over a gray drape suit and a shirt with a broad "Mr. B." collar, a style made popular by Billy Eckstine. My own sense of style had been formed by the Sears Roebuck catalog until, in the Army, I saw trumpet player Gene Kent's civilian clothes, box-back suits from Fox Brothers Tailors in Chicago. Before I was discharged, I wrote to them and ordered a flashy brown plaid suit and a sport jacket, and Gene suggested I also get a dark blue suit in case I found any gigs at home.

The blue suit turned out to be the most outrageous of the three. Its broad lapels were deeply notched and hand-stitched around the edges with baby blue yarn. They swept down from wide, padded shoulders to four pale blue buttons sewn in a tiny square at crotch level. The trousers came up over my ribs, heavily pleated and draped above tight, pegged cuffs.

That sort of drape suit looked great on Gene's square, muscular body, but I wasn't built like that. On my 110-pound frame, my new suits hung like curtains. Still, I thought they were wonderful, the hippest clothes I had ever seen. Fox Brothers had even sewn a little secret pocket in the armpit of the left sleeve of each jacket, in case one needed to stash anything.

If I had arrived in New York with that wardrobe two years earlier, I'd have been the cat's pajamas. But the zoot suit era was passing, and

soon every musician but me was wearing slim Oxford gray suits with
no shoulder padding. I had to keep wearing my Fox Brothers suits for
another year or so until I could afford something that looked more
like Brooks Brothers.

At the bus station in New York, Buzzy and I said goodbye to Porcino
and took a cab to the Hotel Bristol on Forty-eighth Street, just east of
Seventh Avenue. I didn't even unpack. After five days of riding, I was
happy to just collapse into a bed.

The Bristol, on a block lined with music stores, recording studios,
and instrument repair shops, was popular with traveling musicians, but
it was too expensive for more than one night. The $8.00 daily rate
would have quickly depleted the small roll of bills I had brought with
me. The next day, Buzzy moved in with Betty in an apartment she had
found in Brooklyn Heights, and advised me to find a cheap furnished
room on the West Side. I checked out of the Bristol and walked up
Broadway, looking for a home.

Just north of Fifty-second Street I passed the Birdland marquee. A
sandwich board propped in front of the door announced that Charlie
Parker and his quintet were appearing there. After memorizing the
location, I circled around the neighborhood, looking for signs advertising rooms for rent. I saw one, "FURNISHED ROOMS," in a ground-floor
window at the corner of Fifty-third Street and Eighth Avenue, a dilapidated old five-story building next to the fire exit of the Gay Blades
skating rink. (The rink was converted to a ballroom in late 1956, when
Roseland, one jump ahead of the wrecker's ball, moved there from its
old location between Broadway and Seventh Avenue near Fifty-second
Street.)

My room rented for eight dollars a week, and that was the only good
thing to be said for it. The dim hallway was painted a slick, gloomy
dark green and the stairway was steep and rickety. The pervasive smell
of roach spray was overwhelming to me, but not to the roaches. That
third-floor room was just big enough for a sagging bed, a flimsy cardboard dresser, a threadbare rug, and a stained and faded, shapeless
easy chair. The single grimy window overlooked a dark air shaft. I
moved in because it was cheap, and it was just a block from Birdland.

The landlady gave me my first experience with the sour demeanor
of some New Yorkers. She looked at me with suspicion and disapproval, never smiled, never said "hello." I was completely intimidated
by her. One night I left my key in my room when I went out. The door
had a snap lock. When I returned at four A.M. and discovered I was
locked out, I was afraid to wake the landlady and face her certain wrath.

I couldn't think of any indoor place where I could afford to spend the night, so I went down into the subway, a safe place in those days. I got on an E train and rode groggily back and forth between Brooklyn and Queens until it was late enough in the morning to ask the landlady to let me into my room.

I had a lot of time to kill every day until Birdland opened. I would walk over to Charlie's Tavern in the old Roseland building, hoping to see some of the musicians I'd met through Buzzy. One of them was Dave Lambert, an unemployed jazz singer. Dave knew everyone at Charlie's, and through him my circle of acquaintances quickly grew. One day Dave introduced me to Neal Hefti, whose name I knew from arrangements like "The Good Earth" and "Wild Root" that he had written for Woody Herman's band. After that, whenever I saw Neal in Charlie's, we would say hello.

About a year later Dave hired me to sing in a vocal group on a demo that Neal was putting together for his wife, singer Frances Wayne. As we walked into the rehearsal studio at Nola's, Dave greeted Neal and said, ". . . and you know Bill Crow."

I held out my hand, but Neal looked completely baffled.

"Bill Crow?" he protested. "Then who's Brew Moore?"

He'd been saying hello to me for a year, thinking I was Brew.

chapter 7

Charlie's

Charlie's Tavern became a clubhouse for musicians during the big band era. If you gave up your room while you were on the road, your mail could be sent to Charlie's. When you were out of work, Charlie would run a tab for you, and he'd cash your checks when you got paid. A musician could park his wife or girlfriend in a booth at Charlie's before a job and know that nobody would bother her until he got back.

Charlie Jacobs, the owner and chief bartender, bore a resemblance to Wimpy, the character in the Popeye comic strip, but he was no wimp. Once a circus strongman, Charlie was nobody to fool with. He knew his customers and encouraged outsiders to find another bar. He took care of the cops who dropped in, but he didn't like them to hang around. They made his customers uncomfortable. He'd pour a drink or make a sandwich for a bluecoat if he came in when it was quiet, but if one arrived when the place was busy, Charlie would meet him at the door and walk him back out to the sidewalk, slipping him the obligatory gratuity as he ushered him out.

I hung around Charlie's as much during the day as I did at Birdland at night. I couldn't afford to drink at Charlie's, but since I didn't enjoy alcohol, I didn't mind as long as Charlie didn't. He just ignored anyone who failed to order something. I stood around talking with other musicians as long as I wasn't in the way. Any time I felt I was taking up space that could be occupied by a paying customer, I moved on.

In 1950, Charlie was horrified when the *Daily News* ran a photo of his bar on the front page, identifying the tavern as a haven for dope pushers. Evidently somebody had been arrested for possession and under pressure from the narcs had told them he'd bought the drugs from someone at Charlie's. The *Daily News* story painted Charlie's as some sort of opium den.

Charlie knew nothing about drugs. His clientele were drinkers. Sometimes a junkie would come in and sit nodding in a back booth, but Charlie had always ignored that sort of thing. Now he made a new rule: No more junkies! All sleepwalkers were told to get out.

Trumpeter Don Joseph nodded off in a booth one night and Charlie threw him out. The next day I found him sitting outside the tavern on Brew Moore's tenor case, waiting for Brew to come out.

"What's the matter, Don?" I asked. "You look unhappy." Don gave me a piteous look.

"I'm banned from bars," he said, "and I'm barred from bands!"

Bored with peering in at his friends through Charlie's front window, Don decided to have a little fun. He waited until Charlie was at the cash register with his back turned and quickly sneaked in the tavern door. Crouching low, he ran the length of the bar and hid in the back phone booth, where he dialed the number of the front phone booth.

When the phone rang, Charlie came out from behind the bar and answered it.

"Hello, Charlie, this is Don Joseph. Please, can I come back in?"

"No, by God, I don't ever want to see you in here again!"

"Please, Charlie. Just give me one more chance."

While Charlie continued to angrily yell into the phone that it would be a cold day in hell before he ever let Don back in, Don ran up and tapped on the window of Charlie's phone booth. As Charlie gaped, Don waved goodbye and skipped out the door.

One afternoon before Charlie's ban went into effect, I was sitting with Don in one of the tavern's booths, listening while he told me how difficult it was having an addiction to heroin. I sympathized, but at one point I said, "I don't know much about it, but isn't there a doctor or a therapist in New York who could help you?"

Don sat back with a frown. Then he raised a finger and an eyebrow and declaimed, "Millions for junk, but not a cent for therapy!"

A l Thomson was a famous regular at Charlie's. He found intermittent work playing tenor saxophone with road bands. When someone at Charlie's introduced Al to a musician he hadn't met before, he asked him, "What have you been doing?"

"Scuffling."

Al looked interested.

"Is there an opening?"

O n an out-of-town job Thomson got acquainted with a parrot that belonged to one of the entertainers in the show. When the parrot was not being used on stage, its owner parked it in a cage in the bandroom, where Thomson had plenty of time to teach the bird to say "Fuck you!" The parrot made Al's efforts worthwhile one night when he repeated the new words loudly and clearly right in the middle of the show. The entertainer knew immediately who had sabotaged his bird, and nearly killed Al right on stage.

While standing at the bar in Charlie's tavern one night, Thomson listened patiently to a musician who was crying the blues about his inability to find work. Then Al, unemployed himself, waved an imperious hand and ordered:

"Charlie! Give this cat a gig! And put it on my tab!"

On a snowy night Thomson and trombonist Johnny Messner were draped across a pair of bar stools in Junior's, another musician's hangout that once graced West Fifty-second Street. The bar was a few steps below street level. Around two A.M. the door opened and in came alto player Gene Quill, already well lubricated. He missed the top step, slid down the others and landed flat on the floor in front of the bar. Al, an avid baseball fan, leaned over Gene with his arms spread like an umpire, and wheezed,

"Safe!"

A famous Charlie's tavern story involved two trumpet players, Ziggy Schatz and Nick Travis. Ziggy, while having a taste one night with a few friends, overheard Nick's conversation at the other end of the bar. Nick's wife had just left him, and he was bemoaning his plight while he drowned his sorrows. Ziggy could sympathize, since the lady in question had originally been his wife; she had left him to marry Nick. Ziggy shouted down the bar, "Hey, don't worry, Nick. I may get married again!"

Songwriter Roy Alfred's smiling face and shining bald head were frequently seen at Charlie's. He always stopped by on his way home from a hard day at the Brill Building. He became the center of attention for several hours one day when he walked in wearing a brand new toupee. Each newly arriving customer would comment on Roy's rug, stimulating a new wave of comic speculation along the bar. Roy took it all with good humor and even bought a few rounds of drinks.

When Roy left, I walked out with him.

"You took that pretty well," I said. "I was surprised that you stayed around so long, with everybody ribbing you like that."

"It was a test," said Roy. "I knew if I could wear this rug for three hours in Charlie's, I could wear it anywhere!"

There was a strange little guy that hung around in front of Charlie's late at night. He would accost the musicians as they left the bar, holding up a piece of clothesline rope and saying, "Tie me up! Please, tie me up!"

He fancied himself an escape artist, and hoped for small contributions after he freed himself from his bonds. We occasionally obliged him, tying his wrists with his rope and watching him work his way loose. He wasn't particularly skillful at it, but he was persistent, and always eventually managed to slip free.

A couple of musicians got tired of this guy's demands to tie him up. One night they brought a longer piece of rope, and after tying his wrists with his own rope, they bound him hand and foot with the longer piece. They even enlisted the assistance of some passing sailors to make the knots difficult. The poor guy lay on the sidewalk struggling unsuccessfully to free himself for an hour before they finally untied him. He stopped coming around Charlie's after that.

It was in Charlie's tavern that Dave Lambert introduced me to Aileen Armstrong, who became my wife several years later. She was studying acting and dance with various private teachers in New York, and supporting her education by working as a nightclub camera girl. She took photos of the customers at the Havana Madrid on Fifty-eighth Street, in the jazz clubs along Fifty-second Street, and later at Birdland.

Aileen was standing by the bandstand at the Three Deuces with a Speed Graphic camera in her hand on the night in 1949 when Fats Navarro got mad at Bud Powell and bashed him over the head with his trumpet, but she was too surprised to take the picture. She did photograph many of the jazz musicians who worked in those clubs and kept the negatives on file, but when the darkroom man quit his job he took all those negatives with him.

Prints of many such photographs survived for a time at Charlie's tavern. The walls above the booths and behind the bar were covered with nightclub photos, studio portraits, and snapshots of musicians. Over the cash register, next to an old postcard that Brad Gowans had sent Charlie from Mexico, was a photo of a man wielding a shovel. He had a Clark Gable mustache and a devilish grin, and he wore shorts, sneakers, and a fantastic suntan. It wasn't until thirty years later that I found out that Merv Gold was the man with the shovel. Merv is a trombonist and an avid amateur photographer. He had sent the picture to Charlie while he was on the road with Sammy Kaye.

Charlie died in 1956, and the tavern closed soon afterward. When they were getting ready to tear down the Roseland building a year or two later, Merv Gold took the last picture of the tavern, closed and boarded up, bearing a sign, "THIS BUILDING TO BE DEMOLISHED." A few years ago Merv gave me a copy of that picture. It hangs framed on our wall at home, a souvenir of happy times.

chapter 8

Jam Sessions

When I moved to New York, I knew my nightly idylls at Birdland couldn't last forever. When my money was gone, I went downtown to a printing trades employment agency and they found me a job at Bergen Press, a print shop in the Bronx. I had learned printing in Kirkland, working after school and on weekends for seventy-five cents an hour in the print shop of the *East Side Journal,* our weekly newspaper. The money was no better in New York: Bergen Press paid me thirty dollars a week to hand-feed a job press for them.

To stretch that pittance, I moved in with A. C. Bannister, a drummer from Virginia who was studying painting at the Art Students' League. We split the twelve-dollar weekly rent for a furnished room on West Eighty-first Street. I started taking music lessons and, on Buzzy Bridgford's recommendation, began seeing Dr. Alan Cott, a Reichian therapist, to see if I could learn to loosen up a little. After paying for these essentials and my food and transportation, there was nothing left of my weekly salary for anything else.

I lived as cheaply as possible, often walking home from work through Harlem and Central Park to save the nickel subway fare. Ace and I lived on hamburgers that we cooked on a hot plate in our room, but even so, I could no longer afford the admission to Birdland. That didn't keep me away from the place. I'd go there every night and stand halfway down the stairs where I could hear the music, even if I couldn't see the band. And, outside on the sidewalk, there were always musicians to talk to.

When Joe Lopes first arrived in town, someone introduced him to a

couple of us who were loitering in front of Birdland. He asked if we
were going downstairs to hear the music, and was amazed when we
said we didn't have the price of admission.

"You mean they don't let musicians in free?"

When we told him you had to be well known to get in without paying, Joe frowned and pulled the door open.

"Come on, I'll get us in."

He strode down the stairs and we followed, assuming he had connec-
tions. Joe went by the ticket window and on down the last flight of
steps, where Pee Wee Marquette said, "Yes, gentlemen?" and held out
his hand for the tickets.

Joe brushed his hand aside and growled brusquely, "It's cool!"

Pee Wee looked surprised, but made no protest as we walked in and
sat down in the bleachers. Joe looked so tough that I guess Pee Wee
took him at his word. The music seemed especially good that night.

I always kept an ear out for word of jam sessions. All we needed was
a usable piano and enough space for a few musicians to gather around.
There were several midtown rehearsal studios that could be rented by
the hour, but we could rarely afford them. A bass player named Dante
Martucci told me about a bar in the Bronx called the Bolero, where
the owner let musicians use the back room free of charge. There was a
piano of sorts and plenty of room, but there was no heat. The few
times I took the subway up there during my first winter in New York,
we kept our coats on while we played. It was so cold that I could see
my breath condensing into steam as it came out the end of my valve
trombone. I felt sorry for the rhythm section. By the time ten or twelve
tenor saxophone players and I had each taken several choruses on a
tune, Dante and the pianist and drummer were worn out.

The first jam session I ever played in New York was during that three-
day pass from the Army in late 1948. Jack Zini, our drummer in the
Second Army Band, told me to call an alto player named Bob Mintline
when I got to town.

"Bob knows where everything is happening in the Apple."

Mintline gave me a friendly welcome and offered me a couch to sleep
on. Then he took me to a session at Nola's studios. When we walked
in, drummer Jack Davis and pianist Sylvia Gardner were playing with
Brew Moore, who was lying on the floor with his head propped against

the wall. Brew had his tenor sax laying beside him where he could play it without having to hold it up. His florid complexion and the nearly empty half-gallon of wine in the crook of his arm indicated the reason for his supine position.

Brew was drunk, but he still sounded good. He hadn't removed the cigarette from the corner of his mouth when he began playing, and as he blew into his mouthpiece, sparks flew from the end of the cigarette. I stood there, saucer-eyed, thinking, "Wow! This is really far out!"

Mintline unpacked his alto and I got out my valve trombone. On the next tune I began to riff softly behind Brew's second chorus. Icy stares from the other musicians let me know that this was not proper behavior. Riffs were passé. I took a couple of choruses when it was my turn, but I was too intimidated to play with any confidence.

Later, I followed everyone over to the Royal Roost to hear Dizzy Gillespie's big band. Brew knew the guy at the door, so we got in without paying. Dizzy's musicians wore berets, and their band uniforms were fake Tarzan-style leopard skins draped over their suits. We stood at the back of the club and listened to a set. The band was roaring on charts like "Emanon" and "Manteca." I had never heard anything so wonderful.

I had some of Dizzy's records and knew what a good trumpet player he was, but at the Roost I discovered that he was also a great dancer. Dizzy conducted his band with every part of his body, improvising funny, wonderful movements that fit every nuance of the music. To bring in the brass, he might make a fantastic spinning leap into the air, hitting the floor right with the section's entrance. Or he would throw his handkerchief into the air, spin around, and snatch it again right with an accent in the music. During a long conga solo by Chano Pozo, Dizzy danced continuously, wonderfully.

With better information than I had on my first visit to New York, I found Fifty-second Street the next day, but I was too late to hear any modern jazz there. Times had changed, and the crowds of jazz fans and wartime revelers had abandoned Swing Street. The Onyx was still open, but it only had a disc jockey, Symphony Sid. The Three Deuces featured an unknown blues singer. The other modern jazz joints on the block had either become Chinese restaurants or strip joints. But Jimmy Ryan's was still in business, with a traditional jazz band.

I went in and sat at the bar, where I met Sidney Bechet, Tony Parenti, Wilbur and Sidney DeParis, and Lips Page. I bought Lips a drink and got him talking about the good old days in Kansas City. Bunk Johnson came in, sharply dressed in a new pearl-gray suit. He opened the trumpet case he was carrying and showed Lips a brand-new silver and gold trumpet, still in its cellophane wrapper, nestled into the form-fitting blue plush interior of its case. He had left his new false teeth at home, so he didn't play, but he happily showed the horn to everyone and let them buy him drinks.

Before returning to Fort Meade, I went up to Maurice Grupp's studio above Klein's Gymnasium on Seventh Avenue and took a lesson. Grupp was a specialist in helping brass players with embouchure problems. Then I went to hear Buddy Rich's band at the Paramount. I was surprised when he walked onstage with his left arm in a sling. I found out later that he had broken it while playing handball.

He didn't cancel any bookings because of the injury. He continued to work while the arm healed, playing with just one hand. At the Paramount he played amazingly well, booting the band and taking a blazing drum solo. He substituted his right foot for his left hand and played spectacular figures between the snare and bass drum.

Buddy's price was too high for anyone else to hire him for long, yet as a bandleader he was reluctant to hire high-priced side musicians, given his taste for expensive living. Throughout his career he showed little respect for the musicians he could afford, and he often vented his anger on them for the imperfections he perceived in their playing. Hearing the contempt in the way he played for his band, critics often downgraded Buddy's ability, which infuriated him even further. He was at his best when sitting in with musicians he admired. I heard him play like an angel one night, sitting in for Gus Johnson with the Basie band.

Max Roach got a lot of good press when he was with Charlie Parker, and one jazz critic published the opinion that Max had topped Buddy Rich as the world's greatest jazz drummer. John Robinson, another drummer, told me he was walking up Broadway with Max one day when Buddy came driving around the corner at Fiftieth Street in an expensive sports car with the top down. Buddy was dressed to the nines, and had a spectacularly beautiful young woman sitting beside him. He saw Max and yelled:

"Hey, Max! Top this!"

chapter 9

Scuffling

Lennie Tristano was the only jazz teacher that I knew of in New York. As soon as I got my first paycheck from Bergen Press, I got Lennie's number from Betty Christopher and called him.

"I'd like to study with you."

"Why don't you come out and play for me? Then we'll see."

Lennie told me how to find his house in Flushing, and I took my valve trombone out there on the subway one evening after work. I sweated and suffered as I stood in the famous blind pianist's living room, playing a few choruses on "I Got Rhythm" changes while he accompanied me. I was very nervous, and found myself gasping for air. I hated the sound I was getting and despaired at the banalities I heard myself playing. When I stopped, Lennie nodded and said, "Yeah, I think you'll blow."

He asked me a few questions and I told him that I played by ear. I could read notes, but didn't know the names of any of the chords I heard.

"So, we'll start you out with two different exercises," he said. "I want you to learn these chords." He dictated a series of them, and I wrote them down.

"And I want you to choose a Lester Young solo and a Charlie Parker solo. Memorize them exactly the way they're played on the records. First sing them, and then play them on your horn."

That was a task I understood. When Ray Baram had taught me the traditional jazz repertoire in the Army, it was his custom and our practice to always begin a set of choruses on a particular tune with its definitive recorded solo before attempting our own. For example, if we were playing "Dippermouth Blues," one of us would always play Louis Armstrong's famous chorus first. It was done out of respect, as an acknowledgement of where we came from.

I left Lennie's studio feeling excited about having some music to work on. At my job, I practiced my lessons while feeding my printing press, singing to the rhythm of the machinery. The print shop was a noisy place. I could barely hear my voice over the rumble and clank of two job presses, the clatter of a folding machine, the crunching of a paper cutter, the banging of a compositor hammering down his frames of type, and the screaming of the boss's wife at the secretary and the stock boy. But I got on the boss's nerves. He yelled, "Knock off the singing! It's driving me crazy!"

I liked printing, but the constant crabbiness of the people at Bergen Press finally got to me. One Monday morning, as I headed up West Eighty-first Street toward the subway that would take me to work, I looked back toward Riverside Park. The trees against the blue sky had tiny new green leaves, and the smell of spring was in the air. I looked toward the subway and thought of the pressure and the gloom and the yelling at the print shop. Something turned over gently inside me, and I said, "Not today."

I walked over to the park and ambled south along the Hudson, watching the boats on the river, savoring the balmy air. I felt as if a heavy weight had been removed from my heart. I walked all the way downtown and over to Monroe Street on the Lower East Side, where Dave Lambert lived in a cold-water flat with his wife, Horty, and their four-year-old daughter, Dee. I talked with Dave and Horty, played with Dee and stayed for dinner.

Several people dropped in to visit. Interesting discussions took place. We laughed and talked late into the night, and I found a place to sleep across the street at a loft belonging to some friends of the Lamberts. My intention had been to skip a day's work, but I found it difficult to leave Monroe Street. I was so interested in the group of musicians and artists I met there that I didn't get back to my room on Eighty-first Street until a week later.

I had decided not to return to my job, and I had come to tell my friend A.C. that I couldn't afford to go on sharing the room with him. He had been looking for me to tell me he was moving out. Having heard nothing from me, he was just getting ready to put my clothes and trombone in storage with the landlady. I had no money for the week's rent I owed, so I left a valise full of old Army shirts and shoes with the landlady as security and took the rest of my clothes and my trombone back to Monroe Street. It was several months before I got my hands on the six dollars I needed to retrieve that valise.

I fell in love with all three of the Lamberts. Dave was warm and funny, Horty was beautiful and brilliant, and little Dee was delicious. My feet had taken me to their apartment without any conscious guidance. Once there, I just followed the action wherever it led. Theirs was a world of music and laughter, mixed with interesting discussions of art, psychology, and politics.

One day while both Dave and Horty were working, I agreed to babysit with Dee. I took her midtown to listen to Gerry Mulligan's rehearsal band. Gerry, who was also starving around New York, found it easy enough to assemble a band, but since the musicians didn't have enough money among them to rent a studio that day, they decided to rehearse in the park. I hadn't met Gerry at the time, but I knew two of his saxophonists, Brew Moore and Alan Eager, and one of his trumpet players, Tommy Allison. No drummer turned up that day, but there were two bass players, Phil Leshin and Harry Bugin.

It was a fine day, and Gerry's music sounded great outdoors. People gathered around to enjoy the free concert. Rowers on the lake beached their boats and listened. Gerry scheduled another park rehearsal for the following week, but at someone's suggestion moved it to the other end of the lake near the boathouse, where there was a men's room. During that rehearsal the men's room attendant complained about the music to a policeman, who asked Gerry if he had a permit. It hadn't occurred to anyone that they would need a permit to give a free concert. The policeman made them stop playing.

I had no income, but I never considered going back to the print shop in the Bronx. Though broke, I was beginning to live the life of an artist. I shared communal meals with friends on the Lower East Side, and did odd jobs whenever I could find them to pick up a dollar or two. The people I was with all seemed to be happy even though they had little money, so I was sure I'd get along somehow.

When I got hungry midtown, I eked out my nickels at the Automat, the La Salle Cafeteria, or Jimmy the Greek's lunch counter in the Brill Building, and I took full advantage of the "bottomless cup" at the B & G coffee shop. I tapped the musicians' grapevine every day at Charlie's Tavern, keeping an ear out for possible work or jam sessions. I got to know all the Tavern regulars and began to be accepted into the family of New York musicians.

One night at Charlie's, Bill Harris came in. He was in town with the "Jazz at the Philharmonic" tour. Beneath Bill's dignified appearance lurked the heart of a vaudeville clown. As he approached the bar, he surreptitiously loosened his belt, holding his trousers in place with his elbow. He ordered a shot of whiskey, and when Charlie poured it for him, Bill raised it to his lips and downed it in one swallow, releasing his elbow as he did so. His pants fell to the floor with a dramatic whoosh. Wiping his lips, Bill said, "Charlie, you pour a damned fine drink!"

Sometimes I spent an evening with Dave Lambert and a couple of other singers reading through his vocal arrangements. Having a low voice, I sang the fourth or fifth part. Dave got me on a record date because producer Rudi Blesh had asked him to find some musicians who also sang. Mary Lou Williams had written vocal group arrangements on two of her own tunes, "Cloudy" and "Walkin'," but the harmony parts seemed to be too difficult for the singers Blesh had first tried. Mary Lou's lines didn't lead well for singers.

"She wrote the way she would write for horns," said Blesh. "If we find musicians who sing, maybe they'll be able to stay with Mary Lou's parts by thinking about how they would play them on their horns."

Dave was willing to try. He hired me, trumpet player Norma Carson, saxophonist Bob Newman, and someone else I can't remember. We rehearsed with Mary Lou until she was satisfied and then made a very nice recording of the tunes. It was my very first record date. I don't know why, but Blesh never released those sides.

One night Horty Lambert took me to a party at Larry Rivers's loft. In those days Larry was spending equal amounts of time with an artist's palette and a tenor saxophone. He knew all the musicians, painters, and Bohemians in New York, and his loft was big enough to accommodate what became a sizeable party that night. Later that night I joined Rivers and Johnny Carisi and a few other musicians in a jam session in Larry's back room.

I met a lot of interesting people at Larry's party, including the blind street drummer Moondog, who sat in midtown doorways and played 5/4 and 7/8 rhythms that he called "snake time" on a small homemade square drum and assorted small percussion items. I also met the painter Gandy Brodie, and had a long chat with the legendary poet Joe Gould

("Professor Seagull"). Joe wrote the famous couplet called "My Religion":

In the winter I'm a Buddhist.
And in summer I'm a nudist.

chapter 10

Dave Lambert

David Alden Lambert became well known to the jazz world twice during his life. First during the mid-'40s, when he and Buddy Stewart recorded "What's This," a bebop vocal, with Gene Krupa's band, and again in the late '50s when he and Jon Hendricks invented the vocal group Lambert, Hendricks and Ross. In between those periods of success, Dave did a lot of scuffling.

Though Dave was having trouble making ends meet when I first met him, he seemed to be enjoying life. He showed me where a lot of free fun was going on in town. I followed him around to different people's apartments. There always seemed to be a party going on somewhere. If there wasn't, Dave walked in and started one.

Buddy Stewart had become Dave's closest friend while they were singing together with the Gene Krupa band. (Buddy's sister, Beverly, was also a good singer, and a dear friend of Dave's. She became Stan Getz's first wife.) After Krupa reduced the size of his band, cutting out the vocal group, Dave and Buddy occasionally sang together at the Royal Roost, and they remained very close. Buddy's death in an automobile accident in New Mexico in early 1950 was a terrible blow to Dave.

While he was still with Krupa, Dave married Hortense Geist, a young woman from Paterson, New Jersey. Dee was born later that year, in October 1945. When the Krupa job ended they had some very lean times, living in New York on West 106th Street.

In 1946 and 1947 Dave led a vocal quartet in a Broadway show, *Are You With It?* The regular salary got the Lamberts out of debt and into a better apartment, but Dave found the repetitiveness of the job maddening and was glad when the show closed, even though it meant he was broke again.

Gil Evans lived in a basement room at the Gotham Hotel on West Fifty-fifth Street, behind a Chinese laundry. He befriended Dave and Horty as well as several other scuffling musicians. The Lambert family, Miles Davis, Gerry Mulligan, Charlie Parker, and pianist Sylvia Gardner all stayed at Gil's when they had no place else to live, taking turns sleeping in his bed.

Gil's nurturing nature attracted many other musicians to that apartment. Max Roach, Dizzy Gillespie, George Russell, John Lewis, Lee Konitz, John Carisi, and Blossom Dearie contributed to the rich musical atmosphere there. A cooperative musical effort developed at Gil's that resulted in the Miles Davis nonet. They worked a few nightclub gigs around 1949 and made some fine recordings, later gathered together on an album called *The Birth of the Cool*.

Dave told me he was so poor in those days that he stole food from the supermarket in order to survive. He would put his old army field jacket on little Dee, put her in a shopping cart and wheel up and down the aisles, filling her pockets with various foodstuffs. He'd pay for a couple of items at the checkout counter and wheel her outside. She would be so loaded down with purloined canned goods that she could barely stand when he lifted her out of the cart. Recalling those days, Dave told me, "I just realized, I was feeling so poor then that I always stole oleomargarine. I was too poor to steal butter!"

Horty said that Dave was the only person she knew who had dreams with punch lines. One morning he woke up laughing, and told her this dream:

A high school class is putting on a Christmas play, the Nativity scene. On a simple auditorium stage a few flats indicate the stable, and a wooden manger holds a doll representing the infant. Students stand beside it in the costumes of Mary, Joseph, and the three wise men. As Mary kneels to look adoringly at the child, there is a commotion backstage. Loud noises and thumps are followed by the collapse of one of the stage flats. The young actress portraying Mary looks up with annoyance and says—
"Jesus Christ!"

Horty was working as a secretary in a music publisher's office in the Brill Building when she met Dave. Someone told her there was a guy sitting at one of the office pianos, making weird noises. Horty went to look. There was Dave, poking out chords on the piano and whistling his vocal lines through his teeth as he wrote them down. Later, when she went to California, a friend took her to visit the Krupa band, and she renewed her acquaintance with Dave. Romance blossomed, and they were married soon afterward.

Horty remembered an interview Dave had with Stan Kenton, who thought he might hire Dave to form a vocal group for him. Dave stopped by Stan's dressing room at the Paramount Theater in New York, and they talked it over.

"Of course, you'd have to shave off your beard," said Stan, pointing to the Vandyke that Dave wore at the time.

"I couldn't do that," said Dave.

They agreed to disagree, and joked a bit about the possibility of Dave wearing a beard that was removable, like a toupee. As Dave rose to leave, Stan also stood up. The difference in their height was remarkable, and Dave's parting shot as he stared into Kenton's shirt-front was:

"Well, I'm sorry we can't see eye to eye."

Dave was born in Boston in 1917, and attended grade school in Malden. He told me about a teacher there who had a drinking problem. Every now and then the kids would find him at his desk in the morning looking terrible, unshaven, rumpled, hung over, and maybe even asleep. The kids would take care of him. One would shave him, one would run his suit down to the cleaner and have it pressed, one would get him coffee, and the rest would keep an eye out for the principal. Dave said they wanted to save him from being fired because they liked him. He reciprocated their kindness by not being too fussy about their schoolwork.

Dave had an older brother, Henry, whom I never met because he was living, I think, in Australia. Dave told me about a time when he and Henry still lived in Massachusetts. Dave was walking down the street with a girlfriend and met his brother. He started to introduce the girl to him, but couldn't think of his brother's name!

Henry left the house one night, saying he was going to get a ginger ale, and never came back. The family got a card from him a few weeks later from Barbados. He'd met someone who was off to see the world, and had just tagged along. He never did return home, though Dave heard from him once in a great while.

Dave studied the drums for a year when he was ten, but had no other formal musical education. He played a few summers at the shore with a pianist named Hughie McGinnis, who gave him a lot of practical experience. Dave said Hughie always chewed an unlit cigar, with only an inch of it protruding from his mouth. When he would sing, he'd pull the wet beavertail of chewed cigar out of his mouth and whack it on the front of his upright piano, where it would stick. His song sung, Hughie would peel the cigar off the piano and stuff it back in his mouth. The front of the piano had a large crusty brown stain that had built up over many summers.

Dave spent a year in the Civilian Conservation Corps, worked as a tree surgeon in Westchester for a while, and then joined the Army in 1940. He trained as a paratrooper and saw some active duty. It was in the Army that he fell in love with vocal group singing, listening to records of the Merry Macs, the Modernaires, and other good groups of the day. After his discharge in 1943, he got his friend John Benson Brooks to show him how to write out the vocal parts he heard. He sang with Johnny Long's band for a year, joined a group called Hi, Lo, Jack and the Dame for a while, and teamed up with Buddy Stewart on the Krupa Band in 1944.

After leaving Krupa, Dave signed with Capitol Records and made a couple of sides for them, but the company decided that bebop was not going to be the next popular novelty craze and allowed the contracts of all their bop artists to lapse.

I learned from Dave how to survive in New York without a steady income. He had four basic rules of honorable scuffling:

1. Be ready and willing to do any kind of work.

2. Scrupulously keep track of your debts, and repay all loans as soon as you can. But don't go to the same well too often.

3. If you borrow anything—a car, a tool, an article of clothing, an instrument—always return it when you promised, in better condition than you got it, so the owner will be happy to lend it to you again. (Dave always returned a borrowed car washed and gassed up. Tools were sharpened and cleaned before returning them. A borrowed tux went to the cleaner before it went back to its owner.)

4. Give fair exchange to anyone who feeds you. Make a party for them however you can. Make music, sing songs, tell stories, let the good times roll.

Dave and I made a few dollars one day painting the front of Charlie's Tavern. Charlie supplied a bucket of Chinese red paint and paid us fifty bucks apiece. When we finished the job, Charlie drew us each a beer. Dave was small but wiry and strong. He grabbed the edge of the bar and rolled his body forward until he was balanced over his hands. Then he pressed up into a full handstand, picked up his beer glass with his teeth, tilted it up and drank his beer upside down. When he let go of the glass he flipped back to his feet, right where he had been standing. Of course, he got a big hand from the regulars at the bar.

My wife, Aileen, remembers a party where Dave danced all night long walking on his hands. He loved parties, and was the life of most of those he attended. During the days when he was having the most trouble making ends meet, he received an invitation to a masquerade party. He couldn't afford a costume, so he cut two large fig-leaf shapes out of an old green plastic placemat and glued them together to form a pouch, which he slipped over his genitals. With contact cement he fastened the top of the front leaf to his skin, just below his navel. Then he put on his shoes and overcoat and went to the party as Adam. He had a wonderful time, although he shocked some of the guests.

Dave was just as inventive when it came to the simple problems of daily life. When he had trouble getting his neighborhood laundryman to leave the starch out of his shirts, he quickly saw the solution. Since the laundry always stamped a customer's last name inside his shirt collars to identify them, when Dave brought in some new shirts to be washed he told the laundryman, "My name is Dave Nostarch."

One night I went with Dave to a party at the Village apartment of photographer Joe Covello. The place got so crowded that Joe moved the party to his new studio in Long Island City. While driving me and songwriters Alan Jeffries and Jack Segal there in a borrowed car, Dave said that it would be nice if we walked in singing. He chose "Pennies from Heaven," and taught us our parts by rote, four bars at a time. We ran the song down again in Joe's parking lot, and we walked in, singing in modern harmony. With that kind of spirit, everyone was always happy to see Dave coming.

Jack Segal was a good friend who helped me through some lean days. I often visited Jack and his wife Lillian and enjoyed the warm welcome they always gave me. We would sing songs, read plays, laugh, and tell stories for hours together. Jack always made sure I got something to eat while I was there, and a couple of times when I was looking particularly seedy, he slipped a five into my pocket as I left. A true friend in need.

With no income, I had to stop taking lessons with Lennie Tristano. I'd lost a little of my enthusiasm for him as a teacher, probably because I expected too much from him. I wanted him to wave his magic wand and make me into a Lee Konitz. But I began to feel that Lennie wasn't too interested in teaching me when, after I waited over an hour past my appointed time one evening while he finished with earlier pupils, he told me, "I've got to start getting ready for work. We're playing at Birdland this week. You go ahead and start your lesson while I take my bath."

He went into the bathroom and closed the door. As I began playing what I'd worked on that week, I could hear the water running in the tub. Whenever I paused, Lennie would yell, "Yeah, that sounds good," or, "Okay, keep going."

When my time was up, I packed my horn, left the money on the table, shouted goodbye through the bathroom door and left.

When I called Lennie and told him I couldn't afford to continue studying for a while, he wished me luck. I didn't break off quite so cleanly with my therapist. Dr. Cott continued seeing me for a couple of weeks on credit, but finally said, not unkindly, "All you're giving me to work with is your guilt about not paying me. I think you should stop coming here until you can afford it. Go out and live your life. Find out what you're going to do."

It took me a while, but by the end of that year I found out I was going to be a bass player.

chapter 11

Tupper Lake

Playing the bass wasn't my idea. It was Buzzy Bridgford's. While I was drifting penniless around the Lower East Side that first spring in New York, Buzzy was also trying to get something going for himself. He found a few short gigs, but Betty's piano playing was paying the rent

on their apartment. Buzzy sat in a few times with Gene Roland's rehearsal band, and in June, Roland hired him for a summer job he
found for a quartet in the Adirondacks. Buzzy came over to Monroe
Street to say goodbye, and said he'd be at the Altamont Hotel in Tupper Lake, New York, for the next two months.

A few days later, he was back in New York, brimming with excite-
ment. On the first night of the job, Roland had a big fight with the
hotel owner's wife and walked out in a huff. When Buzzy discovered
that Gene had packed up and left town, he went to the owner and said,
"There's no reason for you to be stuck without music. I'll go to New
York and put a good band together for you, and we'll be back next
week."

Buzzy tried to sell him a quintet, but the owner wouldn't pay for a
bass player.

"Another rhythm instrument? It's a waste of money!"

Buzzy hired Marty Bell, whose trumpet playing reminded him of
Buck Clayton's. He persuaded John Benson Brooks to end several years
of seclusion writing songs in his Riverside Drive apartment to be his
pianist. And Freddy Greenwell agreed to fly out from Seattle.

On the evening Freddy was to arrive, Buzzy, Dave Lambert, trumpeter Neil Friel, and I were at Buddy Jones's furnished room on
Broadway across from Birdland, listening to some of Buddy's tapes.
Buzzy wanted to meet Freddy at LaGuardia Airport and asked Dave
the best route on the subway. Dave said, "The subway isn't any way to
meet someone who's flying all the way from Seattle! Wait a minute."

He consulted the phone book and called a nearby limousine service.
After a short discussion on the phone, he told us, "We can get a chauf-
feured limo to take us out and back for fourteen dollars. Can we get
that up?"

We all turned out our pockets. The cash among us added up to a
little over sixteen dollars.

"Great," said Dave. "That'll cover the fare and a tip. Let's do it."

He gave the dispatcher Buddy's address and hung up. When the
black Cadillac limousine pulled up at the curb downstairs, the elderly
uniformed chauffeur looked doubtful as our shabby group approached
his car. Dave affirmed that he was the Mr. Lambert who had called,
and we were off to LaGuardia.

Freddy was delighted with the limousine. As the driver stowed his
tenor and his suitcase carefully in the trunk, we all got into the back
seat and began filling Freddy in on what was happening in the Apple.
On the Triborough Bridge, Dave tapped on the driver's window.

"Would you take the scenic route back downtown? Through Central Park?"

The driver nodded and headed for the park drive, and we all agreed that Dave did things with style.

The entrance to Buddy's building was next to the marquee of the Broadway Theater. Our limousine pulled up to the curb right at intermission, when most of the well-dressed audience was out on the sidewalk, smoking and chatting. They all looked to see who was arriving so fashionably late.

The driver opened the passenger door and stood at attention while our unkempt group straggled onto the sidewalk. As we got Freddy's things out of the trunk, Dave filled the driver's white-gloved hands with our collection of dollar bills, quarters, dimes, and nickels. He stuffed it all into his pocket without counting it and quickly drove off. We all went up to Buddy's apartment and celebrated Freddy's arrival until late in the morning.

Before Buzzy returned to Tupper Lake with his quartet, he told me, "If you can find a way to get up there, I'll put you up for a couple of days. You can have a nice weekend in the mountains."

Being stone broke, I had no hope of taking him up on his offer. But later that week Dave's friend George Vetsis, a handsome young singer, told me that Buzzy had called to offer him a job as vocalist and master of ceremonies at the Altamont Hotel for the summer. Buzzy had convinced the boss that he needed someone like George. I asked him how he planned to get there.

"Hitchhike," he said. "It's the Fourth of July weekend. There'll be lots of cars going to the mountains." I mentioned Buzzy's offer to put me up for a few days, and George said, "Great! We'll go up together."

I met George early the next morning with my suitcase and my valve trombone. We took an A train to the George Washington Bridge, walked across to Fort Lee, and stood there by the side of the road for a long time before getting our first short ride. We discovered that two young men with luggage were not the most desirable prospects as hitchhikers. Our progress was very slow. Neither of us had any money, but George was carefree.

"That's one good thing about being Greek. Almost every restaurant in the country has a Greek in the kitchen. I'll find us something to eat."

Sure enough, when we got hungry, George walked into the kitchen of a diner in Kingston, New York, chatted in Greek with the chef, and got us a free meal.

By the time we reached Lake Placid it was getting dark. We walked through town and a long way into the countryside before catching a ride to Saranac Lake, and another ride from there only took us to a farm turnoff a few miles out of town. Even though it was July, the mountain air was cold at night, and we weren't dressed for it. We sat on our suitcases, shivering in our shirtsleeves in the dark for several hours. None of the few cars that passed would stop for us. Finally, in the morning, a farmer in a pickup truck took us the last fifteen miles into Tupper Lake. The 300-mile trip had taken us twenty-six hours.

We found the Altamont Hotel, a big, homely wooden structure near the lake. Buzzy let me collapse in his bed, where I slept all day. In the evening I got a bite to eat and then took my valve trombone to the bandstand to sit in on the first set. The guys in the quartet seemed happy to have an extra horn, and I had a great time playing.

Later that evening Buzzy took me aside and said, "I had a talk with the boss. I told him you were a busy New York studio player, but your doctor discovered a spot on your lung and said you had to spend the summer breathing the fresh air of the mountains. I told him I thought he could get you if he made you an offer."

I was amazed at Buzzy's inventiveness, but doubted the boss would believe his story, as rumpled and unbarbered as I looked.

"What did he say?"

"He said, 'See what he says to room and board and fifteen bucks a week.' "

"I'll take it!"

I moved into a room of my own and began eating regularly again. I didn't have to wait long for my next surprise. When I got on the bandstand the next night, I saw a yellow plywood Kay bass leaning in the corner behind the drum set. I asked Buzzy, "Did you get them to hire a bass player?"

"No, I rented the bass for the summer from a kid here in town. Whoever isn't taking a chorus has to play it. I can't make it without a bass player."

That "whoever" was clearly to be me, since neither Marty nor Freddy were interested in the bass. I knew nothing about playing one, but was willing to try. Buzzy explained what he wanted:

"Try to get a long fat sound, like Ray Brown. Hold the strings down hard with your left hand and make each note ring into the next one."

I figured out the tuning and located the notes I heard by trial and error. It never occurred to me that there might be a fingering system, or ways to adjust the string height to make playing easier. I got blisters on my fingers and played with adhesive tape on them until they hardened up. I learned a little more every night, and before long my fingers got stronger and more accurate, and I was able to play simple bass lines.

I didn't get to play the trombone very much. Whenever I'd put the bass down Buzzy would suffer and complain. He did have me play one or two ballads on the horn every night just to keep the boss from realizing he'd hired a bass player.

During the day, John Brooks would come down to the bandstand and show me chords, and Freddy would sometimes take me up to his room to play me passages from the previous night's work that he had captured on his wire recorder.

"Listen to this," he would say, "You sound like a real bass player on this chorus!"

Buzzy continued to instruct me on the way a good rhythm section worked. Back in Seattle, when I first met him, he heard me playing drums. Later, when we were listening to records in his room, he asked me, "What do you think about when you're playing?"

"Keeping the time steady."

"How about swinging?" he asked.

"I'm not sure how to do that."

No problem. Buzzy took his own beat apart for me, explaining how each element fitted the other. Then he played me records like "Tickle Toe" and "Avenue C" by the Basie band, and "Jumpin' Punkins" and "Cottontail" by Duke, while he showed me what the drummers were doing to enhance the swing. He danced out the figures, accenting some of them with little kicks of his foot and others with taps in the air with his fingertips. His eyes shone with delight as he let the music move him around the room.

As I watched, I saw exactly what Buzzy meant by "swing." He gave me a clear image of the sound and feeling of it. For years, whenever I was trying to get some swing into the music I was playing, I would think of Buzzy's dance that night, and of the way he played. He didn't know how to read music and had very little formal technique, but, as the older musicians used to say, he could swing you into bad health.

Buzzy would have found his way onto one of the good jazz groups that were working out of New York in those days if he had been able to stay there and concentrate on music, but like so many young musicians of the late '40s and early '50s, he became sidetracked by narcotics. He had no illusions about heroin. He knew how dangerous it was, but he couldn't seem to resist flirting with it. He had learned about drugs in his teens.

Buzzy's father, a doctor and a pillar of the community in Olympia, Washington, had hoped Buzzy would forget about jazz and study medicine, but he did buy him the drum set he wanted in high school. Buzzy also persuaded his father to buy him a juke box, the only playback system in those days that could come close to simulating the volume and presence of a live band. Buzzy told me he learned to play by drumming along with Basie, Henderson, and Ellington records on his Wurlitzer.

He did study medicine, after a fashion; when he found out about chemical stimulants, he read all about them in his father's medical books. And while still in his teens, Buzzy was arrested in Tacoma for possession of marijuana. The car he was driving was confiscated, and it cost his father a lot of his political capital to keep him out of jail.

Deciding that enforced discipline would straighten out his wayward son, Dr. Bridgford packed him off to a military school in northern California. Buzzy, already developing the glibness of a con man, went to the head of the school and, in his most charming manner, told him something like this:

"Look, I'm never going to be able to soldier for you people, so if that's the only way it can go, you might as well accept failure and send me home now. But if you want to keep my father happy and keep his checks coming in, why not let me study music here? Jazz is the only thing I'll ever be interested in."

When he was told there were no music courses at the school, Buzzy talked them into letting him set up his own curriculum:

"It will be an experiment in modern education!"

He made *Down Beat* and *Metronome* his study material and spent his weekdays in a room by himself playing the drums and listening to records. Then, on weekends, he was driven down to San Francisco in the school station wagon to listen to the music at the ballrooms and jazz clubs there.

As a result of those field trips, Buzzy made contacts that led to his being hired to play drums on Jimmy Zito's band as soon as he was eighteen and free of school. He moved on to Jan Savitt's wartime youth band, which took him to the East Coast, and there he joined Randy Brooks. When Randy broke up his band to travel as a featured soloist with Ina Ray Hutton's orchestra, Buzzy stayed around New York and began hanging around with the young heroin users who were emulating Charlie Parker. In 1949, a heroin-related auto accident fractured Buzzy's skull and sent him home to Olympia. He stayed off drugs pretty much until he returned to New York.

I thought a summer in the Adirondacks, far from the ready supply of heroin in New York City, would be good for Buzzy's health, but I forgot about the mail. Buzzy arranged to have a friend in the city send him a little something every so often. Fortunately he couldn't afford a large enough supply to get hooked too badly. When he ran out, a day or two of feeling shaky would bring him back to normal, until the next package arrived.

One afternoon I noticed the little package in his room that had come from New York in the afternoon mail, and saw that Buzzy was high. He came for a walk with me down by the lake shore, and when a mosquito landed on his forearm, instead of brushing it away, Buzzy said, "Watch this."

The mosquito drove its proboscis into Buzzy's skin and began to pump itself full of blood. Before long it began to quiver spastically, then it jerked its little beak out of Buzzy's arm and fell lifeless to the ground. Buzzy positively gloated at being poisonous to mosquitoes.

chapter 12

More Scuffling

The fifteen dollars a week that I earned during my summer in Tupper Lake was a small salary even in those days, but I was only spending money on breakfasts, so I came back to the Apple with some cash in my pocket. I made a beeline for Birdland to hear Charlie Parker's group with strings. Bird seemed to enjoy mirroring the dignity of the classical musicians he had hired. He conducted the introductions and endings of the arrangements with a serious mien, and when he made announcements, his voice took on a cultured tone. But he hadn't become too dignified to swing. Even though the strings sounded a little stiff with a jazz rhythm section, Bird played gloriously.

I moved into a little hotel called the Radio Center on Fiftieth Street on the short block between Broadway and Seventh Avenue, one flight

above the Gypsy Tea Room. It was cheap, and it was near Birdland
and Charlie's Tavern, and only a short walk from Local 802's exchange
floor over on Sixth Avenue. I visited all three places regularly, looking
for work.

There wasn't much happening for a valve trombone player, but I
occasionally found a Saturday night job on string bass. When one turned
up, I'd rent a bass for the weekend for five dollars from Noah Wulfe's
string shop on Sixth Avenue. At Jack Silver's down the block, another
five would rent me a tuxedo. The jobs usually paid fifteen dollars, so I
would clear five, on which I could eat for a week.

While I was gigging around town on rented basses, I kept an eye out
for an instrument of my own. I found a bass player in the Bronx with
a plywood Kay that he was willing to sell for seventy-five dollars. I could
only give him fifteen at the time, but he let me owe him. I had hopes
of paying off the balance when John Brooks began rehearsing a trio
with me on bass and Buzzy on drums, but John had trouble finding
work for us.

Buzzy and I completed our transfers from the Seattle musicians' union
to Local 802. I felt optimistic about the future, but Buzzy fell into a
despondency that I couldn't seem to help him overcome. Drugs began
to make financial demands on him that he couldn't support, and Betty
was back working with an all-girl band in order to pay the rent.

By the end of the year their relationship had begun to come apart.
Then Charlie Parker asked Betty to play piano with him on a New
Year's Eve gig. At first she was thrilled, but then I guess she became
terrified. Without any warning, she packed up and went home to Chicago, leaving Buzzy a farewell letter. I later heard that she left the jazz
world completely, married a Chicago professional man, and moved to
California.

Pianist Johnny Knapp, who loved Buzzy's playing, was trying to find
a job for him, but Buzzy doubted that anything would turn up. With
Betty gone, he threw in the towel. He told me he was going back to
Seattle. When I went over to his Brooklyn Heights apartment to help
him pack, he handed me his key, saying, "You might as well move in
here. The landlord has a month's deposit that I'm sure he won't return,
so just stay here for a month and move out before the next rent is
due."

After I saw him off at Penn Station I walked uptown to Charlie's
Tavern, where I met Johnny Knapp.

"Have you seen Buzzy?" he said.

"I just put him on a train to Seattle."

"That's terrible! I just found a job for him!"

I only saw Buzzy once more after that, when I went home to visit my folks in 1954. I borrowed their car and drove down to a club in Tacoma where Buzzy, Freddy Greenwell, and Neil Friel were working. Buzzy and Freddy weren't speaking to each other that night because of a fight they'd had over a girl, but they came over separately to chat with me at the bar. They both invited me to sit in, and as soon as the music began, they put aside their differences and played together like the close friends they were. I went back to New York, and a couple of years later, word reached me on the musicians' grapevine that Buzzy had died of pneumonia in September 1956.

When the month at Buzzy's apartment in Brooklyn Heights was over, my pockets were empty again. I sat on the curb in front of Charlie's Tavern one day, holding my last nickel in the palm of my hand and thinking, "If I use this to call someone for help and don't get it, I won't be able to take the subway back to Brooklyn Heights. And if I use it to go home, I won't be able to get back to Charlie's again."

A friend came along and told me about a blood bank on Forty-second Street that would pay for donations. I went over and let them extract a quart of my vital fluid, but felt so hungry afterwards that I spent four of the five dollars they paid me on Chinese food. Clearly this was no way to survive.

John Brooks had a large apartment at 136th Street and Riverside Drive where he lived with his wife and their two young daughters. There was a small unused room off the entrance hall where John and Helen let me stay for a few weeks until I got myself together and found another furnished room. I especially appreciated having the use of their music room during the day, where a grand piano was surrounded by a huge record collection.

John had been an arranger in the 1940s, writing for Eddie DeLange's band, and had some success as a songwriter. "You Came a Long Way from St. Louis" and "Just As Though You Were Here" were his best-known recorded tunes. Later he had become interested in American folk songs. He admired the work of Woody Guthrie, and was trying to write with that sort of simplicity and directness. His song "The Happy Stranger," which had been recorded for Columbia Records by Claude Thornhill's orchestra a couple of years earlier, was released while I was staying with John. Gil Evans had done the arrangement. I got a copy of the record and took it back to John's apartment, and he put it on the turntable. As we listened to Gil's lovely introduction, John snatched the tone arm from the record.

"That sonofabitch!"

"What's wrong?"

John sighed as he restarted the record.

"I sweat for a month to find a melody that fits the simple character of that lyric, and Gil does it better in a four-bar intro!"

One afternoon Dave Lambert steered me onto a babysitting job for Dick Buckley. Dave explained that Buckley was a nightclub comedian who billed himself as "Lord Buckley" and affected a British accent on and off stage. Buckley was no snob. He generously elevated all his friends to the peerage as well, addressing everyone as "Sir" or "Lady." I called the number Dave gave me, and Buckley asked me to come to his apartment at nine P.M.

Dave filled me in on Buckley's sense of humor. His best bit was a ventriloquist act in which he used members of the audience as dummies. He would seat three or four of them on stage and put funny hats on them. They were instructed to move their mouths when he poked them in the backs, while he created outrageous dialogue for them.

Buckley was fond of put-ons. Dave said he once threw open his front window and pushed his wife out over the sill, clutching her by the throat and waving a butcher knife in the air as he screamed, "I'll kill you, you bitch!"

When the police arrived, the door was open. Inside, they found the Buckleys dressed in evening clothes, listening rapturously to a recording of a Mozart quartet while sipping tea from Spode cups. They politely inquired, "What disturbance, officers?"

Buckley was once passing through the lobby of the Waldorf and through an open door heard Sammy Kaye's band rehearsing for a benefit show that evening. He walked in and rehearsed the band for half an hour, giving them many complicated cues for his routine, and then went on his way. He wasn't around for the payoff that night when Kaye realized that Buckley wasn't on the show, but he savored it in his imagination.

At the appointed hour I arrived at the Buckleys' ground-floor apartment in a brownstone building in the West Seventies. Lord Buckley, a slender man with a trim, waxed moustache, greeted me at the door.

"Welcome to the Castle!"

His bogus British accent and twinkling eyes gave him the air of a bunko artist. He led me down a hall past several small rooms and out into what had once been the backyard of the building.

A wide living room had been built there with a ceiling of opaque glass and a floor of red tile. In the center of the room was a small reflecting pool surrounded by ferns and philodendrons, with a stone cherub in the center, pouring water from an urn. Bookcases and paintings lined the walls, and pleasant indirect lighting gave the whole place a charming glow.

"Now, Sir Crow, come into the bedroom and meet Lady Buckley and the prince and princess."

I did so. The children, Richard and Lori, were already in bed, and his wife, Elizabeth, was putting on her evening coat. Buckley performed courtly introductions and then led me back to the living room.

"Make yourself comfortable. The TV is in the cabinet in front of that easy chair, the record player is over on the sideboard, the records are in the bookshelf, and the pot is in the lacquer box above them. Help yourself to the bar, or to anything in the refrigerator. We'll be home by three."

I made myself a sandwich and spent a pleasant evening reading and listening to records. When they came home, Buckley slipped me my salary and bade me a formal farewell. After that, whenever I ran into him, he always greeted me as "Sir Crow," and promised to remember me to his family.

A few years went by during which our paths didn't cross. Then, one day when I was waiting to cross Sixth Avenue at West Third Street, along came Lord Buckley.

"Ah, Sir Crow!" he cried, and clasped my hand warmly. His clothes looked a little seedier than when I'd seen him last, but his regal bearing was intact. He beamed with enthusiasm.

"I've been on the West Coast, and I've developed a new routine that's going to knock everyone's arse off! Have you a moment to spare?"

"Come on up to my place and tell me about it. I'll make us some lunch." I had my own Village cold-water flat by then.

Buckley's new routine was the story of Jesus of Nazareth told in the argot of a hipster. He called it "The Nazz," and eventually recorded it. It was funny, and at the time (pre–Lenny Bruce), quite outrageous. I couldn't imagine where he'd be able to perform it without either puzzling or offending his audience, but I knew he'd break up the band. He gave me samples of other routines that he was developing in the same vein: a hipster's versions of Shakespeare and of Roman history. We spent a pleasant afternoon lunching and laughing, and I noticed

when he said goodbye that I had received a promotion. He shook my
hand and said, "Farewell, Prince Crow."

John Brooks finally booked a couple of jobs for his trio, with Harold
Granowski on drums. (He is now Hal Grant, the jingle producer). I still
couldn't make any payments on my bass. I was just barely paying the
rent. We played at one place in Fort Lee, New Jersey, called the Mile-
stone, owned by an overweight ex-madam who *demanded* that the band
swing. She sat in front of us and, loudly on the afterbeat, smacked her
fat, jewelled hand on the bar top, urging us on.

Our most interesting job was a concert at Town Hall with the Weav-
ers, four folk singers who had been very successful until the McCarthy-
era blacklists destroyed their careers. Pete Seeger was their lead singer.
This concert was their first appearance in several years, and they didn't
want to do it all by themselves. Our group was engaged to play in between the two halves of their program.

John decided to expand our trio to a sextet for the concert so he
could write some jazz arrangements of folk songs. He used Taft Jordan
on trumpet, Bennie Green on trombone, and Budd Johnson on tenor
sax. It was thrilling to hear our music in that lovely auditorium. I especially admired Taft's beautiful tone and phrasing when he played
"Shenandoah."

John ran out of bookings for the trio, and Mike Riley asked him to
be his pianist on a few out-of-town jobs. Mike told him he was looking
for a singing drummer. John knew that I could sing and had once been
a drummer, and he also knew how badly I needed a job, so he set me
up an audition for Riley. I borrowed a set of drums for the audition
from my friend Maurice Mark.

At the audition, John and I accompanied Mike as he played vigorous
Dixieland trombone, and I sang a ballad to Mike's satisfaction. After I
agreed to be his straight man on his comedy routines, he hired me. I
was about to receive a crash course in being an entertainer.

chapter 13

"The Music Goes 'Round and Around"

My dad shipped my old drum set to me from Kirkland in time for my first job with the Mike Riley Trio at a bar and grill in Elmira, New York. I recently looked up Mike's vital statistics and found that he was born in Fall River, Massachusetts, in 1904, so he was forty-seven years old when I joined him, but he was a boyish old leprechaun, built like a tree stump. His long, vertical nose erupted sharply between a pair of intensely blue eyes. His fierce red hair had turned gray, but he dyed it back to its original color.

Mike had been doing knockabout comedy in a Dixieland setting for years. During the 1930s, he and trumpeter Ed Farley had a band on Fifty-second Street at the Onyx Club. They claimed to have written their big hit song by chance. Farley had an antique flugelhorn with circular tubing that he kept on the bandstand because he liked the way it looked. Mike told me that Ed was showing it to an interested lady one night, and said, "You just blow through here, and the music goes 'round and 'round, and it comes out here."

Mike claimed he told Farley, "You've got a song there," and they wrote it together.

I discovered through further research that the song really originated with Red Hodgson, a trumpet player who came up with the idea when he was working with Ernie Palmquist's band on the West Coast. Evidently a girl who came into the Onyx one night sang it for Riley and Farley, saying she'd heard it in Chicago. Riley and Farley added a few things of their own to the tune and began doing it regularly at the Onyx.

When "The Music Goes 'Round and Around" became a hit, there was a dispute over the rights. The Decca recording of the tune had a label that read "Reilly-Farley," and the Victor label read "Hodgson-Farley-Riley." The sheet music also bore all three names.

The song took off when Riley and Farley played it on a live radio broadcast from the Onyx on New Year's Eve, 1935. Radios in a large number of American homes were turned on for dance music that night. Millions of people heard "The Music Goes 'Round and Around" and liked it.

For those too young to remember that runaway hit, the lyric went like this:

Verse:
        One night, while playing in the band,
        A girl came up; she said, "You're grand."
        So I replied in words low-down,
        "Now, this is how the music goes 'round:

Chorus:
        I blow through here,
        The Music Goes 'Round and Around,
        Whoa-ho-ho-ho, ho-ho,
        And it comes up here.

        I push the first valve down
        The music goes down and around,
        Whoa-ho-ho-ho, ho-ho,
        And it comes up here.

        I push the middle valve down,
        The music goes down around,
        Below, below, below,
        Deedley-ho-ho-ho,
        Listen to the jazz come out!

        I push the other valve down,
        The Music Goes 'Round and Around,
        Whoa-ho-ho-ho, ho-ho,
        And it comes out here.†

The demand for the sheet music during the next month outstripped anything ever published before. Mike said the main reason was the melody on the bridge. Nobody could remember how those "belows" fit the meter, so everyone bought the sheet music to learn it.

Riley and Farley did a lot of comedy to entertain their customers and hired sidemen that knew how to be funny. They preferred low comedy, like the large pocket watch and chain that drummer Mousie Powell would extract ceremoniously from his trouser fly when he wanted to check the time.

Mike continued the burlesque tradition after his partnership with Farley dissolved. He had a successful bar in Hollywood during World War II called Mike Riley's Madhouse, where his combo played. The club featured sight gags and practical jokes. In the men's room was an oil painting of a nude lady, with a hinged wooden fig leaf over her pudenda. If you raised the leaf, red lights flashed outside the door and a siren went off, so everyone at the bar knew what you'd been up to. A similarly rigged painting of a male nude hung in the ladies' room.

The Madhouse did so well during the war that Mike decided to open a bigger club out on the Sunset Strip, with a ballroom and a dance band in the back and his combo at the front bar. After he spent his whole bankroll renting the place and fixing it up, someone challenged the club's compliance with the zoning rules. He wasn't allowed to open, and his investment was lost.

When I met Mike, he was in New York putting together some jobs to pay off what he owed his agent. To keep his expenses down, Mike decided to work with just a trio. He had one-week bookings in Elmira and Troy, New York; Monessen, Pennsylvania; and some other towns of a similar size. He paid me $90.00 a week, with only transportation provided. We lived in cheap rooming houses and carried hot plates and skillets in our suitcases so we could cook in our rooms.

We were billed as "Mike Riley and His Musical Maniacs," but John and I weren't much help with the comedy. We kept looking for ways to make the job more musical. Mike was used to working with a six-piece band of comedians. With us he had to carry most of the show himself.

"You gotta do comedy if you want to make money," he told me one night on the bandstand. "Listen, this is a high F!" He jammed his horn to his mouth and played a loud one. "You think anybody out there gives a damn?"

I was inexperienced, but I tried to be a satisfactory straight man. As a teenager I had watched burlesque routines at the Palomar Theater in Seattle, and I'd done skits and Spike Jones–type material in high school, but Mike would get me into routines that I didn't know. Sometimes he didn't know them so well himself. He would start some bit that one of his sidemen used to do, but wouldn't remember how it was supposed to end. I'd try to think of something funny to help us get out of it, but I quickly learned that Mike hated for anyone else to get the laugh. I was supposed to do the straight lines, and he was supposed to get the laughs.

Some of my duties consisted of handling Mike's props. When he sang "I Cried for You," he put on an oversized pair of glasses frames made from copper tubing. A rubber tube hung over his shoulder from the right earpiece, and I had to blow a mouthful of water through it so that "tears" would come spraying out of pinholes in the frames of the glasses as he sang.

When Mike sang "With the Wind and the Rain in Your Hair," we put on raincoats while he hoisted a magician's water jar onto his shoulder. Each time he sang the word "wind," he'd blow loudly into the microphone. Each time he sang "rain," he'd upend the water jar and pour what seemed to be the entire contents over his head. The joke came with the repetition of the words. There was always more water in the jar because a baffle inside it only allowed half of the contents to be poured out each time. The amount of water decreased with each pouring, but there was always some left.

Mike's best number was a clown routine on "I Got Rhythm." Wearing a shapeless old hat with a floppy brim and a wonderfully dilapidated long red circus ringmaster's coat with tarnished gold braid and a few missing buttons, he'd announce that he was going to emulate stripper Sally Rand. But he said that instead of taking his clothes off while he played, he would take his trombone apart.

We'd start playing "I Got Rhythm" at a furious pace. On the second chorus Mike would disconnect the bell of his horn from the slide section, pull the tuning slide off of the bell, hang the three parts together in a disconnected tangle and continue playing. The tubing wasn't continuous that way, but you could still hear "I Got Rhythm" coming from the leaky assemblage.

Roaring with manic laughter, Mike would discard the tuning slide and connect the main slide to the bell section where the tuning slide belonged, so that when he played toward the floor, the trombone's bell pointed at the ceiling. As he pumped his slide vigorously at the floor, John would leap up from the piano and pour a pitcher of water into the upright bell as it protruded behind Mike's head.

Pretending not to notice John's action, Mike would rest his slide on the floor in an extended position while he removed and discarded the bell section. He would then put his lips to the mouthpiece and blow hard while pulling the water-filled slide up to its closed position. The result was a huge eruption of water from the open side of the slide, right into Mike's face. As John and I continued the frantic accompaniment, Mike would do dripping, laughing takes to the audience. Then he'd repeat the melody, just on the slide section of his horn, getting a gargling sound because of the water still in it.

Mike would then discard the slide and play the tune on just the mouthpiece. Then he'd attach a long piece of rubber hose to it and, holding the open end of the hose up to the microphone, he'd again play the tune. A tiny, silly sound would emerge, still recognizable as "I Got Rhythm." Then he'd begin spinning the hose slowly over his head as he continued to play, letting a little more of it out with each spin. As the hose got longer, the audience could hear the melody coming around and around over their heads. A storm of laughter would build up as Mike charged around the stage like a madman, shouting and singing and springing his surprises on the audience.

For his final variation, Mike would discard the mouthpiece and hose and grab the bell section of the trombone, still minus its tuning slide. There was a small rim on the tube where the tuning slide fit in. Using this as a mouthpiece, Mike would sound a loud, resonant "doh-SOL! doh-SOL!" like a hunting horn. After all the thin, leaky melodies he'd just played on all the other parts of the horn, the effect was astonishing.

The Wagnerian horn call always brought a cry of delight from the audience, and Mike would race among them, shouting, "Didja *hear* that? Didja *hear* that?" and would bang people lustily on the shoulder with the bell of his horn. He'd mug and sing and carry on a while longer, but that was essentially the end of the routine. It always brought the house down, and was the one number John and I always enjoyed—a classic piece of clowning.

On or off the stand, Mike kept up a constant stream of terrible one-liners. He'd shout, apropos of nothing:

"It was dinner time in Russia, So-vee-et!"

"It looks like a cruller, do-nut?"

"Church on fire! Church on fire! Holy Smoke!"

"What are those holes in the floor?"

My line: "Those are knot holes!"

"That's funny, I could have *sworn* they were holes!"

He wore a pair of empty glasses frames while he was working. He'd poke a finger through them from the inside and waggle it at someone while laughing insanely. He'd shove his chin into his glass of beer and do Santa Claus jokes while wearing a beard of foam. He moved at a frantic pace, and he never stopped trying to get a laugh.

Away from his audience, Mike lost his merriment. He moaned to us

about his financial and family troubles. He suffered terrible guilt because the lovely woman who traveled with him was not his wife. His
wife back in California was "a saint," and his son was in a Jesuit school
studying to be a priest. He said he didn't deserve such a wonderful
family, and that no one had ever been through as much hell as he had.
I'd try to sympathize, but Mike would tell me, "You can't understand
what it's like. You're too young."

He often admonished:

"The only thing that's worth it is the laughs. If you can't have the
laughs, you might as well forget it."

Sometimes Mike was unable to wait until the nighttime job for the
laughs. He'd get John and me to go into a store with him in the afternoon. He'd pull a woman's silk stocking over his head to flatten his
nose and deform his mouth; the stocking seam looked like a terrible
scar across his cheek. With his hat brim low and his coat collar turned
up, he looked like a monster from a horror film. He loved watching
the store clerks try not to stare at him as he shopped for ties and gloves.

At work Mike wanted me to sing once every set. I liked singing, but
he never let me choose the song. He'd pick the hit tune of the week,
saying, "What are you going to sing, Billy? . . . 'If!' Billy's going to
sing 'If.' "

And I'd be stuck with singing a song I couldn't care less about. Sometimes he'd announce that same song on two or three consecutive sets. I
think he did it out of a desperate impatience. He couldn't stand to wait
a moment while I chose a song, and he was afraid I'd pick something
too esoteric for his audience.

Since so many of Mike's comedy bits resulted in his getting wet one
way or another, the prop hat he wore was usually heavy with moisture.
It was a bulky hat anyway, one of those rustic Irish wool jobs, and when
wet it must have weighed three or four pounds. On a punch line, especially during the routines where I acted as straight man, he would
whip off the hat and whack me on the arm with it. It was like being
clubbed with a sock full of sand. Sometimes when he hit my arm while
I was playing, my hand would involuntarily open and drop the drumstick.

Nearly every night, I'd plead with him to take it easy with the hat; I
was getting bruised. He'd promise to remember, but when he got wound
up in a fast-paced routine, the hat would come down hard again. I
found ways to fend it off, but it was still a drag.

When I had saved enough money to make the last payment on my
bass, I was eager to get back to playing it. I gave Mike my notice, telling

him it was nothing personal but I wanted to go back to New York and be a bass player. Of course, he took it personally and put me through a terrible scene. It was as if I were a son leaving home.

"I know what's wrong. It's because I hit you with the hat!"

"No, Mike, really. I just want to play the bass. You need a real comedian. I'm just an amateur."

"You're good, Billy. The audiences love you!"

"I really want to go back to New York."

"I'll let you do some of the jokes. You can have some of the laughs!"

"No, thanks, Mike. Really."

"I tell you what. I'll give you ten dollars more a week."

"Now I'm mad. If you could afford that, how come you've been telling me you could barely manage ninety?"

And on and on. I finally got out of there and went home to New York, ending my career in comedy. That was the last I saw of Mike. Before long he moved back to California.

Mike Riley was an original, a powerful spirit and a great clown. I learned a lot about being in front of an audience while working with him. And I certainly learned a lot about taking care of myself. Now that he's gone to his reward, I remember him with great fondness. I hope he's resting peacefully. But still getting the laughs.

chapter 14

West Tenth Street

Not long after I left Mike Riley and returned to New York, I moved in with Dave Lambert. He and Horty had separated, and Dave had found a basement room in Greenwich Village at 145 West Tenth Street, behind Jerry Francis's typewriter shop. Dave needed help with the rent, and I needed a home.

Our entrance was through a dark hallway under the stoop of the building's main entrance. The large single room, originally used for storing coal before the building installed oil heat, had rough stone walls and a concrete floor, with a single air shaft window that provided a tiny bit of air and light. There was a bathroom with a shower and a sink, but no kitchen.

Dave had installed a bed, an old refrigerator, and a two-burner hot plate. We found a rug and the rest of our furniture at the Salvation Army and on the street. An old couch became my bed. Dave salvaged a semicircular banquette seat upholstered in red plastic that the Spanish bar across the street had thrown out when they redecorated. We put it in one corner of our basement room next to a little upright piano he had rented. A vocal group could sit there comfortably and sing. On the street, Dave also found the discarded top of a round poker table, covered in green felt, which he installed in front of the banquette using milk crates for table legs. It became our music rack and our dining table, and also served as Dave's orchestrating desk.

To cheer the place up, we bought a bolt of cheap green burlap and covered the stone walls with it. In the corner behind Dave's bed we hung an old venetian blind and draped burlap around it like a valance and curtains. Behind the closed slats of the blind, Dave put a shadeless bridge lamp holding a clear two-hundred-watt bulb that was always kept on. It looked like a window with the blind closed against the afternoon sun. As a result, people lost track of time down there. Hours would go by, music would be played, songs sung, and stories told, and our afternoon guests might be shocked to discover upon leaving that it was late at night.

We always managed to pay the rent, but sometimes we chose to buy food instead of paying our electric bill. When Con Edison shut off the juice, we turned it back on again at the meter. When they removed the fuse, we replaced it. Finally they removed the entire meter. By this time our bill was substantial, and we couldn't get our hands on the kind of money we needed to settle it, so we ran an extension cord into Francis Typewriters and borrowed our electricity from Jerry. Whenever we got an extra five bucks we'd lay it on him to defray part of his electric bill. Jerry was very understanding.

People dropped in at Dave's basement at all hours to party, sing, jam, or watch the giant projection TV set that belonged to George Vetsis. George had grabbed it as it was being discarded from the lobby of the Roxy Theater. Since it was too large for his furnished room but too good not to salvage, he hauled it down to Dave's. George was handy with electronics, and it only took him a day or two to figure out how to get it working again.

Dave and George and I developed a sort of a work cooperative. Dave called us the Three Gnomes, which he pronounced Ga-NO-mees. We let it be known that we were handy and willing, and we took any odd jobs that turned up. In between our occasional musical work we painted apartments, moved furniture, built shelves, repaired appliances and TV sets, babysat, and minded cars for a couple of people who lived midtown where there was no on-street parking.

George Vetsis was a great finder. Besides the TV set, he brought us the guts from an old juke box to use as a record player. And one day he took us outside and proudly showed us his latest acquisition, a 1941 Cadillac Fleetwood limousine, with running boards and a convertible top over the chauffeur's seat in front. A glass panel could be rolled up between the driver's seat and the passenger compartment, which was upholstered in soft gray velour and had folding jump seats and a microphone for communicating with the driver.

The car had once belonged to disc jockey Art Ford, but had been registered in his manager's name for tax purposes. To collect some money he felt Ford owed him, the manager sold the car to a Greek friend of George's who, while driving a fare to the Catskills in it, fell asleep at the wheel. The resulting accident only put a small dent in the limo's heavy fender as it clipped off a light pole, but the owner was afraid to drive it again, so he sold it to George for a hundred dollars. George didn't have the hundred, but he promised to pay the man as soon as he earned some money with the car. The man trusted George because he had an honest face, and because the negotiations took place in his native Greek.

Dave loved driving George's Cadillac. It cornered well for such a big car, and it had plenty of power. Dave showed me all the things he'd learned from cab drivers about getting around New York. In those days, when the avenues were still two-way, you could zig-zag all the way across town on a certain pattern that would let you catch all the lights green. It only worked at night when there was less traffic to slow you down. Our best record was a run we made one night all the way from the Lower East Side to Charlie's Tavern without missing a green light.

Whenever we parked out in front of Charlie's, the car would soon be filled with curious musicians. Dave would take up a collection of small change, buy some gas, and give everyone a ride around Central Park and back to Charlie's. That would leave us with enough fuel to get through the next day or two. The back seat was so big that we could pull out the seat cushions and use the car to haul refrigerators and dressers when we did moving jobs.

George got rid of the Cadillac about a year later when it began to develop mechanical problems he couldn't afford to repair. He sold it to someone for a hundred dollars and then paid the man he'd bought it from. He'd had a luxury limo for a year free of charge.

I met Ward Cole, my Seattle friend, walking up Seventh Avenue one summer evening. Ward had left Ted Weems and was playing lead trumpet with Fred Waring. When I told him I'd learned to play the bass and was doing some vocal group singing with Dave, he gave me the name of a bandleader friend who was looking for musicians who doubled.

"Why don't you give him a call?"

I thanked Ward and found the nearest telephone. The bandleader was a trumpet player named Glen Moore, who hired me for a week in Toronto with his quintet. Then we came back to New York to work on the filming of a pilot for a television variety show featuring his wife, who was a dancer, and comedian Eppy Pearson.

When the filming was finished, Glen wanted to keep the band together until his agent had a chance to sell the show. The agent also booked bands for the passenger ships of the Moore McCormack line, so he installed us on the S.S. *Uruguay* for one run to Argentina and back, a thirty-eight-day trip, with stops in both directions in Trinidad, Rio, Santos, Montevideo, and Buenos Aires.

I was all packed to go, but Dave Lambert and I were in the middle of a job we had contracted, painting John Benson Brooks's Riverside Drive apartment while John and his family were in Maine. We had been working on it for a couple of weeks, sometimes taking off to do other short jobs that turned up. Painting John's place took us much longer than we had estimated because the huge apartment was crammed with books, records, music and family possessions that had to be moved around and covered as we painted. We worked there such long hours that I became confused about what day it was.

I went to John's place by myself on a Friday morning to continue painting while Dave was busy working with a songwriter. I wanted to finish the last ceiling before I left for South America. We were to sail on Saturday morning. As I dipped my paintbrush, I glanced at the newspaper spread beneath my bucket. It said, "Friday, August 3, 1951." I suddenly realized that this was yesterday's newspaper! That meant that today was Saturday, not Friday! The boat sailed today at eleven A.M.!

It was nearly ten, and there I stood on a ladder at 136th Street and Riverside with a wet paintbrush in my hand. I leaped down, threw my brush in a pail of water, scribbled an explanatory note for Dave, and ran for the subway. It seemed to take forever to get to the Village. I dashed to our Tenth Street basement, piled my instruments and my suitcase into a taxi, and got to the ship just as the gangway was being hauled in. They lowered it again, and I was on my way to Argentina.

chapter 15

S.S. *Uruguay*

I took all my instruments with me on the S.S. *Uruguay*. When we played on deck as the ship was going in and out of port, I played valve trombone. During the evening dance sets I played both bass and drums: bass on the American tunes and drums on the Latin ones. I knew how to play tangos, rhumbas, and sambas, but I had to be taught the *baion* by a passenger, a Brazilian lady. When the guy she was with complained that we weren't playing authentic Latin music, I told him, "Wait 'til you hear this next one. It's called 'Caveat Emptor.'"

Before we reached our first port of call, Trinidad, we ran into some bad weather. I was awakened early one morning by a metallic rumble that repeated every few seconds. In the dark, I couldn't imagine what it could be. When I turned on the light, I saw that it was the metal drawer under my bunk, slowly sliding open and closed. I had hung my trousers on a hook over my bunk, and they were slowly swinging from horizontal to vertical. I realized that the ship, large as it was, was rolling alarmingly.

My first thought was for my bass, which I had left lying beside the piano in the ballroom on the promenade deck. I threw on some clothes and tried to run up the gangway, but the wallowing of the ship made running difficult. When I reached the outside deck, I couldn't believe the change in the ocean. It had been blue and flat the day before, but now the waves were black mountains, higher than the ship. The sky was an ominous purple, the wind was screaming, and the ship was reeling drunkenly. We were in a hurricane.

When I got to the ballroom, my heart sank. The piano, fastened down with nautical cleats, hadn't moved, but everything else had fallen off the bandstand. My drums were rolling back and forth across the dance floor, and my bass was sliding around among a jumble of upset sofas, armchairs, and tables. The drums were unhurt, but the bass looked strangely askew. I rescued and secured everything and then examined my bass. The neck had pulled loose and was leaning forward at a strange angle. Amazingly, the bridge and sound post were still in place, and the body of the instrument was unbroken, but with the neck pulled loose, the instrument couldn't be played.

Bracing myself against the pitching and rolling of the ship, I loosened the strings to relieve the tension on the neck and saw that I might be able to reseat it if I could pull it back into place and glue it, but I would have to improvise a clamp of some sort. I got a bottle of Elmer's glue from the ship's carpenter and swabbed some into the space where the neck had pulled away from the body of the bass. Then I removed the A-string, hooked its bottom loop over the end pin and ran it up the back of the bass and over the top of the scroll. Threading the end of the string back into the tuning machine, I tightened it until it pulled the neck back where it belonged.

We couldn't play that evening. The ship was rolling too much for dancing, even if there had been anyone who wasn't seasick. We got into calmer waters the next day, and when I loosened my A string, the neck of my bass was solid and the fingerboard was back where it belonged.

The music we played on the S.S. *Uruguay* wasn't very satisfying; it was like being on a dumb club date that lasted for a month. Every night after the job I'd go up to the deserted gymnasium on the top deck and pummel the punching bag furiously until I was exhausted. Then I'd cool off in the swimming pool and collapse in my bunk. When I awoke, I'd pretend I didn't work there, lounging around the pool all day like a first-class passenger. When a steward informed me that, as a crew-member, I should stay in second class until it was time to play at night, I told him, "Fire me. Please!"

The band was off when we were in port. I brushed up on my high-school Spanish so I could explore our ports of call on my own and listen to the bands in the local nightclubs. The rate of exchange for Argentine money on the black market in Uruguay was very high, so I arrived in Buenos Aires with a pocket full of pesos. During the several days that the ship laid over there, I checked into a first-class hotel and lived elegantly. I kept asking for *el mejor,* the best of everything. It was a startling change from my accustomed standard of living in New York. I shopped like it was Christmas, and came home with presents for all my friends.

A few days after I got home, Dave Lambert told me that he had enjoyed living alone while I was away, and was beginning to earn enough money to be able to afford it. He asked if I would find a place of my own. I had been happy sharing his basement, but I understood how he felt. Neither of us had had any privacy for quite a while. Since I had saved most of the money I made on the ship, I moved out right away.

I knew that Teddy Cohen was living at the Prescott Hotel, just above Columbus Circle on West Sixty-first Street, so I called there and found that they had a small room that fit my budget. I became a member of the family of musicians who lived at the Prescott whenever they weren't on the road. Teddy, Eddie Shaughnessy, Luis Barreiro, John Ross, and Alan Jeffreys were the core group. Frequent visitors included Charlie Mingus, Oscar Pettiford, Frank Socolow, John Carisi, and comedy writer Max Grant. (Max was the inventor of the lint suit that picks up blue serge.) The arrival of a visiting musician at the Prescott would usually generate a party or a jam session, which might move from room to room as it got larger. Sometimes we all walked down to see who was in Charlie's Tavern, or to hear the music at Birdland.

One night at Birdland the Basie band was playing the last set of the night. Eddie "Lockjaw" Davis was down front taking a solo, but his attention was over at the bar. A woman was getting ready to leave, and Jaws was trying to get her to wait until he was off the stand. While playing a perfunctory chorus, he carried on quite a conversation with her by wiggling his eyebrows, rolling his eyes, and motioning with his head.

Basie sat at the piano on the top riser, next to Gus Johnson's drums, scowling at Davis. Finally, he grabbed a sheet of manuscript off the piano, wadded it into a ball, leaned over bassist Gene Ramey's shoulder, and pitched it at the back of Lockjaw's head. It hit squarely, and Davis's eyes flew open with surprise.

Jaws got the message immediately. Without even looking around, he switched into high gear. He finished his chorus with great energy and a different kind of body language that was clearly saying, "Look, Basie, I'm taking care of business now!"

Walking to and from Charlie's Tavern, I usually cut through an arcade that ran through the Roseland building. There was a marquee for the ballroom at each end of the arcade, one on Seventh Avenue and one on Broadway. One night I saw that the larger marquee on Seventh Avenue proclaimed in huge, backlit letters: "THE XAVIER CUGAT ORCHESTRA, featuring vocalist ABBE LANE." On Broadway, I glanced up at the smaller marquee on that side. The guy who did the signs must have run short of letters. It read: "XAVIER CUGAT, with ABE LANE."

In Charlie's one night, a guy ran in and yelled, "I need a bass player right away!" I was the only bass player there, but I had left my instrument at John Brooks's apartment at 136th Street.

"What time is the job?" I asked.

"As soon as you can get there. The Hotel Pierre roof garden. The band has already done three hours of overtime, and they want to go home."

I said I'd take it. Dave Lambert had driven to Charlie's that night in George Vetsis's Cadillac and offered to lend it to me for the evening. I drove to the Prescott to ask my neighbor, Alan Jeffreys, to lend me his dark blue suit. Alan wasn't in, so I went out on the fire escape, climbed in his window and got the suit, scribbling a quick note to explain. I hurried to my own room and got dressed, then sped up to John's place, grabbed my bass, and was at the Pierre within the hour.

A huge wedding party for the daughter of a Greek shipowner was in full swing. A bouzouki-playing singer stood on the dance floor in front of the bandstand, sweat streaming down his face as he sang Greek songs, chorus after chorus. Passing dancers plastered five and ten dollar bills on his forehead, where they stuck in the sweat until he wiped them off and stuffed them in his pocket.

I was going to wait until the band took a break, but as soon as the bass player saw me he waved me to the stand and carried his instrument into the lobby. As I took his place, I looked over the pianist's shoulder at the music he was reading. The title was in Greek, and the time signature was 7/8, which I had never seen before. I could hear the simple chord changes, so I fitted a bass line to the rhythmic pattern that the drummer was playing.

I got through the job okay, and when I got back to Charlie's I saw Alan Jeffreys sitting in a booth with some friends. I explained about borrowing his suit and said I hoped he didn't mind. Alan laughed.

"I'm staying with my girlfriend this week so I could let my sister have my room while she's in town. You're lucky she didn't come in while you were climbing in her window."

Alan and his girlfriend eventually moved into one of the larger rooms at the Prescott. One night there were about ten musicians gathered around Alan's piano. Someone had brought a set of drums, I had my bass, John Carisi had his trumpet, and John Ross his trombone. Teddy Cohen rolled his vibes over from his room across the hall and we began to play a little. Max Grant came in and began playing some funny things on the piano, though he was no piano player. To even things up for Max, we all switched instruments and, with each of us playing an instrument he didn't really know how to play, we began to improvise "modern classical" music. Alan turned on his tape recorder.

We enjoyed the musical joke. There were some fortunate accidents when two or three musicians found compatible phrases, but the spirit of the evening was one of musical satire. John Carisi took the tape to his composition lesson with Stefan Volpe the next day and asked him, "Who do you think wrote this?"

Volpe accepted it as the work of some modern composer and tried to guess who it might be. He was amazed when John told him how the music had been created.

Alan Jeffreys was a songwriter in those days, but before I came to town he had been a hot young trumpet player on the New York scene. The modern way of playing, which hadn't been named "bebop" yet, had begun to spread downtown from Harlem. Alan picked up on it and was a regular player at midtown jam sessions. At one of those sessions he met a nice young man from Kansas City named Charlie Parker. Charlie had bummed his way to New York to see the sights, but didn't have a horn with him. He didn't even tell Alan he was a musician. Charlie had no place to stay, so Alan put him up at his apartment. He expounded to Charlie about the new music, and Charlie listened with interest to everything Alan told him.

They got word of a jam session on a night that Alan had a club date. He told Charlie to go ahead, saying he'd meet him there after his job. When Alan walked into the session, Charlie was on the bandstand, playing a borrowed alto. Alan went into complete shock. His roommate not only was a jazz musician, he was the best one he had ever heard. Alan was so unnerved that he left his trumpet in its case that night. He said to Charlie later, "You play like that, and you didn't tell me? How could you do that to me?"

Alan was deeply shaken by his discovery of Parker's genius. He had considered himself a player, but now he felt like a rank beginner. Overwhelmed by the gulf that had suddenly opened in front of him, he decided to leave his trumpet on the shelf for a while. He never took it out again.

chapter 16

Gigging Around

Glen Moore wasn't able to sell his television pilot, and his work petered out after our boat trip. But, through the musicians at the Prescott Hotel, I began to find a few jazz gigs. I met New Jersey pianist Billy Triglia, who hired me once in a while for jobs that he found west of the Hudson, from Englewood, New Jersey, to the Club Paradise in Nyack, New York.

Billy often used Tony Fruscella on trumpet. Tony played beautifully but very softly; Charlie Barnet fired him after only one night on his band because he couldn't hear him. I loved the way Tony played in a small group, but he nearly lost us the gig at one Jersey club when the boss overheard his reply to a customer who offered to buy him a drink:

"Well, I'm already stoned, and the bread is pretty light on this gig, so would you mind just giving me the cash?"

At Charlie's Tavern I met Les Elgart and his manager, Dick Raymond. The handsome trumpeter had not been doing much since his big band had broken up in the late 1940s. Dick had found him a week in a saloon in Pottsville, Pennsylvania. They wanted a small Dixieland band, and when Dick heard that I doubled on bass and valve trombone, he hired me and asked me to write out some hot choruses for Les, who wasn't an improviser. Dick told me we'd meet at Charlie's Tavern the following Monday.

"Just bring dark pants and a white shirt," he said. "Les has band jackets."

We squeezed ourselves and our equipment into Les's ancient Packard sedan and drove to Pottsville, but found no trace of the club. Les phoned Dick, who reread the contract and told us that the job was in Potts*town*,

Pennsylvania, about sixty miles away from Pottsville. With slow traffic on narrow farm roads and a little car trouble outside Reading, we managed to get to the job just half an hour late.

"I'll go in and cool out the owner while you guys set up," said Les. "Bill, will you get the jackets out of the trunk?"

It was getting dark, and I couldn't see into the old-fashioned vertical trunk very well.

"I don't see them," I said. "Are they in these old gunny sacks?"

Les looked puzzled. "What gunny sacks?"

Right. The "gunny sacks" were the jackets. They'd been wadded up in there since the last time Les had a job.

"Let's play in our shirtsleeves tonight, and get these cleaned and pressed tomorrow morning," I suggested.

"Oh, no!" said Les. "We've got to be in uniform! It wouldn't look professional!"

So we were uniformly rumpled and disheveled on our opening night.

Back in New York, I began to get occasional calls for Monday nights at Birdland, when the regular bands took the night off and lesser-known groups were hired. The salary for a Monday night was ten dollars, cash. On one Monday I played there with pianist George Wallington and drummer Arthur Taylor. I don't know who gave George my name. I had heard him play and knew that he wrote hard tunes, so I prepared myself as well as I could by listening to his records.

On the big night, A.T. and I set up and waited for George to arrive. He came in just before starting time and handed me a few sheets of manuscript paper. He had written out his tunes and chord changes in a tiny hand with a red ballpoint pen. I put my parts on top of the piano.

George kicked off the first tune, "Liberty Bell," at a very fast tempo. I had to follow his sketch carefully because the melody and the chords were unusual. Halfway through the first chorus, emcee Pee Wee Marquette decided to improve the bandstand lighting. He turned on a bank of red floodlights overhead, which turned my music paper the same color as the notes on it. All I could see was blank music staves! I don't know what I played for the next ten minutes, but I'm sure it wasn't what George had in mind.

I began rehearsing with Teddy Cohen's trio at the Prescott, with Don Roberts, a good guitarist from Chicago. I replaced Kenny O'Brien, who had taken a steady gig somewhere. Teddy taught me bebop tunes and chords I didn't know. He found us a few jobs during 1952, and in between them we rehearsed every day and hoped for more work.

On our fast numbers, Teddy would play furiously until he could barely lift his mallets, Don would burn up his strings until he nearly dropped his pick, and then they would both turn to me and say, "Bass solo!" My fingers would already be falling off from accompanying them, so I would just continue to walk a bass line for another chorus and hope they wouldn't give me two.

We were well received by the audiences in jazz clubs like Squeezer's in Rochester and the Town Tavern in Toronto, but Teddy didn't have a big enough name to get us steady bookings on the jazz circuit. His manager, Ray Barron, tried to open up some new territory for us. Ray worked for the McConkey Agency, which provided entertainment for small clubs all over the East Coast. He got us bookings in Troy, New York; Portland, Maine; and Ocean City, New Jersey, in places that usually hired pop entertainers.

Our repertoire was straight bebop, but we sometimes did a little light entertaining. Don Roberts would pretend to be electrocuted by his guitar while he took a solo. Teddy did a frantic bebop parody of the old piano warhorse "Dizzy Fingers," and laced his announcements with schtik he'd learned on Chubby Jackson's band. It was inside humor aimed at musicians and jazz fans. The audiences in Troy just gave us blank stares. In Portland, we were closed out of a two-week booking at the end of the first week.

Teddy decided that the name "Cohen" might be holding him back. He called me one day and said, "I'm changing my name to Charles."

"That sounds good," I said, "Charlie Cohen."

"No, I mean it," he laughed. "Charles is my middle name. From now on, we're the Teddy Charles Trio."

Teddy was following the example of several other successful jazz musicians; Julius Gubenko was doing well as Terry Gibbs, Don Helfman was working steady as Don Elliot, and Herbert Solomon had become successful as Herbie Mann. But Teddy's new name didn't seem to get us any more work than the old one had.

We found our audience in Toronto, a town that supported two or three jazz clubs. While we were at the Town Tavern, Dizzy Gillespie opened at the Colonial Tavern around the corner. Percy Heath had just left him to join the Modern Jazz Quartet, and Dizzy came to Toronto looking for a bass player. He asked Herbie Spanier, a good Canadian trumpet player, for a recommendation. Herbie told Dizzy he played bass himself, and took the job.

Herbie played enough bass to get through a tune or two at a jam session, but he had no calluses on his fingers. By the end of the first night with Dizzy he was in trouble. Dizzy's quintet was playing hard, and Herbie developed some painful blisters. When I heard that he needed help, I ran over between our sets every night and sat in.

I thought that Dizzy's drummer, Al Jones, played awfully loud. Basses were unamplified then, and a loud drummer could make it hard for a bass player to hear what he was doing. But the acoustics at the Colonial Tavern were good, and my hands were strong from working with Teddy. I could hear my notes, and I enjoyed sitting in. Dizzy was working with a five-piece band, with singer Joe Carroll. Bill Graham played alto, and the pianist was a nineteen-year-old kid named Wynton Kelly.

Dizzy asked me to take the train down to Buffalo on my day off and play a one-nighter with him there. Early that morning I took my bass and met the band at the Toronto railroad station, feeling happy and lucky and glad to be alive. My euphoria evaporated in Buffalo when we set up to play. The hall was cavernous and echo-y, and every sound bounced endlessly back and forth, creating a cacophony that nearly drowned out the music. I could barely hear what I was playing, and I couldn't hear Wynton at all.

Dizzy yelled chord changes to me on the tunes I didn't know, but I depended on my ears. I played all night with my right ear in the open top of the upright piano Wynton was playing, trying to hear his chords. It was a long, miserable night.

When the job was over, Dizzy said, "Let me know what I owe you," and headed for his dressing room.

I didn't know what to say; I always just took whatever I was offered. I asked Bill Graham, "What should I ask for? What does a gig like this usually pay?" Bill laughed.

"You got him over a barrel! Ask for whatever you want. He's got to pay you."

That was no help. I needed to know what was customary. I didn't want to embarrass myself by asking for too much or too little, and I wished Dizzy would just hand me some money. Anything would have been fine.

"How does thirty dollars sound?" I asked Bill. "Do you think that's too much?" I had made thirty dollars on a recent jazz concert.

"Ask for anything you want," said Bill. You heard him say to tell him what he owed you." So I told Bill thirty dollars, and he got it from Dizzy. As he handed me the money, he said, "Dizzy wants to know if you want to stay on the band."

That really turned me around. I thought about it for while and then thanked him and said no. On the train back to Toronto, and many

times since, I regretted that decision. But I didn't want to hang Teddy
Charles by leaving on such short notice, even though he didn't have
anything booked after Toronto. I was also a little scared of Dizzy, and
I knew he wouldn't keep me on his band once we got back to New
York where there were much better bass players available.

Later I discovered that Dizzy was a wonderful person and a natural
teacher. I regret having turned down the opportunity to learn from
him for however long that job might have lasted.

chapter 17

Slim Gaillard, Stan Getz

I went back to Toronto and finished out Teddy Charles's last week at
the Town Tavern. With nothing else booked, we were ready to return
to New York and scuffle until something else turned up, but then Slim
Gaillard arrived in Toronto to do two weeks at the Colonial Tavern,
and he came without a rhythm section. Slim had been traveling with a
bassist and drummer from the West Indies. They discovered at the
Canadian border that if they left the country, they would have to start
their U.S. immigration process all over again. Slim sent them back to
New York and came to Toronto looking for a bass player and a drummer.

Teddy had worked with Slim before. He suggested that he and I take
the jobs. (Teddy was a drummer before he switched to the vibraphone.) We agreed to put our salaries together and split three ways
with Don Roberts, so our trio could stay together. Slim, agreeable to
the plan, rented Teddy a set of drums and told him to bring his vibes
as well.

Slim was twice as tall as Teddy. He made comic use of this contrast
when they played vibraphone duets. He would reach over Teddy to
play distant notes, would chase him around the vibes while they continued to play, and sometimes would capture Teddy's head under his arm

while they both hammered madly at the bars. After the first night, Slim said, "I like having you at the vibes. I think I'll get a local drummer and keep you up here."

Teddy had a better idea:

"Bill used to be a drummer, and Don Roberts can play some bass. If you can make it that way, it will keep our trio working."

Slim was willing, and that was how we finished out the job.

Though he was principally a singer, Slim played guitar and a little piano.

"If I wasn't so lazy," he told me, "I could have been really good on the guitar. But when I get things to where they're just okay, I quit working on them. Like that amplifier over there."

He pointed to an unfinished plywood box with a naked speaker cone peering through a sawed-out circle on one side.

"I made that myself, and it works fine, but I just never got around to finishing the cabinet to make it look nice."

I knew Slim from his 1938 hit record with Slam Stewart, "Flat Foot Floogie," and I had seen his act many times at Birdland. He was a natural entertainer, very much at home in front of an audience.

One night at Birdland I saw Billie Holiday and a friend walk in and sit down at a table in front of Slim. Billie looked beautiful, tired, and a little drunk. Slim was singing a nonsense tune with his rhythm section when he saw her. He immediately stopped and acknowledged her presence, telling the audience that the world's greatest singer was in the house.

As Billie smiled and took a bow, Slim asked her if she felt like sitting in. Billie handed her chihuahua to her companion and allowed Slim to help her onto the bandstand. She gave him her key and sang two perfect choruses of "Them There Eyes." It was as if twenty years of her hard life had suddenly fallen away. Her voice was sure, her natural swing irresistible.

Billie accepted her applause and began to sing "I Cover the Waterfront." At the slower tempo the liquor she had been drinking began to undermine her control. Her voice wavered slightly off pitch on sustained notes, and she lost the ebullience that had carried her through the first tune. Billie began to look uncomfortable. She took the song out at the end of one chorus and during the applause looked sadly at Slim.

He stepped quickly to her side, put an arm around her and began to improvise a ballad: "Billie Holiday, I Love You." The lyrics were simple doggerel, but the sentiment was genuine and touching. As Slim sang his love and admiration, Billie recovered her composure. Glowing with appreciation, she gave Slim a kiss on the cheek and returned to her table as the audience applauded.

One of Slim's favorite jokes was to turn his palms upward and play a few bars of Debussy's "Claire de Lune" with the backs of his fingers. And he liked to make facetious announcements, like:

"Drinks on the house tonight! All drinks on the house. They got plenty ladders outside, and you can go up and have your drinks on the house, right after you pay for them."

He had invented comical nonsense words like "vouty, roony, reeny-mo," and "vouse," and would make up impromptu songs using them. He occasionally threw in a smattering of Spanish, but in Toronto I was surprised to discover that Slim spoke Greek like a native. One night he overheard a group of people speaking that language among themselves while they were being seated near our bandstand. To their amazement and delight, Slim did the rest of that set's songs and patter in Greek. He kept the rest of the audience happy with asides like, "Don't worry, we just talkin' 'bout cheeseburgers."

"Where did you learn Greek?" I asked him later. He told me that when he was a boy his father, a merchant seaman, had left him in the care of a family on an island in Greece for several years.

It was during that gig with Slim that I first heard a Fender bass. Teddy and Don and I went to hear a matinee performance that Lionel Hampton's band was playing at a theater in Toronto. The bass player was holding what looked like a large electric guitar, and his notes popped out through the band in a way we'd never heard before. He sounded wonderful.

I loved the energy and swing of the band, but I was a little put off by Hamp's antics on stage. He played well, but he was embarrassingly servile to the audience. Black musicians called that sort of bowing and scraping "Uncle Tomming." We discovered that Hamp wasn't unaware of the term. As Milt Buckner, his pianist, was playing a lively solo, he hit a heavy block chord, leaped to his feet, ran around his piano stool with exaggerated urgency and sat back down again just in time to play the downbeat of the next measure. As the audience laughed and applauded, Hamp ran over to the piano and shouted, "Buck! Stop Tommin'!"

When I looked up at Hampton's trumpet section, there sat Quincy Jones. After I left Seattle, Hampton had passed through town needing a trumpet player. He hired Quincy because he was recommended to him as a good arranger. I found Q. backstage after the show. He was pleased that Hampton was using some of his charts, but he was disappointed that his solo efforts hadn't made much impression on Hamp.

"You have to juggle and tap dance on this band in order to get any solos," he told us.

When our gig with Slim Gaillard came to an end, Teddy got on the phone to see if Ray Barron had found us another booking. Teddy and Ray had designed a code to inform us of any new jobs while avoiding the cost of the call. Ted would call Ray's number in New York and tell the operator, "I want to place a person-to-person call to Teddy Charles." When Ray answered, he might inform us of our next gig by telling the operator something like this:

"Teddy's not here, but he can be reached at Squeezer's Bar in Rochester between June seventh and thirteenth."

Or, if there was no job, Ray would tell her, "Teddy will be back in New York next week."

Since the operators always left the line open while talking, Teddy would get the information free of charge.

We were making so little money that it often took all we had just to check out of our hotel and buy gas to get to the next gig. On the first night of a new job we would usually make an advance against our salary to buy food, but in Ocean City, New Jersey, a surly club owner refused to let us have any money before payday. We had to hock a pair of bongos, a camera, and a suit in order to eat that week. When we got our money at the end of the job we paid for our rooms, stopped by the pawn shop to ransom our belongings, gassed up the car and got back to New York with just enough money left to check in again at the Prescott.

Art Mardigan was in town for a short stay. He was playing with Woody Herman, who had a booking at Roseland. When Art drove into town he parked for a moment in the loading zone in front of the Taft Hotel, where Woody had told him he'd be staying. He went into the lobby, called Woody on the house phone and said, "I'm here. I'm going over to Roseland to set up."

He went back out to the car and found it had been broken into and his drums stolen while he was on the phone. Art called Phil Arabia and arranged to borrow his drum set in time for the job at Roseland that night. The next day he went to work and found an empty space on the bandstand where the drums had been. He asked the janitor where he had put them.

"What do you mean?" was the answer, "You came and got them this morning!"

Art thought that having two sets of drums stolen in two days established some sort of record.

Teddy Charles met a singer named Amanda Sullivan, who billed herself as "The Blonde Calypso." Her husband and manager, Bob Phillips,
hired us to play for her on a show called "Fun and Fashions" that ran
for a couple of months on WPIX-TV on Sundays at eleven P.M. Since
an airline was the sponsor, Teddy sometimes got paid in plane tickets,
and had to find buyers for them in order to get our money. I spent
much of my salary fixing up a cheap cold-water flat that I had found
at 22 Cornelia Street in Greenwich Village.

Wanting a New York showcase for Amanda, Phillips made a deal
with the owner of the Wigwam Bar in the Iroquois Hotel on West Forty-
fourth Street. He arranged to put Amanda and our trio in the back
room, a space that now houses a club called Judy's. The Iroquois sat
next to the legendary Hotel Algonquin, where the *New Yorker* writers
of the 1930s had their famous Round Table, but none of the Algonquin's elegance had rubbed off on its neighbor. The Wigwam Bar in
the Iroquois had neon Budweiser signs in the window.

In those days the back room was decorated to look like the inside of
a log cabin, with logs made of the same dark brown leatherette that
covered the banquette seats in the booths along the walls. Fake cabin
windows between the booths looked out onto painted scenes of Indian
warriors on horseback (certainly not Iroquois) circling Conestoga wag-
ons. The boss gave us permission to redecorate if we could cover the
original decor without harming it.

Bob Phillips wanted to call the place "The Bermuda Room," and asked
me what I thought we could do to suggest the tropics. I thought that
the easiest way to cover the fake log walls was to hang bamboo blinds
on them. I offered to do the decorating myself for a hundred dollars
plus the cost of materials. Bob gave me some spending money and said
he'd settle up with me after the job was finished.

The Yellow Pages led me to a dingy little shop on Water Street near
the Fulton Fish Market where bamboo blinds were very inexpensive.
They also had mats woven from palm leaves. I bought a few to cover
the bandstand wall. In the back of the shop I found some halves of
bamboo tree trunks that had been there since they were used to decorate the lobby of the Chrysler building when it opened. The guy prac-
tically gave them to me just to get rid of them. They made perfect
edging for the "windows" and the bandstand area.

The bamboo and a sky-blue paint job on the ceiling brightened up the room very nicely. Now I needed to cover up those Indian massacre scenes in the windows. I got some free scenic photos from the Bermuda Trade Association and had two of them blown up to the size of the false windows. Mounted there, they completed the illusion that the room was a bamboo hut on a tropic island. With straw gels in the stage lights to give a sunshine effect, the place looked quite nice, and I just managed to pay for everything with the money Bob had given me. On opening night all our friends came, including Tony Bennett, a young singer I'd met through songwriter Jack Segal. Amanda did her calypso numbers and we played jazz in between.

I was intrigued with the possibilities of the Fender bass. I bought one and used it on this job. Teddy jokingly called it a "bassophone." A reporter for the *International Musician* took him seriously. He wrote, "Bill Crow, bass man with the Teddy Charles Trio, is one of the first musicians in the East to feature the Bassophone, a new type of bass fiddle resembling the electric guitar."

Things went along swimmingly for a couple of weeks, and then, when we came to work one night, we discovered that we had been thrown out of the club. The owner told Teddy that Bob Phillips had hired a couple of B-girls to sit at his bar and talk his customers into moving to our back room to spend their money. He was outraged, the deal was off, and the gig was over. I never got paid for decorating the place.

While we were at the Bermuda Room, Don Roberts was offered a job with Benny Goodman. He left the Teddy Charles Trio, and Jimmy Raney replaced him until the place closed. Jimmy had been playing guitar with Stan Getz's quintet, but Stan was on the West Coast for a couple of months, leaving Jimmy at liberty. When Stan called Jimmy for his next gig, a week at the Hi-Hat in Boston, he asked him to get a bass player, and Jim hired me.

Stan and I were nearly the same age, but he was light-years ahead of me in talent and experience. He had left the high school he was attending in the Bronx when he was fifteen to go on the road with Jack Teagarden's band. By the time I got out of the Army, he had already been through the bands of Bob Chester, Stan Kenton, Jimmy Dorsey, Benny Goodman, Randy Brooks, Herbie Fields, Butch Stone, and Woody Herman, making records along the way that made him famous as a virtuoso of the tenor sax. While I was learning to play the bass in New York, Stan was touring and recording with his own group.

In Boston, Jimmy Raney introduced me to Stan and the other members of the quintet: Roy Haynes, our drummer; and Jerry Kaminsky, our pianist. We set up on the bandstand at the Hi-Hat, a small room packed with jazz fans. Stan kicked off an up-tune, and in the middle of the second chorus my D-string snapped. I tried to find the notes I needed on other strings, but I was making a lot of mistakes.

There was another bass under the piano that belonged to the bassist with the intermission group. I quickly laid my bass down and grabbed it, missing only a couple of measures in the process. But as I began to play, I discovered that there was such a thing as a left-handed bass! Its strings were set up in reverse order. I tried to rethink my fingering in mirror image, but I played more wrong notes than I had been playing on my own crippled instrument. I'm afraid I didn't make a very good first impression with Stan on that tune.

Jerry Kaminsky was a wonderful pianist with a lovely touch. He delighted us every night with his sensitive accompaniment and imaginative solos, but for some reason he was sure that no one liked his playing. No matter how much we praised him, he remained convinced that he wasn't making it, and he spent most of that week's intermissions sitting morosely in the bandroom, comforting himself with pints of Christian Brothers brandy.

Terry Gibbs told me that when Jerry worked for him, one of the highlights of each set had been the featured solo he would have Jerry play. After one set a customer called Terry over to his table and raved about Jerry so much that Terry hurried backstage with the good news.

"Jerry," he said, "there's a guy out there who's thrilled with your playing! He wants to meet you. He says you're the greatest thing he's ever heard!"

Jerry looked up gloomily.

"Yeah, one guy!"

When our week at the Hi-Hat ended, Stan asked me to stay with the quintet, and we opened at Birdland two days later. Roy Haynes wanted to stay in Boston, so Stan hired Frank Isola to replace him on drums. I was excited about playing at Birdland with Stan, but nervous about my lack of experience. I had played a few Monday nights at the club, but this was the headline group, and everyone would be expecting dynamite players. To make matters worse, there was a live radio broadcast on opening night.

As I carried my bass onto the bandstand and removed the cover, I looked over toward the bar. There stood Oscar Pettiford talking to Charlie Mingus. A little farther down stood John Simmons chatting with Curly Russell. In the bleachers I saw Gene Ramey, Tommy Potter, and Clyde Lombardi. To my eyes there seemed to be nothing but bass players waiting to hear our first set. My stomach sank a little, but I said to myself, "Well, this is me. I can't play as well as any of these guys, so I'll just have to do the best I can."

I got through the first number without being denounced as a charlatan by the assembled bassists, and since our band sounded good, I relaxed a little. But I never faced a tougher audience than the one at Birdland that night.

chapter 18

Pee Wee Marquette

Whenever musicians talk about the old Birdland, they always mention Pee Wee Marquette, the master of ceremonies. William Clayton Marquette, three feet nine inches tall, was usually nattily dressed in a brown pin-stripe vested suit and a floral tie, or a dark green velvet suit with a large bow tie. On special occasions he wore tails. His miniature suits were fairly zoot. His belt line was at his armpits, his trousers were heavily pleated and tightly cuffed, and his box-back jackets featured extra-wide lapels.

Pee Wee wore one of two facial expressions while performing his duties as master of ceremonies: a superior, disapproving frown that indicated the importance of his office, and an exaggerated toothy grimace that he usually reserved for mooching tips. Not just from customers—Pee Wee expected a gratuity from each bandleader that worked at Birdland, and since he announced the name of each musician before each set, on payday he let it be known that he expected a dollar per musician for the publicity.

When Terry Gibbs first took a group into Birdland he was told that Pee Wee expected to be taken care of. Feeling embarrassed about the idea of handing Pee Wee cash, Terry bought him a nice pair of cufflinks and had them gift-wrapped. When Terry gave him the package at the club, Pee Wee said suspiciously, "What's this?"

He opened it, and frowned.

"Cufflinks!" he snorted loudly, pushing the box back into Terry's hand. "Man, I got cufflinks! Don't give me no cufflinks, GIVE ME THE BREAD!"

Bob Brookmeyer was offended by Pee Wee's cupidity. When he took a quintet into Birdland in the mid-'50s, Bob refused to tip Pee Wee and instructed his musicians not to give him anything either. Pee Wee retaliated by refusing to announce the band. Morris Levy, the boss, finally laid down the law. Pee Wee had to announce the musicians, tip or no tip. His subsequent announcements of Brookmeyer's group dripped with disdain.

Pee Wee had one of the first adjustable butane cigarette lighters on the market. He used it to ostentatiously light the large cigars he sometimes smoked, but he carried it mainly as a service to patrons at Birdland. To compensate for his height he would adjust the lighter for maximum flame length. It was an unnerving experience in a dark nightclub to put a cigarette in your mouth and have a two-foot flame suddenly shoot up from waist level with Pee Wee leering hopefully at the other end.

Pee Wee's voice was high-pitched and brassy. Though he did his best to enunciate carefully, he frequently slipped into the dialect of Montgomery, Alabama, his birthplace. He would climb laboriously onto the Birdland bandstand, pull the microphone down to his chin and shout officiously:

"AND NOW, LAYDUHS AND GENTLEMEN, BIRDLAND, THE JAZZ CORNAH OF THE WORLD, IS PROUD TO PRESENT, THE ONE AND ONLAH. . . ."

After laboriously naming the bandleader and all the musicians and asking for a "large round of applaw" for the band, he would climb back down to floor level and admonish piercingly, "All right, now, fellas, let's get right UP heah! We don't want no LULLS 'roun' heah! No LULLS!"

Pee Wee often had trouble with names. He usually consulted his notes, but that didn't prevent him from announcing Dinah Washington as Ruth Brown on one occasion. Most musicians counted themselves fortunate if he merely made their names unrecognizable. Teddy Kotick would grind his teeth with fury every time Pee Wee announced Charlie Parker's quintet:

". . .and on the BASS, Teddy KO-TEX!"

"Just don't say my name at all!" Teddy would hiss.

With the Stan Getz quintet, Pee Wee did fine with "on the PIANO, JE-

ruh Ka-MIN-skuh, on the GIT-tah, JIMmuh RAYnuh, on the BASS, BEAL
CROW . . ." But then, frowning at the piece of paper in his hand, he
continued doubtfully, "and on the DRUM . . ."

He puzzled a moment over Frank Isola's name. I whispered the pro-
nunciation to him, and Pee Wee continued with supreme confidence,
"and on the DRUM, . . . PHIL BROWN!"

Phil had been Stan's drummer at a previous appearance at Birdland.

One night during his announcement, Pee Wee put together a particularly pompous phrase filled with multisyllabic adjectives. He paused
and looked craftily behind him at the band.

"Ol' Pee Wee's gettin up into the BIG woids tonight! And, when I
gets up into the BIG woids, sometimes y'all don't undah-STAND me! But,
I'm IS tellin' you, this band is the GREATEST!"

A Birdland jazz tour featuring the Basie band once used Pee Wee as
emcee. Benny Powell, then a member of Basie's trombone section, played
me a tape of one of the concerts on that tour. As the applause waned
following a number, Pee Wee's voice began with strident importance:

"And NOW, ladies and gentlemen, befo' the band play this next NUM-
BAH, I just want to SAY, how HAPPY we all are to BE heah in, uh . . . in,
uh . . . uh . . ."

His voice dwindled. Loud whispers from the saxophone section
prompted, "Topeka! Topeka!" Pee Wee surged back to full volume:

"Heah in POTEEka!"

Pee Wee's tongue often fell prey to spoonerisms and malapropisms.
He once announced the presence in Birdland's audience of Mr. Marlo
Brandon. On another night he announced that Duke Ellington had
won the *Down Beat* poll, and that "the man from *Down Beat* magazine
will now step up to the bandstand to award the PLAGUE to Duke Ellington!"

After a few years' absence from Birdland I returned for a week in
1961 with Quincy Jones's big band, subbing for Buddy Catlett. Pee Wee
met me at the door when I arrived with my bass.

"Beal Crow! You used to work here in the old days! With Stan Getz!"

He named the other members of Stan's old group, and somehow
Jimmy Raney's name became embedded in his mind. When he announced Quincy's band, Pee Wee included in the roster, ". . . and Jimmah RAYnah on the bass!"

I told the rest of the band not to say anything to Pee Wee so we
could see how long he'd continue with the mistake.

At the end of the week I was still being announced on every set as
Jimmy Raney. As I got off the bandstand after the penultimate set,

Jerome Richardson, the band manager, was getting the payroll ready in the back room, and he handed me my money. I went out into the house to chat with Sarah Vaughan and Dizzy Gillespie, who were at a corner table. Soon Pee Wee began rounding up the musicians for pay-day.

He came by our table twice to announce, "Say, Jimmah, Jerome's paying off in the back room."

I'd say, "Okay, Pee Wee," and go back to my conversation. It was nearly time for the last set, and Pee Wee was getting worried.

"Say, Jimmah, Jerome wants to see you in the back room!"

"That's okay, Pee Wee, he already saw me."

Pee Wee's eyes became round with concern.

"Well, you know, when he sees you, YOU SEE ME!"

I pretended innocence. "What for?" I asked. Pee Wee began to fawn.

"Now, Jimmah, you remembah in the old days, you always took care of old Pee Wee at the end of the week!"

I leaned across the table and looked him in the eye.

"What's my name?"

Pee Wee's face was a study in confusion. He gaped at me for a min-ute, and then trotted over to Drayton, the headwaiter. There was a whispered exchange between them, and then Pee Wee scurried back to where I was sitting. He was all smiles.

"Beal Crow! How come you let me say the wrong name?"

To correct matters, and to earn his dollar, Pee Wee hurried to the bandstand. He announced Quincy and the entire band, saving me for last. Then he gave me the full treatment: ". . . AND, on the BASS, one of the GREATest BASS playahs of ALL TIME, a musician of GREAT renown, the GREAT, the ONE and ONLAH, . . . BEAL . . . CROW!"

As Pee Wee left the bandstand, I hurried to the microphone before the rest of the band came up.

"Ladies and gentlemen," I said, extracting a dollar from my wallet, "I would now like to present this one dollar bill, legal tender, United States currency, to our inimitable master of ceremonies, Pee Wee Mar-quette. Not because he has earned it. Not because he deserves it in any way. But simply because he has asked me for it."

I yanked rhythmically on the ends of the dollar bill as I held it up to the microphone, making a popping noise over the speakers. Pee Wee came scuttling between the tables and chairs, his hand stretched high over his head.

"Don't put your business in the street!" he cried as he snatched the bill from my fingers and tucked it into his pocket.

chapter 19

Papa Jo

The Stan Getz quintet joined several other jazz groups for a concert at Carnegie Hall in the fall of 1952. Charlie Parker's group went on first, and I was surprised to see a stagehand walk out in front of them and plant an old-fashioned bird-cage microphone at the front of the stage. With the wonderful acoustics at Carnegie, amplification seemed unnecessary. We listened from out front, and I whispered to Stan, "That mike is terrible! It's loud, and it's distorting the sound."

Stan said, "Let's not use the damn thing."

When we were announced, he turned the mike off and we were able to enjoy the natural acoustics of that beautiful hall. Duke Jordan sounded especially good. We didn't always get to hear him play on such a fine piano. There was a live mike somewhere in the hall, though. Years later a couple of the tunes we played on that concert came out on a bootleg record album.

Stan Getz had been recording for Teddy Reig's Roost label, but he signed with Norman Granz just before I joined the group. Our first recordings for Granz were a set of standard ballads that, because of the new formats in the record industry, were released three ways. There were 78 rpm versions on the Mercury label, 45 rpms on the Clef label, and 10–inch LPs on the Norgran label. Jerry Kaminsky, still convinced that Stan didn't like his playing, left the quintet just before we recorded. Stan hired Duke Jordan to replace him.

Teddy Reig talked Stan into doing one last date for him. He was having all his artists record George Shearing's "Lullaby of Birdland" as a tie-in with the club and Symphony Sid's radio disc-jockey show, which it sponsored. To make it possible for Stan to record the tune for him, Teddy told him he would report the session as having been done before the starting date of Stan's contract with Granz. Discographies show that last Roost date as having taken place on December 5, 1952, but it was actually done around December 17th. We recorded "Autumn Leaves," "Fools Rush In," and "These Foolish Things," along with "Lullaby of Birdland."

After we made our second album for Granz, Stan changed drummers in a surprising way. We finished a short road trip and came home to New York one Sunday night with a week's layoff before our next job. Stan called me on Monday to say that he'd been able to fill in the week with a last-minute booking at Birdland, starting the next day. When I arrived at the club I found Kenny Clarke setting up his drums, and assumed that Frank Isola, our regular drummer, had booked something else for the week. But an hour after we played the radio broadcast on the first set, I saw Frank sitting in the bleachers beside the bandstand. I went over on the break.

"What's happening, Frank?" I asked. He grinned wryly.

"I turned on the radio and discovered that I was fired!"

Frank worked with Stan again later, but not until after I had left the band.

Kenny Clarke and Duke Jordan ("Klook and Duke") hit a nice groove together, and they taught me some good things about rhythm section playing. Klook introduced me to a pair of my heros, Lester Young and Jo Jones, who often visited Birdland. I stood listening to Jo and Lester talking, but I couldn't understand a thing they were saying. They spoke a special language that they had developed when they were together on the Basie band. I knew most of the more common terms of "hip-talk," the argot of jazz musicians, but it took me a while to learn enough of Jo and Lester's figures of speech to make any sense of conversations with them.

I went to visit Jo when he was playing at Snookie's. He had his own special way of "signifying" to the audience. As he played, his sparkling dark eyes would register admiration of his hands as they flashed effortlessly about the drum set with the sticks and brushes, or sometimes with palms and fingertips tapping the drumheads. His eyebrows would raise and lower flirtatiously, matching the subtleties of his musical punctuation.

Sometimes Jo would turn while playing and make some inaudible but clearly delightful remark to Gene Ramey, the bass player standing at his elbow. I envied Gene and wished I were playing in his place. A few years later I got my wish. I was on a bandstand next to Jo, playing along with his lovely cymbal beat. It was just as much fun as I had thought it would be.

As the band settled into a pleasant groove, Jo turned his thousand-watt smile on me, raised his eyebrows significantly, and said something like, "Sa, voos-da hazzumou. Vazzazza?"

It was absolute gibberish, but, to the audience, it looked like he had made a witty inside comment. I was disappointed and somewhat disillusioned.

The older generation of musicians felt a lot of pressure when bebop came along. Some of the younger players thought Jo was old-fashioned, a has-been. The worst I ever heard him play was in a group with Oscar Pettiford on bass. Oscar kept yelling at Jo on a very fast tempo:

"Come on, old man, keep it up there! This ain't no Kansas City blues we're playing!"

Jo worked himself into a frenzy, his usual confident smile frozen on his face like a death rictus as he bashed murderously at his top cymbal and wiped Oscar out with a loud four-four on his bass drum. There was little love on the bandstand that night.

When Bob Brookmeyer hired Jo in 1956 for a Storyville album with Zoot Sims, Hank Jones, and me, I spent the set-up time chatting with Jo, letting him know that we loved and respected him and were proud to have him on the date. He responded by playing with great imagination and finesse. When I complimented Jo on something he played, he passed it off with a shrug. He said, "Walter Page! Walter Page taught me that!"

Page was a band leader in Kansas City before he became the bassist in the "All American Rhythm Section" of the original Count Basie band, and Jo said it was Walter who established the character of that section, with the bass and guitar walking a four-four line together, the piano decorating sparsely, and the drummer giving the bass and guitar a chance to be heard by using light cymbal sounds to propel the band. Jo called it "giving the music a chance to breathe." Walter died of pneumonia in 1957, an illness that got its start when he spent a couple of hours standing with his bass in a snowstorm, unable to get a taxi to stop for him.

Jo had been a tap dancer in his youth, and he always wore a pair of tap-dancing shoes (without taps) when he played. Those shoes became an integral part of his equipment. He carried them in his trap case and slipped them on when he sat down at the drums. They became shabby over the years, but he still wore them. When I was playing at the Town Tavern in Toronto I noticed an ancient pair of patent leather shoes in a cubbyhole in the checkroom. Sure enough, they were Jo's playing shoes. He was working there with a local band that alternated weeks with traveling jazz groups.

Sam Berger, the club owner, told me that earlier in the month he'd gone through a terrible experience. Jo had finished his week's work and had parked his shoes in the checkroom. When Jo came back to work the following week, his shoes were missing. He raised a cry of alarm that set off a full search. Sam called the cleanup man, who remembered throwing them out, thinking they were worthless. Jo wouldn't accept Sam's offer to buy him a new pair. He folded his arms, closed his eyes, and refused to play until he got his old shoes back.

Sam found a substitute drummer for the night, and the next morning he took a crew of searchers out to the city dump. The dumpmaster was able to tell them the general area where trucks from downtown Toronto had emptied their loads on the fateful day, and after hours of searching, they actually found the shoes, tidied them up and returned them to Jo. I believe he used them to the end of his career.

As he grew older, younger musicians, out of respect, began calling him Papa Jo. I was happy that he accepted me as a friend. He called me "Section," meaning I was a member of his rhythm section family. Whenever I saw him in his later years, he would seize my arm and exhort me for several minutes about something that was clearly a burning issue with him, but as he often spoke in a private language of symbolic allusion, I couldn't always make out the details of what he was saying.

It was clear that Jo felt his contribution to jazz was being overlooked. He didn't understand how someone who had been so at the center of things could wind up broke, working as a schlepper in Frank Ippolito's drum shop. I didn't understand it either.

During the late 1970s, when it became fashionable for men to wear decorative gold medallions of various designs on gold neck chains, Papa Jo began to wear a miniature Zildjian cymbal. When he met someone wearing some other medallion, Jo would jab a finger angrily at his chest and say, "I *earned* mine, daddy! Where did you earn yours?"

He certainly did earn his. His cymbal work established a lasting standard for other drummers. Many of them are unaware of it, but the present generation of drummers is still playing a lot of Jo Jones.

chapter 20

Stan the Man

Stan Getz was the fair-haired boy of the jazz world, but his life got complicated. Like many of the musicians on Woody Herman's famous Four Brothers band, Stan had begun using heroin in the 1940s, and the drug haunted him for many years. Drugs were an on-again off-again thing with him during the time I was with him. Consequently, though his playing was beautiful, I never knew what to expect from him personally.

Heroin had a different effect on Stan than it did on most junkies I knew. The others just became passive and distant when they were high. Stan had a pleasant disposition when he was sober, but when using drugs he could be awash with maudlin sentiment one minute and cold, distrustful, and cruel the next. Discussing him with friends at Jim and Andy's bar one day, Zoot Sims said, "Yeah, Stan's a nice bunch of guys!"

I had a terrifying experience with Stan one night after a concert in the Bronx. He had driven me to the job with my bass, and on the way home he asked if I'd mind waiting while he stopped to visit some friends. He drove to a private house where a party was going on. Stan introduced me to a lot of people, including Blackie, an old schoolmate of his. The lady of the house made me a sandwich and a cup of coffee, and I chatted with her for a while in the kitchen.

Eventually I began to wonder where Stan was, and when he was going to drive me home. I found him in the basement rec room with four or five other guys. He was leaning on the pool table, tying up his arm and getting ready to shoot up some heroin. I said, "Come on, Stan, don't do that. It's time to go home."

"I'll be right with you," he frowned. "I just want to do up one more little taste."

He injected the drug, loosened the tie on his arm, turned pale, and collapsed on the floor. Blackie quickly rolled him over on his back.

"He isn't breathing!"

"Oh, my God!" yelled the host. "Get him out of here! I don't want no stiff in my house!"

"Push on his ribs!" I shouted. "Artificial respiration! He's turning blue!"

Blackie pumped his chest while I pried his mouth open and pulled his tongue forward. After a few tense moments, Stan made a strangling noise and sucked in some air. His color returned, and he began breathing on his own again.

When he opened his eyes, he scowled at Blackie and said, "Man, get off me! You're getting my suit all dirty!"

"Motherfucker! You were dead!" yelled Blackie, jumping to his feet. "I've been pumping air into you! You were blue, man! You were dead!"

Stan got up and brushed himself off. He gave everyone a surly look and said, "Well, I bet I'm higher than any of you."

As they cursed Stan for his ingratitude, I got him upstairs and into his car and drove him to his home in Long Island.

Stan and his wife, Beverly (Buddy Stewart's sister), had a small house on Shelter Lane in Levittown. I often stayed there overnight after driving Stan home. I would spend the next morning playing with the kids, Steve and David, and chatting with Bev.

Stan's habit began to encroach on his music. After he showed up high on a couple of jobs, Jimmy Raney left the group. Kenny Clarke and Duke Jordan and I played with him as a quartet for a few weeks, and then Kenny and Duke also left. Stan began to make an effort to stay away from heroin, and from then until I left him, he seemed to be functioning without drugs most of the time, but later they again dominated his life, and it took him years to get completely away from them.

When Klook and Duke left, Stan told me that he had decided to try a new sound with his band. He had hired pianist John Williams and drummer Al Levitt, and Bob Brookmeyer was going to join us on valve trombone as soon as he worked out his notice: I think he was playing piano with Tex Beneke's band. I knew Bob from jam sessions at Med Flory's apartment on West Seventy-first Street, and was eager to play with him. While we were waiting for him, Stan hired Johnny Mandel to play trombone with us for a couple of weeks in a Baltimore jazz club.

Gerry Mulligan's first quartet record with Chet Baker had been out for a little while. Since we all liked the music, John transcribed some of Gerry's tunes from the record for us. We were staying at the Parkside in Washington, a musicians' hotel that we preferred to any of the accommodations Baltimore had to offer, and during our nightly drives to and from the job, John taught us the tunes he'd transcribed during the day. He also wrote us a couple of his own things. By the end of the gig he had expanded our repertoire considerably. One night Stan said, "Look, John, if you want to stay on the band, I can call Brookmeyer and tell him I've changed my mind."

"No, thanks anyway," said John. "I've got to get back to New York. I never get anything accomplished when I'm out of town."

We were sorry to see Mandel go, but we were delighted with Brookmeyer. His great talent turned us into an entirely different group. Bob wrote several attractive original tunes for us to play, and to match Bob's sound, Stan broadened and deepened his own. We were all excited about our new quintet.

A couple of weeks later, in Boston, Stan told Nat Hentoff how much he admired Mulligan's quartet. He said that his dream would be to bring Gerry and Chet back to New York and have Gerry write for a pianoless sextet with Brookmeyer and himself. He was so specific about the details of this fantasy that Nat thought Stan had discussed it with Gerry. He wrote a story for *Down Beat* announcing Stan's impending merger with Mulligan. In the following issue of the magazine there was a letter from Gerry in which he disowned the idea, and suggested that Stan go get his own band. Actually, the sextet Mulligan put together three years later with Brookmeyer, Zoot Sims, and Jon Eardley was very much the sound Stan had in mind.

Once, when we had a week off in New York between bookings, Stan invited the band to stay at his house rather than check into a hotel. It saved us money and gave us a chance to rehearse some new material. While we were there, Brookmeyer got a call from tenor man Buddy Arnold. Buddy was rehearsing a small band and wanted Bob to write some arrangements for it. They agreed on a price for a few charts, and Bob retreated to Stan's spare bedroom to write them. He delivered them to Buddy at the end of the week.

Bob later discovered that Buddy had left his apartment for a rehearsal carrying his new Brookmeyer arrangements but arrived at Nola Studios emptyhanded. Too late, he realized what he had done. He'd bought a *Daily News* to read on the train and tossed it aside as he reached his station with the music mixed up somewhere in the pages of the newspaper. Buddy never got to hear Bob's charts.

Bob was also working on some tunes for a record date that Stan had set up with Norman Granz. He wrote a couple of originals and said he'd also like to find a standard that hadn't been done to death. I happened to have the sheet music to "Have You Met Miss Jones," which Jack Segal had given me. I loaned it to Bob, and he wrote the tune out

for tenor and trombone. I could always tell when a musician had learned
that song from our record. He would include as part of the melody a
little four-note phrase that Bob added at the end of the first eight bars.

In those days Norman Granz's record labels carried the legend, "Under the personal supervision of Norman Granz." He sat in the booth
during all our record dates. When we recorded our first Brookmeyer
original, Granz called out on the intercom,

"What's the name of that one?"

" 'A Rustic Dance,' " said Bob.

"Great. Let's call it 'Rustic Hop.' "

After recording Bob's next tune, Granz again asked for the title.

" 'Trolley Car,' " said Bob.

"We got a good mix on that one," said Norman. "Let's call it 'Cool
Mix.' "

We thought it presumptuous of Granz to rename Bob's tunes so casually, but Bob just shrugged and laughed. The records were released
with Granz's titles.

Stan booked a concert for us in Pittsburgh that was a disaster. The
Philadelphia promoter who arranged it agreed to provide transportation for us, and told us to meet him at Joe Glaser's office around noon
on the day of the concert. He showed up late, with two cars. The one
he was driving had his overweight girlfriend sitting in the front seat.
There was only room in the back seat for Stan and his horn. Without
our instruments, the rest of us could have squeezed into the other car,
but with a bass, a drum set, and a trombone case, there was no way we
could do it.

Stan owned a station wagon, but it was parked at his mother's house
in Queens. He and I took the subway out there and drove the wagon
back to Manhattan, so our three-car caravan didn't leave for Pittsburgh
until late afternoon. As the Pennsylvania Turnpike ended west of Philadelphia in those days, there was no direct connection to the New Jersey Turnpike, but there was a way to avoid Philadelphia by taking Route
202 to the turnpike entrance at King of Prussia, Pennsylvania. I asked
the promoter if he knew the way, and he assured us that he did. Then
he led us right through Philadelphia at rush hour.

It took us forever to creep through the city and out again. Then, on
the turnpike, we ran into a violent rainstorm. I was driving Stan's station wagon. The rain began to come down so hard that the wipers
couldn't handle it. The wind made the car difficult to steer. In the
middle of all this, the catch on the car's hood broke loose, and the wind
banged it back against the windshield. I was able to steer to the side of

the road and bring the car safely to a stop by peering out under the hood hinge. Fortunately, the windshield hadn't broken. We got out in the rain, bent the hood back down, tied it in place, and forged on, soaking wet. When the rain stopped we made a little better time, but I was exhausted when the long drive was finally over.

We arrived in Pittsburgh an hour late, and found the street in front of the theater crowded with people. Some of them cursed and shook their fists at us when they recognized Stan. With no word from us, the theater had canceled the concert, and had just finished refunding everyone's money. We had to turn around and drive back to New York without playing a note.

chapter 21

Claude Thornhill

In April 1953, Stan Getz changed bass players. He and Brookmeyer decided they would like to try Teddy Kotick, who had worked and recorded with Charlie Parker. Stan broke the news to me at the end of a week we played in Philadelphia. I was bitterly disappointed, but accepted the news realistically. Stan certainly deserved the best bass player he could get. His quintet went on to Kansas City and California, and I went back to New York.

The next evening I looked in at Charlie's Tavern. Winston Welch, Claude Thornhill's drummer, told me that Claude's band was in town, and that Teddy Kotick had left it to join Stan Getz.

"Tell me something I don't know," I said. "Stan just fired me."

"Then you're available! We need a bass player right away."

Winston called Kurt Bloom, Claude's manager, and got me the job. I joined the band two days later on a string of one-nighters that started with a weekend in Erie, Pennsylvania.

Before we left, Kurt told me to go to London Tailors to get measured for a band uniform. They said it would be sent out to me in about a week. I rode up to Erie with Winston and found the band's panel truck parked behind the ballroom. It was the domain of Bobby "Gator" Walters, the band boy.

"Kurt Bloom said you'd have a uniform I could wear until mine arrives from New York," I told Gator. "Can I pick one out?"

"You get your choice of the one I got," he said.

It was some choice. If it was the one Teddy Kotick had been wearing, he must have looked strange in it, too. Teddy was about my height and weight. That suit was made for someone shorter and fatter than either of us. It hung on me like a tent, and my wrists and ankles protruded oddly. I felt ridiculous in it, and tried to hide behind my bass as much as possible, hoping my own uniform would arrive soon.

Road band uniforms were made of strong fabrics that would take a lot of abuse. Claude's were a heavy brown twill that resisted the best efforts of some of his musicians to destroy them. We moved too fast to have them cleaned very often. They were played in, traveled in, slept in, fallen down in, spilled on, abraded, crumpled, and soiled, and still managed to look like band uniforms on the next job.

When my own uniform finally caught up with me in Columbus, Georgia, I put it on and found that it fit me nearly as badly as the one I'd been wearing. The waistband was too large and the jacket was at least two sizes bigger than it should have been. I don't know whose measurements they used, but they certainly weren't mine. I didn't have a uniform that fit until we got to New Orleans, where the hot weather forced us to buy some summer-weight blue suits. Claude picked up the tab and deducted a small amount from our salaries each week until they were paid for. When I left the band, that was my working blue suit for several years.

On that first night in Erie, I didn't get to meet Claude before the job. He arrived just in time for the first tune. Short and nattily dressed, he sat at the piano with a kind of darting manner and a puckish expression. He looked like a man with a devilish sense of humor.

He never looked in my direction while we were playing. During the intermission I tried to say hello, but Claude edged away, avoiding my eye. I was afraid he was disappointed with my work. But the next night Claude arrived early, before the dancers came in, and walked right over to me and shook my hand vigorously.

"Nice to have you here," he said. "I couldn't say hello last night. I didn't want the customers to think I didn't know my own musicians."

I stayed with Thornhill until the end of that summer. It was a very musical band, although cut to the bone and run on a shoestring in those days. Besides Claude on piano, there were five reeds, three trumpets, a trombone, a French horn, bass, drums, and a vocalist. The band had at one time used another French horn, another trumpet, a tuba, a guitar, and a vocal group, but Claude couldn't afford that many salaries on the jobs he was able to book in the 1950s. His arrangements sounded good even with the reduced instrumentation. We were especially fond of the things Gil Evans had written for him.

There was no band bus. We traveled in a caravan of four cars and the panel truck for the instruments. One of Claude's cars, filled with rejects from the other three, was called the Rat Patrol. They always made it to the job, but sometimes just barely. After a dance in Virginia, Kurt Bloom gave us directions to the next town, in South Carolina.

"It's 250 miles straight down Route 1; you can't miss it," he said.

At the hotel in the morning we awoke to discover that the Rat Patrol hadn't checked in. As Kurt was about to send out the alarm, the missing car drove up. Gene Quill, our lead alto man, was driving.

"We were on Route 1, just like you said, but when the sun came up, someone noticed it was on the wrong side of the car, and we realized we were going the wrong way," Gene explained. They'd driven right through Washington and Baltimore without realizing they were headed north.

On another long night trip, Sonny Rich, our third trumpet player, was driving that car. Everyone else was asleep. In the back seat Quill woke up and noticed that the car wasn't moving. They were stopped on a deserted stretch of highway with the engine running, and Sonny was looking blearily through the windshield.

"What's happening?" asked Gene.

"I'm waiting for this light to change," said Sonny.

Gene could see no traffic light, but beside the road was a motel with a NO VACANCY sign that had a lighted red neon NO.

Thornhill was a fine musician. He could get his own lovely sound out of some of the most unkempt pianos I've ever seen. He would size up a piano in the first couple of minutes he was playing it, and by avoiding the worst notes, manipulating the soft pedal, and modifying his touch, he would clean up many of its faults. But I could never understand why anyone would hire a noted pianist and then provide him with an inferior instrument. At one ballroom the piano was so bad that Claude broke off most of the hammers, so that no other piano player would have to be tortured by it.

Tours through the South in the summertime always included some outdoor ballrooms. Night-flying bugs were a problem on such bandstands. At one place, they came in such numbers that we turned off our music-stand lights to avoid attracting them. The dancers' area was already dark, so the only remaining bright light was a pin spot trained on vocalist Paula Martin's microphone. Poor Paula had to step aside into the darkness after every phrase she sang in order to take a breath that wasn't full of moths and other flying things.

The ballroom in Brownsville, Texas, had a band shell in the shape of a quarter-sphere. When I saw it, I remembered a phenomenon that Allen Eager once showed me when we were walking through Grand Central Station. As we went through a side passageway, Allen led me to a corner and stood me facing an inset right-angle in the supporting pillar. "Stand here," he said, "and you'll hear something interesting." He walked away.

I stood there for a minute, and was just about to turn around to see where he had gone when I heard his voice say softly in my ear, "Hi, Bill. Can you hear me?"

Startled, I looked around and saw that Allen was standing clear across the passageway facing another corner pillar like the one in front of me. The angle in the pillars rose to a hemispherical ceiling, and any sound made at one corner traveled up across the hemisphere and down to the opposite corner without interference from the hubbub of hundreds of commuters hurrying between us.

In Brownsville, when I saw the curve of the wall behind the bandstand, I wondered if I could get the same effect. The back row—trumpets, drums, bass, and piano—was set up in a straight line, so only Claude and I on one end and trumpeter Sonny Rich on the other were near the wall. I got Claude's attention and then leaned close to the wall.

"Sonny, your fly's open!" I hissed. Sonny, leaning back against the wall, jumped, checked his fly, looked behind him where he'd heard my voice, and then looked across the bandstand at me, completely mystified. Claude was delighted, and began trying to figure out who he could fool the same way. His target was Al Antonucci, the French horn player who sat in front of Sonny.

Al wasn't close enough to the wall for the trick to work, so Claude began manipulating the musicians sitting next to him, asking them to move over a little. As soon as Antonucci was pushed close to the wall, Claude got him.

"Nooch! Your fly is open!"

Antonucci reacted the same way that Sonny had, and Claude howled

with laughter. Of course, this all went on while we were playing a medley of dance tunes.

Claude had a sense of humor, but he was essentially a shy man. He
wanted a successful band, but didn't want to be a popular bandleader.
Occasionally, when the press had begun to pay too much attention to
him because one of his records was selling well, he'd taken some time
off and gone fishing until things calmed down a little. He hated being
in the spotlight and avoided making announcements whenever he could.

As we were setting up for a one-nighter in Texas, I discovered that
the ballroom's electrician had rigged the bandstand with switch boxes
at the ends of long cables, so each section of the band could control its
own stage lights. I tried them out and gathered up the switches for all
the lights that were aimed at the piano; there were four or five of different colors and intensities. I ran the cables behind my music stand
where I could reach the switches with my foot. That evening, every
time Claude would play two notes out in the open, I'd hit him with a
barrage of spotlights. He looked wonderfully uncomfortable all through
the first set. When we took a break, Claude didn't leave the bandstand.
He hunted around until he found my collection of switches and moved
them where I couldn't reach them for the rest of the night.

Claude put up with a lot of strange behavior from his musicians,
partly because he admired their talent and partly because he appreciated eccentricity. (There was a lot of both on that band.) He seemed
happiest on low-class jobs: roadhouses, servicemen's clubs, rural ballrooms. He got uncomfortable in fancier places like the Roosevelt Hotel
in New Orleans, where we played in July and August that year, for
dining and dancing and for an ice show every night. The piano at the
Roosevelt was good, but the place was crawling with managers. The
atmosphere was much too dignified for Claude. Every day he withdrew
further into himself. He came to work at the last minute, vanished before we finished playing the last set every night, and rarely spoke to
any of us.

Late in the second week at the Roosevelt, Claude came in early one
evening, beaming and shaking our hands as if he hadn't seen us for
months. I said, "What happened, Claude? Did you bet on the right
horse?"

"No," he said, giving me a big smile. "I've been feeling pretty de-
pressed lately because I had such a weird bunch of guys on this band.
But I was looking out my window this afternoon at those people on the
street, and . . . you want to see *weird!*"

We all got new black shoes to go with the blue suits we bought in

New Orleans. On the first night we wore the new outfits, everyone began to suffer in the unyielding new shoes. During the ice show, Claude
noticed that most of us had slipped them off in the dark, hiding our
stocking feet behind our music stands. Claude eased around behind us
and mixed up as many of the shoes as he could reach, causing complete
confusion when we began to slide our feet back into them again.

During a soft, slow dance medley one evening, I heard strange sounds
coming from the piano. Claude was playing "Oh, Katharina" in a different key and tempo, with plenty of stride left hand. He grinned up
at me and explained, "This is the way I used to have to play the steam
calliope on the riverboat when I first ran away from home in Terre
Haute, Indiana!"

I said, "This is a hell of a time to tell me!"

chapter 22

Gene Quill

Claude's band was booked for a weekend in Hull, Quebec, but when
we arrived at the address we had been given, we found the burned out
shell of a hotel. There were charred timbers still standing inside crum-
bling brick walls. We couldn't figure it out. There were sizeable seed-
ling trees growing in the rubble, so we knew the fire hadn't been recent. We finally found the ballroom around back. In a fire several years
earlier, the front part of the hotel had burned down, but the ballroom
and restaurant were still intact, and over them was a floor of undam-
aged hotel rooms that were now used by the traveling musicians who
worked there.

Having the hotel all to ourselves was too much of a good thing. The
party spirit after the job gathered momentum, and by the second night,
the revelers were tearing up each other's rooms after the job. Kurt
Bloom tried to calm things down, but Gene Quill and tenor man Ralph

Aldridge locked him in a closet in his room and proceeded to whoop it up.

Having no talent for alcohol, I had left the party early. Using a set of poster paints that I had with me, I was in my room painting pictures on shirt cardboards. When someone set off a firecracker in the keyhole of my door, I opened it and witnessed a bizarre scene. Gene Quill, who had passed out on his bed dressed only in his undershorts, was being dragged into the hall, mattress and all, by several of the other band members. Gene slept peacefully on.

As the pranksters stood back to admire their work, I stepped over to Gene's recumbent figure and painted "Do Not Disturb" on his chest. Everyone rushed into my room and got jars of paint and brushes, and soon Gene was decorated from head to toe with graffiti, outlines of his internal organs, flowers, and runic designs. A couple of times while he was being painted, he muttered in his sleep and changed his position, revealing new areas of unpainted flesh that were immediately pounced on by the decorators.

When we ran out of bare skin, we painted on Gene's shorts and on the sheet under him. After the artists pronounced the work completed, most of them wandered off to someone's room for a nightcap while I picked up my scattered jars and brushes and went back to my room, leaving Gene still snoring in the hall. Someone remembered Kurt and let him out.

As I was about to go to bed, I heard a soft noise in the hall. Curious, I looked out and found Dale Pierce, our lead trumpet player, standing outside my door in a state of semi-paralysis. The sound I had heard was Dale softly saying "Whew!" every now and then, a comment on the way he was feeling. I steered him to his room and went back to mine, and to bed. In the morning the maids who took care of our quarters took one look at Gene and at the mess in the rooms and quit their jobs. Gene told me that his first thought when he awoke in the hall was, "This is really a long room!"

Claude was staying with friends, so he missed the party. When the manager of the ballroom complained to him about the band's deportment, Claude jollied him into overlooking the whole thing. Having gone fishing the day before, Claude was in a good mood. A huge salmon he had caught was prepared for the band's dinner that night by the restaurant's chef.

When the Thornhill band arrived in Cleveland one Sunday morning we found a parade going up the street in front of the hotel where we were to stay. The entire Cleveland police force seemed to be marching by in dress blues, accompanied by a drum-and-bugle corps. As Winston Welch and I stood at the desk checking in, we saw three or four angry cops rush through the lobby and into an elevator. Later, Dick Sherman told us what had happened.

Dick and Gene Quill had arrived ahead of us and were given a room facing the street. Alcohol was their usual sedative, but they had scored for some heroin in the last town. Gene used some and went to bed. As Dick took his share of the drug into the bathroom, Gene began to notice the noise of the parade. He got up, opened the window and shouted a few salty insults at the passing policemen. As an afterthought, he unscrewed a bulb from a table lamp and threw it at them.

Someone shouted, "It came from that window!," and a few bluecoats rushed up to Gene and Dick's room and pounded on the door. As Dick cowered in the bathroom, trying to hide his drug paraphernalia, Gene opened the outer door and shouted at the policemen, "What's the idea of keeping me awake with all that noise out there?"

"You threw a light bulb out the window!" accused the officers, stalking menacingly into the room.

"You can't prove it was me!"

"Oh, yeah? How come there's no bulb in this lamp?"

"I was just about to call the manager and complain about that!"

"Oh, a wise guy! What's your name?"

"Dick Sherman!"

After giving "Dick" a tongue-lashing, the cops finally left, and the real Dick Sherman had a few more words to say to Gene.

Quill usually played Thornhill's lead alto and clarinet book perfectly. But he was a scrappy little Irishman, always ready to challenge the world, especially when lubricated with ignorant oil. One night he became impatient with the subtle mood Claude had set with a slow dance medley. Instead of playing the soft clarinet lead that was written, Gene stood up on his chair and played his part loudly on alto saxophone. When the chorus was over he scowled at Thornhill, gave him the finger and sat back down. Claude found this highly entertaining.

Gene was usually too preoccupied with various forms of self destruction to bother with the regular maintenance that reed instruments require. Most reed players constantly fuss with their reeds and mouthpieces, wipe out their instruments, adjust their pads, corks and springs, oil their key assemblies, etc. Gene just slapped the caps on his mouthpieces after the job each night and stuffed the instruments in their cases. The next night he'd throw the mouthpieces, with the ligatures and reeds still on them, under a running faucet in the men's washroom for a minute or two, jam them onto his alto and clarinet and play amazingly well.

This lack of maintenance would catch up with Gene now and then. One of the two posts that held the rod that supported his alto's right side-key assembly broke loose one night in Texas. Gene found that the pressure of his right hand kept the assembly in place, so he continued to play that way and put off looking for a repairman. In El Paso, Gene was in the middle of a solo when the post at the other end of that assembly came loose. Gene stopped playing and looked at the handful of keys and rods he was holding. He quickly fitted them back onto his alto and told Red Norman, sitting to his right, "Hold your finger right there."

With Red holding the keys in place, Gene finished his solo. At the end of the number he used a shoelace to tie the assembly onto the horn, and the next day he found a repairman.

During our booking at the Roosevelt Hotel in New Orleans, Gene's girlfriend, Bobbie, came down to visit him. Several of us were sharing a cheap apartment on Pirate's Alley in the French Quarter, overlooking the courthouse square. Gene and Bobbie decided to get married, and made arrangements with the judge at the courthouse. On the appointed morning Winston Welch and I put on our blue suits and were about to accompany Gene to the wedding when Charlie Frankhouser arrived from New York. Charlie was replacing Dale Pierce on lead trumpet. Dale's drinking had begun to worry Claude, so he sent him home to Salt Lake City to dry out.

We invited Charlie to accompany us to the wedding, but he said, "No, it's too hot, and I'm too tired. I just want to get out of these clothes and into bed."

We left him and went downstairs. Halfway across the courthouse square, we heard a trumpet playing. We looked around and there was Charlie, standing on the balcony of our apartment in his red polka-dot undershorts, playing the Wedding March.

Bobbie was lovely, Gene was sober, and the ceremony was brief. When it was over, I saw Gene slip a sealed envelope to the judge who had married them. On the way out, I asked,

"How much did you give him?"

"A hundred dollars," said Gene. "Monopoly money."

I played with Gene many times after we both left Claude's band. He

was a wonderful musician, but his drinking brought out a salty aggres-
siveness in him that he wasn't physically large or strong enough to back
up. He wound up the loser in many after-hours brawls.

One morning after the last Fifty-second Street bar had closed, Leo
Ball and Gene were standing on Eighth Avenue waiting for a cab to
appear when a Volkswagen passed too close to Gene. He cursed the
driver loudly and gave him the finger. The Volkswagen stopped short,
and a large tough guy got out, walked back to Gene, and decked him
with a single punch. As he stood over Gene's recumbent figure, he
demanded, "You want any more, wise guy?"

Gene, holding his hand over a rapidly swelling eye, shouted from the
gutter, "Not tonight, thank you!"

Many years later, after Gene had returned to Atlantic City, his birthplace, to work a job there, he got into one fight too many. He was
beaten nearly to death, suffered brain damage, and lived out his final
years severely handicapped.

As the summer ended, Thornhill announced that he was only going
to be working weekends for a while. Terry Gibbs offered me a full-
time job with his quartet, so I gave Claude my notice. On my last night
with the band in Harlan, Kentucky, Claude left us with an indelible
memory of him.

We were playing for the Black Diamond Coal Festival Ball in the
Harlan High School gymnasium. It was an unbelievably hot, humid
night. Early in the evening Claude told us to shuck our uniform jackets, and he did the same. He was sitting, sweating, behind a high upright piano that he had pulled around so its back faced the band. All
we could see of Claude was a forefinger that occasionally appeared above
the piano top to bring us in or cut us off.

I heard no piano for most of one tune and realized that Claude was
no longer at the keyboard. He had slipped through a nearby doorway
and gone into the back room. A few minutes later he came out in his
shirtsleeves and suspenders, holding a milkshake-sized paper cup full
of ice water. He stood in front of the band as we played, waiting until
we all noticed him. Then he held the cup high in the air and slowly
poured the contents over his head. We broke up laughing, but managed to keep the music going. Claude stood there soaking wet, thoroughly enjoying his joke.

At the end of the night I went over to say goodbye to him. Claude
gripped my hand and said he'd enjoyed having me on the band, but
he kept looking over his shoulder all the time, never once looking di-

rectly at me. I think saying goodbye made him nearly as uncomfortable as making announcements.

chapter 23

Terry Gibbs

My first job with Terry Gibbs was a week at the Rouge Lounge in River Rouge, Michigan, near Detroit. Our quartet included pianist Terry Pollard, who sometimes played duets with Gibbs at the vibraphone, and Frank DeVito, our drummer. We laughed a lot on that group. We had fun playing together, and we enjoyed each other's company off the bandstand.

Woody Herman played a concert in Detroit, and most of the band came out to see us afterwards. Red Kelly, Woody's bass player, was also from the Pacific Northwest, but we hadn't met before. We stood outside the club during a break and got acquainted. When we came back in and passed by Woody's table, Red grabbed me by the back of my jacket and held me up in front of Woody as if he were showing him a beagle.

"Hey, Woody, this guy's from Seattle!"

Woody examined me and nodded gravely, and Red put me back down.

Terry Pollard was from Detroit and had worked with Billy Mitchell's quartet at a favorite hangout on the West Side called the Blue Bird. The night she took us there, I was stunned at the number of good jazz players that turned up. I met three good bass players, Ernie Farrow, Doug Watkins, and Paul Chambers. Tommy Flanagan played the piano for a while and then turned it over to Barry Harris. Elvin Jones and Wilbert Hogan were the drummers. Kenny Burrell played guitar, Thad Jones played trumpet, Curtis Fuller the trombone, Pepper Adams the baritone sax. I was amazed that there were that many first class musicians that I had never heard of. They were happy jamming together in

Detroit, but I don't think they were making a living. As soon as a couple of them joined New York bands, they all moved east.

Gibbs booked a week for us at a club in East Saint Louis in a very tough neighborhood. We were glad to be staying in an apartment above the club so we didn't have to go out on the street after work. The bandstand was behind the bar. The band room, also behind the bar, had a one-way glass window. The idea was to give the entertainers privacy while allowing them to keep an eye on the bandstand and the customers. But the glazier had installed the glass backwards, so the customers could see in, and we couldn't see out. Terry Pollard pasted newspapers over the window to avoid being stared at.

The club owner reminded Pollard, a black woman, that we were in the South, and that it would be a good idea for her not to mix with his customers. Hearing this, Gibbs and DeVito and I stayed in the dressing room with her when we weren't on stage, so we didn't meet anyone in East Saint Louis but the club owner and the bartenders.

After a few weeks on the road, Terry took us into Birdland opposite Count Basie's band. I formed lasting friendships with Basie and his musicians, especially with Joe Newman and Gus Johnson. I worked with both of them in later years, after they left Basie.

A year or so earlier, Birdland had made a deal with Basie to book his band several times a year. To make the sound of sixteen musicians a little less overwhelming in the low-ceilinged basement room, the owners added more sound-absorbent surfaces. Curtains were hung behind the bandstand and Herman Leonard's photo murals were replaced by acoustic paneling. A decorator cut some of those photos into geometric shapes, tacked them here and there on the acoustic panels, tinted parts of them with pink and yellow shellac and connected them with lines of colored twine, making amateurish "modern art" collages with the chopped up photographs.

I heard that Herman Leonard threatened to sue when he discovered what had happened to his murals.

"You can take my pictures down," he reportedly told them, "but you can't mutilate them like that and then hang them back up."

Morris Levy, the boss, had the collages removed and replaced them with painted portraits of jazz stars.

When I took my bass through Birdland's back entrance one afternoon, I saw, tucked behind a row of garbage cans, one of the cutouts of Leonard's cardboard-mounted murals. It was part of a life-sized picture of Charlie Parker, in a plaid suit jacket and a striped bow tie, playing with closed eyes and a slight frown of concentration. I took my bass down to the bandstand, ran back upstairs and stuffed Bird's photo in the Model A Ford that I had borrowed from a friend to transport my instrument. That relic of Birdland is still on my wall at home.

Someone sold Morris Levy a "stereo" sound system for his club. A pair of speakers were hung, one at each side of the Birdland bandstand, but only the front microphone was connected to both channels. The piano mike went to the left speaker and the bass mike went to the right one. When more mikes were added for large groups they were split between the two channels. The music sounded balanced to anyone sitting at a table between the two speakers, but at the bar and in the bleachers the left one predominated.

Since the speaker that carried the bass mike was across the bandstand from where bass players usually stood, it took me a while to notice that whenever I played a low A, something in that speaker enclosure vibrated in sympathy, causing a loud buzzing noise. When I reported the problem to Morris Levy, he said, "Don't play that note."

One of our bookings at Birdland was opposite a honking tenor player from California. He was very successful in his own rhythm-and-blues venue, but he hadn't appeared before at the Jazz Corner of the World. Levy had booked him hoping to broaden Birdland's audience. Oscar Goodstein, who managed the club, viewed the experiment with suspicion.

At the sound check on the afternoon of opening night, the tenor player asked Goodstein, "Where's the runway? I've got to get out in the audience to do my thing."

Goodstein reluctantly moved the center tables aside and had the porters build a low, carpeted runway that extended six feet out into the room from the front of the bandstand.

During the first set the tenor player stepped onto the runway and played a solo that consisted of one simple blues phrase repeated endlessly. As he played, he writhed his body grotesquely. Goodstein watched with stony disapproval.

On his second number he worked himself into a frenzy that catapulted him off the runway into the audience. Honking and sweating, he strutted among the tables while the rhythm section on the bandstand chugged on. He worked his way over to the bar and along it to the rear of the club. As he came hooting around past the entrance stairway, he discovered Goodstein blocking his path. His face livid, Goodstein pointed up the stairs. The tenor player, still belaboring his riff, climbed the stairs and passed out of sight. Goodstein shouted after him, "And don't come back!"

That was the last we saw of him in Birdland. His rhythm section finished out the night. The next evening the runway was gone, and another bebop group played opposite us.

When Terry Gibbs took some time off in early 1954, I made the rounds, passing the word that I was available. In Charlie's Tavern I met Jerry Wald's manager, who hired me for a month at the Embers. Jerry had run out of bookings for his big band and disbanded it. His manager had talked Ralph Watkins, the owner of the Embers, into hiring Jerry with a sextet, with guitar and vibraphone, plus a string quartet. Johnny Richards had written the arrangements.

There was a week of rehearsals before we opened. I went to Nola's at the appointed time and discovered that Teddy Kotick had also been hired. Stan Getz's quintet had broken up in California, and Teddy was back in town. Instead of just telling one of us to go home, Jerry decided to audition us for the bass chair. Teddy and I hated being put in that position, but we both needed the work, so we each played half of the rehearsal. Marty Napoleon was on piano, Nat Ray on drums, Jack Hitchcock on vibraphone, and Johnny Quarra on guitar, plus the string quartet.

Jerry hired me, but the job wasn't much of a plum. After rehearsing for a week without pay, we opened at the Embers, and at the end of the first night Ralph Watkins told Jerry that he didn't want the string players:

"There's more people on the bandstand than there are at the tables!"

The strings were sent home and the rest of us had to stay at the club for a couple of hours after closing time, making cuts in the arrangements. With anyone else, we would have just played head arrangements, but Jerry couldn't improvise; he needed music in front of him at all times. To add injury to insult, the job only lasted one week. We found out that Jerry didn't have a contract for a month's work after all. He had a week with options, which weren't picked up.

At one of Wald's rehearsals at Nola's, Don Joseph dropped in to visit. He had played trumpet on Jerry's big band, but they had parted unamicably. When Don walked in, I saw Jerry turn away, pretending not to see him. We were on a break, so Don chatted with us for a while, and when Jerry said "Let's get back to work," Don headed for the door. As we were about to start the next tune, Don said loudly from the doorway, "Hello Jerry."

Jerry mumbled reluctantly, "Hello, Don."

"I just dropped by to say," Don announced cheerfully, "that I wouldn't work for you again for three hundred dollars a week!"

He waved to us and exited. We swallowed our laughter as Jerry reddened. Before he could give the downbeat, the door reopened and Don poked his head back in.

"Make that four hundred!" he said, and disappeared again.

Don was a melodic player with a lovely tone. Like Tony Fruscella, he preferred jazz that was soft and warm. Several years later he and I were playing with Brew Moore at one of Bob Reisner's Sunday concerts at the Open Door, south of Washington Square. A couple of young drummers were waiting their chance to sit in. When one of them took over and began pouring on the fire and brimstone, Don gave him a pained look and asked me, "What happened to that other drummer we had all nice and tired out?"

chapter 24

The Marian McPartland Trio

I was lucky that the gig with Jerry Wald didn't last any longer than it did; I might have missed a good job with Marian McPartland. I had met her when I was with Terry Gibbs, on a concert we shared with her trio and the Ahmad Jamal Quartet. As I was going into the Embers with Wald, Vinnie Burke gave Marian his notice, and she asked me to join her the following week at the Hickory House.

Marian and I and drummer Joe Morello worked there for several years, with occasional hiatuses when she booked a couple of weeks for us in Chicago, Detroit, or Columbus, Ohio. The Hickory House had featured jazz since 1933, but by 1949, like many of the other Fifty-second Street clubs, it had given up on live music. At the time Birdland opened, the Hickory House was using a disc jockey for entertainment.

In 1951, Jerry Shard reintroduced live music there with a trio, and was followed by guitarist Mary Osborne. Marian started there in February 1952, and I joined her two years later.

More a restaurant than a nightclub, the Hickory House's Fifty-second Street façade was half-timbered, with high windows that were divided into small, rectangular panes. A canvas canopy bore the famous name of the place. As you pushed through the revolving door, you faced a broad expanse of dining tables on the left and a huge oval bar on the right. Along the wall behind the bar were varnished oak booths, and above them hung huge, amateurish oil paintings of sports scenes. In one, a giant two-dimensional football player lunged horizontally in front of another player who seemed to be standing, but the artist hadn't given him any legs.

On the back wall was a massive fireplace. Beside the kitchen entrance, a large window looked into the cold-storage locker where cuts of meat were on display. At intervals around the room, wagon wheels hung horizontally from the high ceiling, above the diners' heads. Two sets of lights were mounted on each wheel, a ring of small yellow bulbs and a pair of bright white floodlights aimed down at the white tablecloths. During the dinner hour, the reflected glare from the tablecloths was intense.

At both ends of the bar, hundreds of liquor bottles were on display in front of square, mirrored pillars, and between those pyramids of booze, in the center of the bar's oval, was the bandstand. When we began playing at nine, Marian had the waiters turn off the bright lights over the dining tables, but John Popkin, the boss, insisted on leaving all the rest of the lights on, including the bright lights in the meat case and on the front of the fireplace. A single pink floodlight over the piano bench did little to focus the audience's attention on Marian.

Since Popkin was ignoring Marian's complaint that the meat was lit better than the musicians, I decided to take care of the problem myself. I located some miniature spotlights in a nearby theatrical electric shop and got Marian to buy them. I mounted them above the bandstand and, with parts from a Canal Street junk shop, wired up a foot-switch box. Marian, Joe, and I each had a spotlight, and I could control any light, or two or three lights at once, with a touch of my foot. When we traded four-bar breaks, I would make the lights switch from one player to another right on the beat. Then I'd make a blackout on the last note of the tune and bring the lights back on again for the applause. A fourth light threw a soft pin-spot on Marian to set the mood for ballads.

The lighting in the rest of the room still worked against us. It could easily have been improved, but I couldn't get Popkin to listen to my suggestions. One night when he was away I turned out all the room lights except a few dim yellow sconces around the walls. I also doused the light in the meat case and the floodlights on the fireplace front. The fire itself looked more dramatic in the darkened room, and the whole place was instantly more intimate and theatrical. The spotlights on the bandstand now made it the center of attention. As I completed my adjustments, the customers said, "Oooh! How nice!"

We played half a set that way, and then Popkin returned. He rushed into the room and accosted Julius, the headwaiter.

"Who put out the lights?" he yelled. "People will think we're closed!"

John Popkin presented jazz at the Hickory House for many years, but I think he was a little puzzled by it. He liked Marian personally and approved of the business she attracted, but he viewed musicians with suspicion, particularly drummers. After Buddy Rich became famous, Popkin claimed to have discovered him, but when Joe Marsala first added Buddy to his band at the Hickory House in 1937, Popkin kept urging Joe to fire him: Too noisy.

When Marian hired Joe Morello, the Hickory House became a mecca for young drummers who admired Joe's superb technique. Joe played at a very tasteful level with the trio, but now and then, when Marian saw that a lot of his fans were in the house, she would give him an extended solo. Popkin often sat at a table near the cash register, perusing the racing news. As Joe pulled out all the stops, we would see the newspaper that hid Popkin's face begin to tremble. Then he would throw it down and rush to the bar, shouting up to the bandstand, "Stop that banging! Stop that banging!"

Morello was a spectacular drummer, but he felt embarrassed when people compared him to Buddy Rich, Max Roach, and Louis Bellson. To fend off such discussions, he invented a mythical drummer named Marvin Bonessa who he said could cut all of them. Marvin was supposedly a recluse who never recorded and rarely came to New York. Marian loved the joke. She and I abetted Joe in it, as did his friend Sal Salvador, to the point that Bonessa began to accumulate votes in jazz polls. Joe still tells some of his young students about the legendary Marvin Bonessa.

Between sets we usually sat in a back booth, where Joe was regularly joined by drummers who came to talk to him and watch his hands. Joe practiced constantly on the table top, using a folded napkin to dampen the sound. Sometimes he would use just the forefinger of his left hand to keep his drumstick tapping at a rapid, controlled speed. On drum solos he would combine that finger trick with wrist accents.

I fooled around with Joe's drumsticks until I got the hang of his finger trick. When his students marveled at his use of it, Joe would say, "Gee, anybody can do that. Even my bass player can do it."

He'd hand me a stick and I'd casually demonstrate, ruining their day.

If John Popkin had bad luck at the track he would begin to worry about his business. He would scrutinize his cash register tapes, and at any perceived irregularity he would aim a tirade at his cashiers.

"T'ieves!" he would cry. "Nothing but t'ieves I got working for me!"

He repeated this too loudly one night, and the chef suddenly loomed large in the kitchen doorway. Cursing in Greek and glowering furiously at Popkin, he advanced menacingly across the room. Popkin's rage completely evaporated.

"Not you!" he cried. "I didn't mean you!"

The chef untied his apron, removed it, and threw it dramatically to the floor in front of Popkin. He snatched his tall white hat from his head and threw it on top of the apron. Then, arms akimbo, he inflated himself with anger and glared furiously while Popkin begged him to return to the kitchen and forget the insult. Finally the chef exhaled and looked around at the customers, waiters, bartenders, and musicians who were all watching.

He stalked slowly over to the bar, and, while fixing Popkin with a glare that dared him to say anything, he seized a silver coffee pot in one hand and a bottle of good scotch in the other. He filled the coffee pot with scotch, slammed the bottle back on the bar, and stalked into the kitchen carrying his prize. A waiter scurried after him with his apron and hat. Popkin heaved a sigh of relief and retreated to his office.

Popkin's bark was much worse than his bite. He never fired anyone. The foot-weary waiters had worked there for years, as had his old cashiers. His headwaiter, Julius, who spent much of his time standing at attention and shouting like a Prussian drill sergeant at the waiters, and Morris, the nearsighted men's room attendant, had always been there. Morris liked to keep busy. When things were slow in the men's room, he would come out and slice the bread for the dinner baskets.

The two bartenders, just beginning to lose their hair, were the youngest employees in the place, except for the musicians, of course. Compared to the rest of them, we were just kids. Marian's British accent and sweet nature charmed them all. She even turned Julius into a pussycat. Marian also charmed our audiences. She developed a community of devotees who felt personally connected to her and who supported her at the Hickory House for many years.

Of course, every customer at the Hickory House was not a jazz fan. Sometimes the stools at the oval bar around the bandstand would be occupied by racetrack types blowing cigar smoke up at us. The club had an excellent exhaust system, so this was only a problem when John Popkin's wife was around. She would get lonesome and come down to sit in the restaurant, but she was terribly sensitive to drafts and always turned off the exhaust fans when she came in. Then the smoke would begin to hang like a pall on the bandstand. I'd slip down and flip the switch when Mrs. Popkin wasn't looking, and the fans would whisk away the smoke before she noticed the draft and shut them off again.

The worst customers were the drunks who felt that their manhood required them to harass the female pianist. Julius would summarily eject deadbeats, but he wouldn't bother a paying customer just because he was insulting. We were usually able to get rid of pests by telling them to get lost, but one big beefy guy just sat there one night and continued to say ugly things to Marian.

Julius wouldn't throw the guy out, so I tried to do it myself. I weighed about 115 pounds at the time and had no experience with fighting, but I was angry enough to move mountains. I told the guy to get out, but he just leered at me drunkenly and repeated his ugly remarks. So I hit him. I hit him in the chest, just as hard as I could. He barely noticed I had done it. My hand felt slightly sprained, and I felt considerably deflated. I climbed sheepishly back onto the bandstand, and the guy eventually staggered out the door on his own.

The years I played with Marian at the Hickory House kept me happy musically, and also kept my bills paid. It was a great place to meet other musicians. Duke Ellington and Joe Morgen, his publicist, ate there frequently, and Duke came up and played with Morello and me a couple of times. We also played with Oscar Peterson, Billy Taylor, Cy Coleman, Barbara Carroll, Dave McKenna, and many other pianists who dropped in. Jackie Cain and Roy Kral heard Joe and me there and used us on a record date, as did Jimmy Raney when he recorded a sextet album featuring an unknown young saxophone player from Springfield, Massachusetts: Phil Woods. Marian jokingly threatened to start charging us an agent's fee on our outside jobs.

Marian was always eager to hear other jazz groups. We would sometimes take a long intermission and run over to Birdland, a block away, or to Basin Street West, in the basement of the old Roseland building.

Our intermission pianist, Ellie Eden, would never cover for us; she would play her regular set and get off, leaving a lull in the room that, when we came running in a few minutes later, would get us the fisheye from Popkin.

When Ellie left, John Mehegan took over the solo piano. John would cover for us when we were late, but sometimes he'd get so involved in his playing that his set would never end. Marian was supposed to play the first and last sets of the night. John would close his eyes and play so long that we would sometimes only have enough time on our last set to play one short tune.

John always apologized, saying he lost track of the time. I fixed that. I bought a cheap alarm clock at the drugstore on the corner. It was one of those loud ones with two large bells on the top, designed to wake the dead. I hid it under the music rack of the piano one night before John's last set, with the alarm set to ring in half an hour. It did, loudly, right in the middle of a complicated chorus John was construct-ing. When I saw the look of absolute panic on his face, I decided I had gone too far.

That didn't stop me from playing one more prank on John a few months later. John kept time by stamping his right foot while he played. On his more vigorous passages he stamped it pretty hard. I had one of those little airline pillows in my bass case. While John was playing, I slid the pillow under his foot while it was in the air. When his foot came down silently, John was so disoriented that he stopped playing altogether.

I was in Birdland on a break from the Hickory House the night Bill Davis presented Count Basie with his arrangement of "April in Paris." Bill was playing the Hammond organ with his own trio opposite Basie that week, and when the band ran down his chart, he played organ with them while Basie listened. Davis booted the band along, playing the figures with them to help them learn the phrasing. At the end, Davis initiated the "One more time" reprise that Basie always used on that arrangement.

After the last "One more time" and several minutes of applause from the audience, Basie climbed back onto the piano bench, pulled the mike over and said, "Thanks for the arrangement, Bill. Now I've got to go out and buy a damn organ!"

chapter 25

Jazz Records

Though *Metronome* magazine named Marian McPartland's trio the Small Group of the Year in 1955, we only made two albums, for Capitol Records. Marian added a harp and cello to a couple of the tunes, an unusual blending of "classical" instruments with a jazz trio in those days. She wasn't thrilled with the condition of the piano at Capitol's Forty-sixth Street recording studio. The action was poor and it was slightly in need of tuning. We were surprised that a major record label would have a mediocre piano. Still, I'm glad to have any souvenir of the way we were playing in those days.

One night a young man sat at the Hickory House bar listening and smiling as we played. When our set was finished, he introduced himself as Victor Feldman. The talented English vibraphonist had just arrived in New York, and had come in to meet Marian. He said he liked the way Joe and I played together.

"I'm doing an album for Keynote," Victor told us, "and I'd like you guys to do it with me. I already sort of promised it to Kenny Clarke, so I'll have him do the first date and Joe the second. I've got Hank Jones on piano."

Both dates went beautifully. Victor had written some attractive tunes, and he and Hank hit it off together right away. We couldn't have felt any more comfortable if we'd been playing together for years. Victor was glad to have the recording finished before he left town to join Woody Herman's band.

The next time I ran into Vic, he told a sad story. The producer at Keynote had decided to delay releasing the album, hoping Vic would become famous with Woody. But the next Keynote recording project ran over budget, and when he needed to raise some cash, the producer sold Victor's master tapes to Teddy Reig at Roost Records. Vic came back to New York, discovered what had happened, and called Reig to find out when he planned to release the album.

"Just as soon as Keynote sends me the tape," said Teddy.

Vic called Keynote to ask when this would take place, and was told the tape had already been sent. A search of both record companies' offices failed to locate the tape, and as far as I know it was never found. It may still be lying in a storeroom somewhere, or it may have been destroyed.

Since Keynote announced the album when we did the date, it was listed in *Down Beat* in their "Things to Come" column, and that information found its way into the Bruyninckx discography, but now that Vic and Kenny are both gone, that music only exists as a lovely resonance in the memories of Joe, Hank, and myself.

Late one night at the Hickory House I got a call from Lennie Tristano. About a year after I stopped studying with him, he had moved his musical activities to a studio on East Thirty-second Street, where he taught and had jam sessions with his students and friends. He wanted to know if I felt like playing after my job. I did, even though I'd already been playing for six hours. I was young.

Because of the growing difficulty of finding a parking place for a car near my apartment in Greenwich Village, I was using a Lambretta motor scooter for transportation around the city. I usually left my bass at the Hickory House every night after work, but when I had to move it I would strap it on my back, get on the scooter and drive carefully to my destination. That night I took my bass down to Lennie's studio on the Lambretta.

When I walked in, I could barely make out who was there because no lights were on in the studio. A dim glow came from a light in the hall that led to a smaller room in the rear where Lennie was busy with a student. In the main studio, Phyllis Pinkerton was at the piano, and Jeff Morton was playing brushes on a snare. There were also a couple of horn players sitting in the gloom.

"Why is it so dark in here?" I asked.

"Lennie didn't turn on the lights."

I laughed.

"Lennie's blind! He doesn't use them!"

I turned on a lamp near the piano and unpacked my bass. We played a few of the tunes that Lennie's devotees liked to play, like "All of Me," "Donna Lee," and a minor-key version of "Pennies from Heaven."

When Lennie finished with his pupil, he came out and took over at the piano. He called one of the same tunes we had just played, but nobody seemed to mind. There was a limited list of tunes that Lennie and his students were interested in playing. During that first tune, Lennie sat down pretty heavily on the time. He comped with dense block chords, and since he was playing a little behind the beat, I had to work hard to keep the tempo from slowing down. At the end of the first tune, I said,

"I couldn't seem to keep the tempo up where we started it."

Lennie shrugged.

"If it feels like it wants to slow down, I just go with it."

I didn't think we ever got a good time-feeling going that night, but it was interesting to build bass lines on Lennie's chords. I went back to play with him several times just for the experience.

Recording engineer Jerry Newman called me one evening on my night off and introduced me to Henri Renaud, the French pianist, who had come to New York to record Al Haig. Al hadn't been heard on record since his dates with Charlie Parker. I think he was working with a society band at the Hotel Astor. Henri wanted to record that night.

I welcomed the chance to play with Al, whom I'd heard several times at Birdland but had never met. I took my bass to Newman's recording studio on Twenty-sixth Street and met Henri, Al, and the drummer, Lee Abrams. Jerry only wanted to use one microphone, which he hung over the strings of the lidless grand piano. He stood me on a small platform in the curve of the piano to get the F-hole of my bass close to the mike, and he kept moving Lee's drums farther and farther away, looking for a balance. Lee's drum stool ended up in the doorway to the bathroom, about twenty feet from the piano.

It was an uncomfortable setup, but Al played beautifully, doing everything in one take. We had no rehearsal; he would play a couple of bars of a standard and ask me, "Do you know this?" I would nod, and we'd record. On some tunes I could have used a second take. I could have matched Al's chord progressions with a better line, once I'd heard what he was going to do. But Al was on a roll, and we quickly finished the eight tunes for Henri's album.

Jerry Newman took off his headphones and said, "That was great. How would you like to do another eight tunes for me? I'll release them here in the States on my Esoteric label."

Al chose another group of standards and we recorded them the same way.

When Newman sent me a check a couple of weeks later, it was union scale for a single date. I called and asked him where the money was for the second album, and he said, "Oh, I thought you understood it was all for the same price. I couldn't have afforded to do the other album it if I had to pay for a second session."

I didn't complain to the union since I didn't think it would do any good, so Newman got away with a free album. I even bought it when it came out. Some years later, in France, Henri gave me a copy of his French release, but I loaned it to Al Haig when I came back to New York, and he never returned it.

chapter 26

Popsie Randolph

Popsie Randolph, who had once been Benny Goodman's famous band boy, often dropped in at the Hickory House. I had first met him when I was with the Teddy Charles Trio in 1952. He had become a show business photographer, and he took our publicity shots. I always enjoyed chatting with him and listening to his stories.

Popsie was born William Seezenais, but Goodman always called him "Pops." He used that name with everyone, but the band members began calling Seezenais "Popsie," and the name stayed with him. He changed his last name one night in Chicago when, discouraged at the prospect of once again having to spell out "Seezenais" for a hotel clerk, he chose the name of the street they were on and said his name was Randolph.

Popsie told me that he started hanging around musicians while he was in high school. He used to skip school and spend his days haunting West Forty-eighth Street, where there were music stores and rehearsal studios. Popsie loved to hear the music and to be near the musicians. He found out where they congregated by following anyone he saw carrying a horn case.

Fearful of being told to stop hanging around, Popsie looked for things to do to make himself useful. He helped drummers carry their equipment from the sidewalk up to the studios. He ran out for coffee and cigarettes. Some of the musicians gave him small tips for the services he performed. One day he arrived early for a rehearsal and saw that all the chairs and stands were still piled along the wall. He knew how that band liked to set up, so he went to work, and when the musicians arrived they found everything in place, ready to go. Pleased with his efficiency, the band leader offered to pay him to set up for every rehearsal. Soon everyone on Forty-eighth Street was taking advantage of Popsie's willing presence, and he began to have a small income.

It was a natural development for one of the bandleaders to take Popsie along when his band went out of town on a tour of one-nighters. He became adept at getting the equipment transported, set up, taken down, and moved to the next job, and his reputation spread. His first big-time job was with Ina Ray Hutton's band.

Popsie loved being a band boy. He was right where he wanted to be, in the company of musicians, and he expressed his delight in the way he knew best, by doing anything anyone asked him to do with a willing alacrity that became his trademark. His greatest challenge came when he was hired in 1941 by Benny Goodman, who had become the hottest band leader in the business. Goodman's reputation for being enigmatic and capricious didn't faze Popsie, who considered it his job to anticipate Benny's every wish. He often went to incredible lengths to please him.

Popsie came to his first rehearsal with the Goodman band prepared with cigarettes and a lighter. Since he didn't know what brand Benny smoked, he bought a pack of each of the major brands and had them in various pockets of his jacket. After he discovered Benny's brand he always carried it. Benny would raise two fingers and make a scissor-like gesture, and Popsie would quickly place a cigarette between them while firing up his lighter.

Besides taking care of the band equipment, Popsie also served Benny as a combination errand boy, valet, and nursemaid. An ex–Goodman sideman told me that while he was in the men's room at a ballroom where they were playing, he noticed Popsie covering a toilet seat with carefully laid sheets of tissue. Surprised at Popsie's fastidiousness, he was even more surprised when Popsie went out and came back with Benny:

"Your toilet seat is ready."

While traveling with Goodman, Popsie developed the custom of writing his name on backstage walls wherever they worked. His signature and the date of the performance were a common sight in the bandrooms of theaters, ballrooms, and nightclubs all over the United States and in many other parts of the world. One musician told me he even saw it written inside an Army C-47 airplane, which must have transported the Goodman band to a job somewhere.

Popsie's innocent good will immunized him to the pettiness for which Benny became famous among others who worked for him. His high opinion of Benny never faltered, and Benny in turn seemed genuinely fond of his amanuensis. He stayed with Benny until 1947, having been promoted to road manager in 1945. When Benny no longer had a job for him, Popsie managed the Woody Herman band for a year or two. After that job ended, Popsie mentioned to Goodman and his wife that he would like to get off the road and try his luck as a photographer. Benny and Alice set him up in a studio in New York, where Popsie specialized in publicity shots for musicians and entertainers.

Since he knew hundreds of people in the music business, Popsie did well as a photographer. He regularly visited all the Manhattan nightclubs, taking pictures of every musician and entertainer who passed through, and he kept the negatives on file. Anyone who needed a publicity photo could call Popsie and get a quick print from his files. The familiar jaunty "Popsie" with which he had autographed a thousand dressing-room walls was always inscribed at the bottom right-hand corner of his eight-by-ten glossies.

My favorite Popsie story took place when he was still Goodman's band boy, on a job at Princeton. Popsie told me that he set up the bandstand and was preparing things in Benny's dressing room when he realized that there was only one cigarette left in the pack he carried for Goodman. He quickly ran outside to look for a place to buy more, but could only see college buildings on tree-lined streets. He had no idea which direction to take to find a store.

"I saw this old white-haired guy walking slowly down the sidewalk," said Popsie. "He was wearing baggy pants and a sweatshirt, and he needed a haircut. I ran over and asked him where I could buy cigarettes. He seemed interested in the way I was dressed. I had on a very hip outfit, a yellow cardigan jacket and pegged pants and a beret. He wanted to know about my clothes, and where I came from. He acted like he thought I was from Mars.

"I sort of fluffed him off. I said I was in a hurry, that I needed cigarettes for Benny. Finally he told me where there was a candy store, about two blocks away. I ran down and got the smokes, and when I came back, one of the kids at the building where we were playing said he saw me talking to Professor Einstein, and wanted to know what he

was saying to me. I said, Einstein! My God, I thought he was the janitor! Imagine! Popsie Randolph talking to Albert Einstein! He seemed
like a nice old guy, but Jesus! Einstein!"

chapter 27

Vic Dickenson

When I joined Marian McPartland's trio, I was still playing the plywood
Kay bass I'd bought in 1951. I had admired finer instruments that I'd
heard being played by other bassists, but I hadn't found one of my
own. Irv Manning, a bassist with an eye for quality in instruments, took
me to the workshop of Sam Kolstein, a bowmaker and bass repairman
on Sixth Avenue. While Sam adjusted my Kay to improve its sound
and action, he let me play some of the fine old instruments that he had
there. They were for sale, but I couldn't afford Sam's prices.

My appetite for a better bass was well whetted by the time Irv came
into the Hickory House one night and offered me a great deal. He
needed to raise some cash to buy a beautiful bass he'd fallen in love
with, a Fendt, that had just been brought to New York by a friend of
his who worked on the Cunard steamships. Irv was willing to part with
an old French bass of his for $150 and my Kay. I knew the bass; Irv
had let me play it once. I didn't need to think it over. I got an advance
from Marian, and Irv delivered the French bass the next day. It sounded
so good and played so easily that my playing improved right away.

I've acquired a couple of other basses over the years, but that French
bass is still my favorite. Over a hundred years old, it's in very good
health. Of course, it has appreciated greatly in value as the prices of
instruments have risen, but that only means that insurance and repairs
on it cost more now; I would never think of selling that bass.

Every so often Marian booked some out-of-town work for the trio.
Billy Taylor, Don Shirley, or Mary Lou Williams would hold the fort at
the Hickory House while we were away. Our favorite out-of-town clubs

were Baker's Keyboard Lounge in Detroit and the Grand View Inn in
Columbus, Ohio. Once in a while Jimmy McPartland came with us as a
featured soloist.

Jimmy was a good golfer, and when out of town, always found a jazz
fan who would offer his hospitality at a local country club. He often
took me along and gave me pointers about the game. He even gave me
his old irons when he bought a new set. I never developed Jimmy's
passion for golf, but I had a lot of fun on the course with him. He was
great company.

When we returned to New York I played golf one afternoon with
Jimmy and Bud Freeman somewhere in New Jersey. Bud didn't have
a strong drive and his iron shots were only fair, but with his handicap
he was usually even with Jim when they reached the green, where Bud,
a pool shark with a putter, was difficult to beat. I was outclassed by
both of them, so I just duffed along and enjoyed watching those two
old Chicago friends courteously play every dirty trick they could think
of, trying to put each other off their game. Jimmy tried to overwhelm
Bud with power, and Bud tried to infuriate Jimmy with cunning. On
one close hole, Bud even whistled a song out of tune while putting, a
ploy calculated to unnerve a musician with a good ear, taken straight
from Stephen Potter's classic manual, *Gamesmanship*.

Jimmy sometimes borrowed Joe Morello and me when he had a job
that didn't conflict with Marian's hours at the Hickory House. It was
on one of these, an afternoon Christmas party upstairs at Toots Shor's,
that I first got to play with Vic Dickenson. I had admired Vic on records for years. He sat next to me all night, playing his unmistakable
trombone sound with a powerful swing. We fell into a happy musical
relationship right away. Whenever Vic gave me an approving look, the
world was my oyster.

I had developed neither the talent nor the desire for drinking alcohol, but I noticed that Vic was drinking straight gin, so I would order
gin, too, whenever someone would buy a round for the band, and I'd
push my glass over beside Vic's. Vic would look at me lovingly and say,
"Ding, ding!" as he downed both drinks.

From then on we were buddies. Whenever he saw me he would smile
and raise his eyebrows. "Ding, ding!" was always his greeting. Many of
his friends called him Ding. He said he got the expression from Lester
Young, who used it to mean many things. It could mean, "You've rung
the bell, I agree with what you just said," or "You just played a prize-
winning chorus." Said without a smile, it could mean, "Your playing
would get you the gong on the Amateur Hour." For Vic, it simply meant,
"Hi, pal," or "Here goes another drink, and I hope it rings my bell."

Vic was always a joy to play with. His lyrical style fit all forms of jazz. Though he played mainly with Dixie and swing groups, he also fit comfortably into more modern settings. His musical ears were large, and his playing was always delightful.

Vic was born in Xenia, Ohio, the seventh of nine children, five brothers and three sisters. His brother Carlos played the alto saxophone—very well, according to Vic. In 1925 they had a band in Columbus they called the Dickenson Brothers. Carlos stayed in Ohio and finished out his years working in the postal service, while Vic took to the road and wound up in New York, but they remained close. Vic always talked about getting Carlos to come to New York and record with him, but he was never able to arrange it.

"I never get to pick my own musicians on my records," he said. "It seems like somebody else has always done the picking."

After a record date one afternoon at a studio near the Hickory House, I took my bass back to the club, got on my motor scooter, and started east on Fifty-second Street, where I saw Vic walking in the same direction, carrying his trombone case.

"Ding! Where are you headed?"

"I'm walking over to Lexington Avenue."

"Hop on, I'll drive you over."

"Nooo, thank you. I rode on a motorcycle just once in my life. It belonged to a friend of mine. I nearly had a fight with that man, he *leaned* with me so!"

I explained that motor scooters were much more docile than motorcycles and I promised not to lean with him, since we were going straight across town and wouldn't turn any corners. Vic looked doubtful, but he let me strap his trombone on the rear luggage rack. He climbed onto the pillion seat behind me with great care, folding the bottom edge of his topcoat under his legs to keep it from flapping in the breeze. He seized the hand grip with one hand and clutched the crown of his fedora with the other. I eased in the clutch and gingerly rolled down Fifty-second Street, doing my best to avoid potholes and manhole covers.

When we stopped at Lexington Avenue, Vic got carefully off the scooter and adjusted his clothes. As I unstrapped his horn case, I said, "That wasn't so bad, was it?"

"No, that was a very nice ride," said Vic. "But I don't believe I'll do that again."

Often I made better time on the scooter than I would have if I had taken a cab, because I could slip through narrow spaces between cars when traffic was stalled. When I drove it to record dates, I would sometimes take it inside the studio with me to avoid parking hassles. Once, when Marian appeared with the trio on a television program on ABC, the studio director was fascinated when he saw me parking my scooter behind the bandstand. He had me go back outside with the bass on my back and drive into the studio through the freight doors, on camera.

Al Avakian saw me go by one day carrying my bass on the scooter. Al, the brother of George Avakian of RCA Victor Records, worked as a movie editor. He called the next day and said, "You're exactly what I need!"

He explained that he was planning a documentary about jazz in New York, and he needed something to visually tie together the different locations where the music was played. He wanted shots of me on the scooter, driving to a gig and going by other New York jazz clubs that would be included in his essay. Al had enough money to make the demo reel he needed to apply for a grant.

He came to my Cornelia Street apartment and filmed me practicing at home, then followed me with his camera down the stairs to the street and onto the scooter. From the roof across the street he got some long shots as I drove away toward Sixth Avenue with the bass on my back, and then he mounted the camera on his car window and filmed me as I scootered past various city landmarks and jazz clubs. Al sent his completed demo reel to Washington with a grant application just at the wrong time. The changing political climate dried up a lot of arts funding money that season, and Al never was able to complete his project. That reel of film may still be lying on a shelf somewhere in Washington.

Vic Dickenson and I were working with Jimmy McPartland's band at Nick's in the Village the week Vic's brother Carlos died. Vic took a night off to fly out to the funeral, but he came straight back to work the next night. We could see that grief was still heavy on him.

His playing that night was filled with emotion, and he seemed to find deep solace in it. He played soft backgrounds behind everyone else's choruses, played heartbreakingly beautiful choruses of his own, and when our band was off the stand, moved over to Hank Duncan's solo piano, sat down on the bench beside him and played along quietly throughout his set. Vic didn't take the mouthpiece away from his lips for more than a minute all night long. It was a remarkable example of the healing power of music. He did all his grieving through his horn and was pretty much back to normal the next night.

Through the years I often found myself on the same bandstand with Vic at jazz concerts and festivals. He loved to share the pleasure of music with his friends; his generous, welcoming smile and cheerful "Ding, ding!" always made me feel like an honored guest at his party. The last times I played with him were during his stay with Red Balaban's house band at Eddie Condon's on West Fifty-fourth Street. By the time that club was ready to be torn down, Vic's age was beginning to show. He moved slower and more carefully, and remained seated on a tall stool while he played. His sound had become much softer. Its unique burry quality was still there, but you really had to stand in front of his trombone bell to hear all of it. He wasn't strong enough to push it all the way out of the horn any more. He had finally become the old man I had thought he was forty years before, and his trombone was still singing the same bittersweet songs.

Vic succumbed to cancer in November 1984, at age seventy-eight. He left far too few records behind. I treasure the one I got to make with him, a Ruby Braff date in 1974, on which he played some fine solos. After a lifetime of consistent, craftsmanly musical expression, he went on his way. But he left the light on for the rest of us. Ding, ding.

chapter 28

Bird

I was working at the Hickory House when I heard the sad news of Charlie Parker's death. It stunned every musician I knew. He was twenty when he first overwhelmed the jazz world with his brilliant playing, and only fourteen years later that Niagara of music had ceased to flow. During my first months in New York I spent every possible hour listening to him, but as I began to live my own musical life I only went to hear him now and then when he played in New York. I felt no urgency; I thought he would always be there.

I had only a few personal encounters with Bird during the five years of his life that remained after I came to New York. I hung around him at Birdland when I first arrived, but I didn't really get to talk to him at

length until he began visiting Jimmy Knepper and Joe Maini's basement on 136th Street.

Before Jimmy and Joe lived there, I was introduced to that basement
apartment by Buddy Jones, a bass player from Hope, Arkansas, who
had been a friend of Bird's in Kansas City. Shortly after I moved to
New York, I was standing in front of Birdland one night chatting with
Frank Isola and a couple of other musicians when Buddy came by and
told us that he had found a great place to play. A sax player named
Gerson Yowell had rented a large basement room that extended beneath the sidewalk and part of the street. Music could be played there
day or night without bothering anyone.

I hurried over to my room on Eighth Avenue to get my valve trombone, and Frank went home to get his drums. Buddy waited for us at
the Fiftieth Street IRT entrance with his bass and three or four other
musicians. Uptown, we trooped after Buddy into the lobby of an apartment building at Broadway and 136th Street. We took the elevator to
the furnace room in the basement and found Gerse's door, but knocking brought no answer. The door seemed to be hooked from the inside. Buddy was puzzled. He had called and told Gerse we were coming
up.

"Maybe his girlfriend came by, and they don't want to be disturbed,"
someone suggested.

Since no one answered our repeated knocking, there didn't seem to
be anything to do but go back downtown. As Buddy rang for the elevator I gave the door one final, heavy thump. It slowly and eerily swung
open. My last knock had shaken the hook loose. In the large, gloomy
room an old upright piano stood in the middle of the floor. Gerse was
on the piano stool with his head on the keyboard and his arms dangling
limply toward the floor. He was sound asleep. An empty gallon wine
jug sat beside him on the floor. We shook him awake and teased him
about drinking all the wine before we got there, and then we set up
and played until late the next morning.

Some time after that, while I was camping out at John Benson Brooks's
apartment on Riverside Drive near 136th Street, I dropped in at Gerse's
basement to see what was going on, but Gerse no longer lived there.
The new tenants were Knepper and Maini, and they were hosting jam
sessions nearly every night.

Bird was among the guests the first night I dropped in. He went
there often to play or to watch Jimmy's little television set. Jimmy also
had a tape machine on which he recorded the music that was played

there. He would later write out Bird's solos to use for trombone practice material.

I was learning to play the bass by then, but I would never have
dreamed of trying to play while Charlie Parker was around. I don't
think Bird even knew what instrument I played. I was just one of several guys who hung around and listened to him. Sometimes I went
back during the day to hear the tapes Jimmy made.

Buddy Jones had a lot of Bird tapes. He played one for me of Parker
at a session with five or six other horn players and a rhythm section.
During Bird's solo, the other horns began playing heavy riffs and sustained chords behind him, filling in all the space. Suddenly Charlie
played a very strong melodic figure a beat earlier than one would have
expected. The other horn players, thinking they had dropped a beat,
stopped playing, leaving Bird in the clear for a few measures. Every
time the horns would find him and come in again behind him, Bird
would play another figure that made them think they were in the wrong
place. He did this for the rest of his solo, always coming back into
consonance with the rhythm section before he lost them, too.

Bird would play musical tricks like that, but I never heard him put
anybody down. He usually encouraged everyone to play. Bird didn't
insult or refuse to play with awkward beginners. He'd been through
those scenes himself when he was starting out. He did come close to
sarcasm one night when a nice young man named Tony, who had fan-
tasies of being a tenor saxophone star but very little understanding of
jazz, played with Bird at a session and then asked him what he thought.
Bird looked at him and smiled.

"Tony," he said, "you're incredible."

Bird filled his solos with melodic themes taken from a wide range of
sources. He was an omnivorous listener, and recycled everything he
heard. If he'd been listening to Bartok or Webern during the day, his
solos that night would quote their themes. If he heard someone practicing finger exercises on the piano, he'd tuck some of them into a solo.
I once heard him play the verse to an obscure pop tune called "My
Little Nest of Heav'nly Blue." The only reason I knew the song was
that it was in a stack of old sheet music on my mother's piano in Kirkland. I'd love to know where Bird learned it.

One night at Birdland, Bird showed up on the bandstand playing an
alto saxophone made of cream-colored plastic. Everyone speculated about
the new instrument, some claiming it was an improvement on a metal
horn, some deprecating it as a toy. Bird played it because the instru-

ment company had given it to him. As they had hoped, people accepted the plastic alto because Bird was playing it.

Though I liked his Selmer better, I thought Bird sounded fine on the plastic horn. He could get his own sound on any saxophone he picked up, whatever the make, mouthpiece, reed, etc. A good horn made it easier for him, but there seemed to be no such thing as a bad horn in Charlie Parker's hands.

I ran into Bird one afternoon in Washington Square Park. He was living way east of the park on Avenue B, and my place was a block west of it. We sat on a bench under the trees and chatted for a while. A little girl came by who was having trouble with a mismatched wheel on her tricycle, and Bird got into a serious discussion with her about possible remedies.

After she pedaled squeakily away, I mentioned that I usually joined a group of friends every Sunday morning at the nearby city swimming pool on Seventh Avenue between Carmine and Leroy streets. Weekday mornings were reserved for children's swimming classes, but on Sunday mornings the Leroy Street pool was our country club. Bird sounded interested and said he'd join us sometime. After chatting a while longer he headed on home.

I hadn't expected Bird to show up at the pool, but the next Sunday morning he was waiting at the entrance with a little canvas gym bag in his hand. We went into the locker room, got into our bathing trunks, and joined the Sunday regulars stretched out on towels on the sunny side of the pool. When we got too warm, we would jump in and get wet and then return to the towels for more sunning and conversation.

Bird wore a thin rubber bathing cap, but he didn't really swim that day. He just floated a little and had some splashing contests with a couple of kids. Once he sank to the bottom of the pool and stayed there so long that we became concerned. I leaned over the edge and looked down at him. He was lying on the bottom, curled up in a fetal position, grinning. I could see the sun twinkling on his gold tooth. When he finally surfaced, he was pleased to discover that he had worried us.

"I can hold my breath a *long* time," he said.

Even though Charlie seemed to enjoy himself at the pool that morning, he never came back. I ran across him now and then in the park, or at the Open Door on West Fourth Street or the Spotlite on West Third. He was always friendly, at ease, a charming conversationalist with a broad range of interests and an optimistic point of view. He made me feel that the possibilities for satisfaction in music and art were unlimited.

I was especially saddened to hear that during his last days Bird was feeling defeated and unappreciated. I like to remember him at the peak of his skill, sure of himself, able to do anything, expansive, kind, generous, flowing with the wonder and delight of his own imagination, secure in the dignity of the master artist deep in his work. It is a tragedy that he lost all that at the end and that his life was so soon over.

Though I hoped to find a memory of him in Clint Eastwood's movie *Bird,* I was sorry to see that, except on the soundtrack, Charlie wasn't there. The movie missed Bird's nature, his confidence, his intelligence, and especially his wit.

Everyone who knew him has their own memories of him, and many have already been published. I wasn't surprised to find Dizzy Gillespie's recollections more appreciative of Bird's fine qualities than those of Miles Davis, who acknowledged Bird's genius, but wrote him off as "one of the slimiest and greediest motherfuckers who ever lived in this world . . ." "(who) never did know when to stop, and that's what killed him." Hard words for the man who Miles also said "treated me like a son, and he and Dizzy were father figures to me."

All of the collected memories of him still don't add up to the complex, fascinating man that Bird was. But even if we fail to tell it all on the written page, even if the movie about him is a caricature, when the last personal memory of him has faded, Charlie Parker's recorded music, that wonderful, beautiful music, will let listeners of the future know that a great artist passed this way. Bird lives. Indeed.

chapter 29

Gerry Mulligan

Stan Getz's quintet broke up in California not long after I left him. Bob Brookmeyer stayed in Los Angeles for a while, sometimes playing with Zoot Sims and Gerry Mulligan, who had both moved out there. Bob eventually became a regular member of Gerry's quartet. Then, on one job, Gerry added Zoot and Jon Eardley, and the Gerry Mulligan Sextet was born.

Gerry, Zoot, and Brookmeyer moved back to New York, and Gerry formed a new sextet with Idrees Sulieman on trumpet. Through Idrees's recommendation, Peck Morrison became the bass player, and Peck brought in Dave Bailey as the drummer. Idrees never recorded with the sextet; when he left in 1955, Jon Eardley came east and took his place.

That winter, Peck left the group and Gerry asked me to replace him. I was happy with Marian's trio, but I loved Gerry's music, and I couldn't turn down the chance to play regularly with Zoot and Bob. I gave Marian my notice and began rehearsing with Gerry in December 1955. The sextet, like Gerry's quartet, used no piano, even though he and Brookmeyer both played that instrument. Gerry built his arrangements for the four horns on just the bass line and the drums.

Marian's lovely harmonic sense and her penchant for playing tunes in unusual keys had drawn me into improving my playing technique, and she had given me room to develop as a soloist. But as soon as I joined Gerry's group I discovered I was in technical trouble. The fingering system I had invented for myself worked fine in the lower register of the bass, but I hadn't figured out how to be accurate in the upper register. I could play high notes if I worked my way up to them, but I couldn't be sure I had my finger on exactly the right spot on the fingerboard if I had to begin a passage on a high note.

I found some of Gerry's bass parts hard to play. I made pencil marks on my fingerboard to help me find troublesome notes, but I saw that it was time that I learned some of the things that other bass players seemed to know. The only time I'd ever heard anyone mention a bass teacher was when Marian's trio had played on a CBS radio show; staff bassist Trigger Alpert had told me that he was studying with Fred Zimmerman. I called Trigger and got Fred's number.

I couldn't have found a better teacher. Fred, the principal bassist with the New York Philharmonic at the time, taught with skill and imagination. At my first lesson I explained that I was self-taught and didn't know the right way to do anything. Fred said, "So, we'll just start you at the very beginning, as if you'd never played before. That way, we won't miss anything, and when we come to things you already know, it will go quickly."

It was discouraging to discover how much I didn't know. For the next several years, I took lessons from Fred whenever I was in New York. He showed me the standard fingering system and encouraged me in my struggle with bow control. His empathy and interest were most helpful.

"I studied with a man who used to hit my hands with a stick when I made a mistake," Fred told me. "I swore then that if I ever became a teacher I would never add any pain to the learning process. The physical problems of playing the bass are already painful enough."

I would always go early for my lesson. Fred's apartment on West Fifty-fifth Street was filled with art treasures that I loved looking at. He had a collection of pre-Colombian gold weights, delightful little figurines. On his walls were Pechsteins, Kirschners, Klees, and several of Fred's own oils. His bookshelves were filled with what looked like a complete collection of the Skira art reproduction books.

When I made progress with the bass, Fred was always enthusiastic. Once he ran into the kitchen, got his wife, and had me replay a passage for her. Fred said, "Isn't that beautiful? And he isn't even serious about music!"

Fred may have felt that a vocation in jazz was frivolous, but he was openminded. One day he had me play a few bars of dotted eighth notes he had copied out. I think it was from a Hindemith piece the Philharmonic was rehearsing. It looked like a swing figure to me, so I phrased it that way. Fred said, "That's not the way it's written."

"No, but that's the way any jazz musician would play it. We play most things that are written in four-four as if they were written in twelve-eight. It's swing phrasing."

"Aha!" said Fred. "I knew the way we were playing it sounded corny, but I didn't know why."

Fred told me excitedly one day that Charles Mingus had called him to do a record date with him. He knew Mingus's reputation as an innovator in jazz, and was eager to play his music. When I saw him the following week, I asked him how the recording had gone.

"It was a fiasco!" said Fred angrily. "Everything on my part was written at the very top of the range of the bass! It was almost impossible to play, and it sounded ridiculous. I told Mr. Mingus if he wanted to write cello parts, he should have hired a cello player! He kept saying it sounded fine. I was never so uncomfortable in my life!"

My first work with Mulligan's sextet was in nightclubs around the Northeast. We squeezed in a record date in January 1956 for a Mercury album that Gerry had begun while Peck Morrison was with him. Then in February we began a European tour. The promoter brought us to Italy on the *Andrea Doria,* the beautiful ship of the Italian Lines that sank the following year after a collision with a freighter. Gerry's

wife, Arlene, came with us as our road manager, and Brookmeyer
brought his wife, Phyllis. We rehearsed a couple of times on the ship,
but I spent most of the trip playing ping-pong on deck with Zoot.

We played concerts in Naples, Rome, Milan, Genoa, and Bologna. It
was Gerry's first European tour, and we were made very welcome. At
a restaurant in Bologna our local guides said we should ask for a special Bolognese delicacy called "pompini." The waitress blushed deeply
when we asked for some, and we realized we had been set up. "Pompini" turned out to be a local slang word for oral sex.

After the Bologna concert we were taken to a restaurant to meet the
members of the local jazz club. We were each seated in a separate booth
with several young Italians who were doing their best to discuss jazz
with us in English. A commotion broke out at the bar, and the fans I
was sitting with hurried me outside. They said some Communist students were trying to create a disturbance, and we would be safer out in
the street.

I searched the throng that had rushed out of the restaurant with us,
but I couldn't locate any of the rest of the sextet, or the Italian promoters who had brought us on the train to Bologna from Milan. Just
as I was wondering how I would get back to Milan if I couldn't find
them, a young man stepped over to me and said, "Say, man, didn't I
meet you in New Jersey at a jam session with Phil Urso?"

He was an American exchange student and a jazz musician. He helped
me find the rest of my party, who had gone out a different exit onto a
side street.

When we arrived to play at one Italian opera house, we saw a huge
banner hanging across the front of the building that read: "Stasera, il
sestetto GERRY MULLIGAN, CON ARLENE MULLIGAN, ROBERT BROOKMEYER,
PHYLLIS BROOKMEYER, WILLIAM O. CROW, e SAMMY DAVIS, JR." Someone
had evidently taken the names from our official papers. They had
transformed Dave Bailey into Sammy Davis, Jr., by misreading Dave's
full name: Samuel David Bailey, Jr.

Since Zoot's name had been omitted, he kept trying to hand his tenor
to Arlene as we went on stage.

"You're the one they came to see," he said.

As we sat in a backstage greenroom during intermission, an Italian
jazz fan who had begged or bribed his way past the house security men
appeared with record albums for Gerry and Zoot to sign. He said to
Jon, "And you are Jon Eardley, from Altoona, Pennsylvania, whose
father played trumpet with Paul Whiteman and Isham Jones and now
works for a finance company?" Jon looked stunned.

"Man, *nobody* knows that!"

I was thrilled about visiting Italy, and I wanted to see everything. I got up at dawn every day and, armed with my Berlitz phrase book and a camera, walked all over every city we visited. When I returned to play the concert each evening, I'd report on the day's discoveries to the rest of the group. Zoot usually didn't venture too far from the hotel, but he seemed interested in hearing about what was out there. On the way to our first concert in Milan, Zoot saw something he liked in the window of a shoe store as we drove by. He asked me, "Do you know how to get back here?"

I did, and offered to accompany him the following day. I was a little surprised that Zoot was taking an interest in Italian shoes; he usually wore casual clothes: corduroy trousers, sweaters, and sneakers.

The next morning, when I tapped at his door, I found Zoot dressed and ready to go. We walked back to the neighborhood where he had seen the shoes he wanted. They turned out to be heavy brown canvas hiking shoes with thick rubber soles and high tops that laced up with hook eyelets. When Zoot tried on a pair his eyes lit up with pleasure.

"Yeah! These are *my* shoes!"

He wore them constantly for the rest of the trip.

When our Italian concerts were finished, the promoters put us on a stiffly sprung little Mercedes-Benz bus with seats as hard and straight as church pews. We slowly chugged across the French border and up to Paris via some very narrow roads. The ride was bumpy, but the scenery was great.

In Paris, we were installed in a pension near the stage entrance to the Olympia Theater, where we were to appear for a three-week run as one of the acts on a variety bill. The show opened with jugglers and comedians. We went on just before the Nicholas Brothers, Fayard and Harold, who closed the first half of the show with their famous tap dancing routine. After an intermission there was a dog act, a dancing violin duo, another comedian, and then the headliner, Jacqueline Fran-çois, the popular French Canadian singer.

When our turn came, the pretty young lady who was the emcee would step in front of the curtain and announce, "Et maintenant, Zhe-REE Mooli-GAHN et son sextette!"

The curtains would part and we would play about three tunes, and that was it for that show. With only two or three short appearances scheduled every day and all of Paris to explore in our spare time, it was inevitable that sometimes, when the curtain opened, someone would be missing. Jon slept through the first show one day, and on another afternoon Zoot stood at the stage door chatting with a friend for so long that our part of the show was over by the time he finally came inside the theater. The emcee would announce, "Et maintenant, Zhe-REE Mooli-GAHN et son . . ." and then she would pause, peer behind the curtain and count heads, and then continue, ". . . son sextette!" or ". . . quartette!" or whatever the number was at the moment. A lecture from Gerry brought us back up to full strength for the remaining shows.

The musicians in Paris made us very welcome. Henri Renaud and his wife Ny introduced us to many of them, and Henri took us to jazz clubs on the Left Bank where we could sit in after our last show. Zoot and Dave and I were jamming one night with Henri and some other musicians in a Left Bank sub-basement. Zoot's admirers had been toasting him liberally, and he was feeling no pain. He was too stoned to stand up, but he still felt like dancing. Slumped in his chair, eyes closed, he blew energetically into his tenor, playing chorus after chorus of his own special brand of whoopee.

On the last couple of choruses Zoot gave up trying to articulate anything intricate. He just swung the same simple riff harder and harder. He finally surrendered to exhaustion and relinquished the tune to the next soloist. Falling back in his chair, he looked over his shoulder and gave me a snaggle-toothed grin.

"You know," he said, "you can have a lot of fun with these musical instruments!"

chapter 30

Duke Ellington

American jazz drummer Kansas Fields was living in Paris, and the Nicholas Brothers had hired him to play their act at the Olympia Theater. Kansas spoke a wonderful mixture of fractured French and Harlem argot, but the locals seemed to have no trouble understanding him. Between shows on our first day at the theater, Kansas took us to a

restaurant in Montmartre owned by American ex–football player Leroy
Haynes and his French wife, Gaby. The cuisine was American soul food
served with French salads, bread, and wine. Haynes and Gaby's became
my favorite dinnertime hangout. Any American jazz musicians or entertainers who were passing through Paris were sure to turn up there.

Another American in Paris, Art Simmons, was playing solo piano at
the Mars Club. Dave Bailey and I spent many evenings there after our
last show. Art used Dave and me on a record date with his quartet,
with Terry Donoughue on guitar, and on another record with American singer Bertice Reading. I wrote some blues lyrics for Bertice to sing
that included a plug for Haynes and Gaby's restaurant.

Bob Brookmeyer's recordings had impressed the trombone players
in England, and when they heard that he was in Paris, four of them
came over to hear him at the Olympia. They attended several of our
performances and hung out with Bob between shows. One of them, Ed
Harvey, charmed us all with his radiant good nature. When we toured
England in 1963, Ed took Bob and me on a tour of all the best pubs in
London.

On the Olympia Theater's day off each week, Émile Cocatrix, the
owner, sent us to play in nearby cities. We played in concert halls in
Lille and Rouen, but in Roubaix we were booked into a movie theater.
We had made the long drive to Roubaix on a cold day in two old Ci-
troëns, neither one with a heater that worked, and we were dismayed
to discover that we had to wait shivering in the parking lot until the
movie was over and the screen was dismantled. There was no dressing
room. The door from the parking lot led directly onto the stage.

Our most bizarre concert appearance took place in Lyon, after the
Paris engagement. We were supposed to play three nights there, along
with a local band that would provide dance music. A special feature
was to be a contest for the "world's champion be-bop dancers." The
weekend was sponsored by the Hot Club of Lyon and the Lyon Be-bop
Club.

Our stage at the Palais d'Hiver, an athletic arena in Lyon, was high
on one wall, far from the grandstand tiers where the audience sat. As
soon as we began to play, a large section of the audience began to
shout, boo, and ring cowbells. One guy even had a battery-operated
klaxon. We stopped playing and looked around, perplexed. The people in the audience were arguing and fighting among themselves.

One of the promoters came on stage and explained to us that there
were many jazz fans in Lyon who felt that anything that didn't sound
like the music of Sidney Bechet or early Louis Armstrong was not jazz.

An anti-bebop group had come to disrupt the concert. Gerry listened to the bedlam in the audience for a moment and then said, "Screw them. Let's get out of here."

He canceled our remaining appearances in Lyon, and we went on to Geneva and spent a few pleasant days there before our scheduled concerts in Switzerland. Zoot and Brookmeyer and I rented bicycles and spent an afternoon in Geneva riding along the lake shore. The Swiss audiences were eager to hear our music, and we met some good musicians at jam sessions there.

We finished the tour in April with concerts in Brussels and Paris before sailing for New York on the *Queen Elizabeth*. When Ny Renaud heard we were returning on a British steamship, her face fell. British cuisine had a poor reputation among the French.

"Oh, you poor things," she said. "Pack a lunch."

Back in New York, Gerry noticed some nice-looking and inexpensive corduroy jackets in the window of the Bond's store on Broadway. The material had vertical one-inch stripes of three alternating shades of gray. We each bought one for a second uniform. The first time we wore the jackets was at a concert uptown at the Audubon Ballroom.

We went in through the front entrance where a line of people were waiting to buy tickets. Bond's must have done well with that corduroy pattern. Half a dozen young men in the waiting line were wearing the same jackets we had on. When they saw us, they rushed over and offered to carry our instruments, telling the ticket taker that they were with the band. We laughed and said, "How many people do you think there are in a sextet?"

Jon Eardley moved to Florida, and Don Ferrara took his place on trumpet. Between jobs we finished the album that Gerry had begun for Mercury Records. Nippon Phonogram reissued this material in the 1980s, and squeezed three twelve-inch LPs out of it by including alternate and discarded takes. There was a blues Gerry played on piano as a warm-up tune before the mikes were set, and Gil Evans's arrangement of Claude Debussy's "La Plus Que Lente," which had originally been shelved because the guardians of the Debussy estate informed Mercury Records that they wouldn't permit arrangements to be made of his work. I'm glad it was finally released. It was the only Gil Evans arrangement we had.

Gerry's last sextet job was a week at the upstairs room of the Prevue Lounge in Chicago. Zoot had begun to work with his own quartet and told Gerry this was the last sextet job he would accept. Don Ferrara wasn't available, so Dave Bailey recommended young Oliver Beener,

who learned the book quickly and did a fine job with us. From then on
Gerry, Bob, Dave, and I worked as a quartet until 1957, when I left
the group.

Gerry took a month off during the summer of 1956, and I filled the
time working with J. J. Johnson and Kai Winding. It was their last
month of bookings before they broke up their quintet: a week at Basin
Street West, a night at the Newport Jazz Festival, and an album for
Columbia Records. The arrangements J.J. had written for the two
trombones had resulted in some very successful recordings, but by the
time I joined them I could tell that both he and Kai had lost interest in
the format. They each had plans for new groups, and were just going
through the motions until this one finished out its last bookings.

On our first night at Basin Street, Dick Katz, the pianist, helped me
learn the arrangements. My old friend Kenny Clarke was the drummer. He wasn't playing with much spirit on the first set. He was suffering with a toothache and was just trying to get through the night.

Then Carl Fontana walked in carrying his trombone. When Jay and
Kai invited him to sit in, Carl faked a rich third part on the opening
ensemble of "It's All Right with Me" and then was given the first blowing chorus. Carl immediately swung the whole rhythm section into life.
Kenny forgot about his tooth and put the pots on. Carl played with
such joyous effervescence that Jay and Kay woke up and began to cook.
The three trombonists traded choruses, eights and fours, then played
a riotous out chorus. The rhythm section was all smiles; this was more
like it! Even after Carl left, we stayed in a good groove. Everyone enjoyed the rest of that week. Kenny Clarke was getting ready to move to
Paris, but he made a record date with us for Columbia before he left
town. Rudy Collins was our drummer at Newport.

We played at Newport on the night of the Duke Ellington band's
electrifying appearance. They were playing exceptionally well, and the
assembled musicians and friends backstage were as excited as the audience. We danced and carried on all night while the band romped
and swung. It was a great party.

Duke always surrounded himself with musicians who provided him
with the sounds he wanted to hear, but that band had a reputation for
idiosyncrasy and capriciousness that outstripped any other I ever heard
of. Some members of the trumpet section weren't on speaking terms
for years. Shorty Baker once told me:

"When I first joined that band, they let me sit there playing wrong
notes for a week without telling me the parts had been changed! Nobody ever marked changes. The trumpet parts were all full of traps. I

wasn't used to that sort of thing. In St. Louis, where I came from, musicians were a family. If your ass was out some kind of way, somebody would pull your coat and let you know."

The saxophone section also had its problems. Years after he'd left Duke, Ben Webster came to hear the band one night at Birdland, and Paul Gonsalves invited him to sit in. Ben took Paul's horn and climbed up onto the bandstand next to Johnny Hodges, who gave him no greeting. When Duke asked him what he'd like to play, Ben chose "I Got It Bad, and That Ain't Good," and rendered it with great beauty. Throughout the entire number, Hodges sat scowling at Ben.

As Paul slid back into his chair after Ben left the stand, I heard Johnny say indignantly, "That was *my* tune! The man *knows* that was my tune!"

I got to play with Duke's band one evening when Gerry Mulligan's quartet was scheduled to share a concert with them at Lewisohn Stadium, an outdoor amphitheater at 135th and Amsterdam in New York. Duke's bass player hadn't arrived, and it was beginning to look like rain. Duke looked at his watch, inspected the sky, and walked over to where I was standing with my bass.

"Come with me," he said, taking my arm and pulling me on stage. I followed him as if in a dream as he positioned me at the left end of his keyboard. When I reached down to get the bass book that was lying under the music stand, Britt Woodman leaned over from the trombone section and said, "Don't do that. That's all been changed."

Meanwhile, Duke was out front announcing the first number. Britt said, "Just hang around in B-flat. We'll tell you when to change."

I'd been listening to Duke's music all my life, and just followed my ears. With the trombone players giving me helpful clues, everything went fine. Duke stayed in front of the band most of the time, but when he announced a ballad I didn't know, he came to the piano. While playing his own part and continuing to relate to the audience, he made sure I had the information I needed. He would point to the piano key that represented my note each time there was a chord coming up that I needed to know about. He never played my note for me. He just pointed to it half a beat before I needed it. I was able to play as if he'd written out a part for me.

I had such a good time playing with Duke that Gerry's nose got a little out of joint. As the quartet took the stage, he grumbled to Duke about "tiring out my bass player," and later said to me, "How come you don't have that much fun playing with me?"

I did, of course, but this was Duke's band! I was quite properly thrilled.

A few months later at a jazz festival at French Lick, Indiana, I was in the hotel lobby waiting for the elevator when the doors slid open and out walked Duke.

"Ah, Mister Crow," he intoned silkily, giving me a courtly bow, "I never had the opportunity to remunerate you for your splendid assistance at the concert in New York."

"Please be my guest," I said, returning his bow. "The pleasure was entirely mine."

He accepted with a smile and a nod and glided elegantly off to the dining room.

In 1963, when I was with a later edition of Mulligan's quartet, we were rehearsing background music for the live broadcast of a dramatic show at the NBC-TV Brooklyn studios. We discovered that Duke's band was in the main studio rehearsing the Ed Sullivan Show. We went over and found the band on a break. After we had chatted with Duke's musicians for a bit, the studio manager called time and they headed back to the bandstand. A fuss arose because a tenor player, new on the band, hadn't come back from the men's room.

Cootie Williams, who was back with Duke after years of leading his own band, made an indignant speech excoriating the man's discourtesy and lack of professionalism.

"This isn't no nightclub!" he said. "This is nationwide television! We got to make time! Time is money!"

When the tenor man came rushing in, abashed to find everyone waiting for him, Cootie dressed him down. Then, as everyone in the studio got ready for the next segment they were rehearsing, Cootie pointedly laid down his horn and walked out to the men's room. If they were going to wait for someone, it was going to be someone worth waiting for! During the entire episode, Duke remained aloof, refusing to notice that anything unusual was going on.

Duke's success in keeping his band together during the years when other big jazz bands were unable to stay in business was a minor miracle. He pumped his ASCAP royalties into the payroll, and he kept salaries as low as he could.

Trumpeter Leo Ball told me he was traveling in Europe during the 1960s and had just cleared customs at the Amsterdam Airport when, as he started down the stairs to the street level, he saw his old friend Rolf Ericson. Rolf was at that time one of Duke's trumpet players. Leo saw that his friend was talking to someone whose face wasn't visible, but as he rushed down the stairs and threw his arms around Rolf, greeting him warmly, the other man melted into the crowd. Rolf said, "Leo, I love you, but I'm not so glad to see you right now. I've been trying for a year to get next to Duke Ellington to ask him for a raise. I finally had him cornered, and because of you he got away!"

chapter 31

Garner & Monk

I enjoyed several weeks of good companionship and a lot of good music when Gerry Mulligan's Quartet joined a tour that included the Erroll Garner Trio, the Miles Davis Quintet, Count Basie's Band, Kai Winding's new four-trombone septet, and Dinah Washington.

One cold day in Detroit, we played in an arena where most of the dressing rooms were unheated. When I heard that Basie's large dressing room was warm, I carried my bass over to wait there for our turn on stage. Several others had the same idea. Basie had an old upright piano in his room, and was sitting at the keyboard, tinkling a little, so I began playing along with him. Freddie Green broke out his guitar, and couple of horn players joined in.

More musicians came in to warm up and to drink some of Basie's scotch. I was having a great time playing until I suddenly realized there were five other bass players among the crowd in Basie's room. With six of us on the tour, that meant that one of us should have been on stage. Sure enough, it was me. I stopped playing in mid-measure and ran with my bass to the stage, where Gerry's Quartet was getting ready to play as a trio without me.

Gerry didn't like the train connection that the tour manager had made for the jump from Detroit to Toronto, requiring us to leave very early in the morning. He decided to fly the quartet there, absorbing the extra expense himself. We got some extra sleep, but bad weather delayed our takeoff and put our plane into a very long holding pattern before we could land. We had to circle the airport for about an hour. To keep

the passengers happy, the flight attendants served everyone complimentary cocktails. I usually didn't drink, but I accepted a martini and
began to feel quite merry, laughing and carrying on. Bob Brookmeyer,
my seatmate, was an experienced drinker. He looked at me grumpily
and said, "That's disgusting. Do you realize it costs me thirty-five dollars to feel that way?"

Wynton Kelly was Dinah's piano player in those days. A wonderful
accompanist, Wynton was also full of fun. He was often the center of
backstage laughing sessions as we told stories on each other. Wynton
had a removable upper front denture. While on stage, if he saw some
of us standing in the wings listening, he would turn around so the
audience couldn't see, give us a stern look, and drop his upper plate
forward onto his lower lip, creating a grotesquely comical effect. Sometimes he heightened it by sticking his tongue out at us over his upper
teeth.

When the tour reached Chicago, Dave and I accepted someone's invitation to attend a party at a Gold Coast mansion. Several musicians
were there, including Roy Haynes, who was in town with Sarah Vaughan.
When we told him about our tour and mentioned that Erroll Garner
was with us, Roy sat down at the piano and did a hilarious imitation of
him. He had Erroll's facial expression and movements exactly right.
Just like Erroll's, his left hand played a steady four-four while his right
hand played phrases that lay far behind the beat. But *all* of the notes
were wrong; Roy just hit any keys that fell under his fingers. Amazingly, because he had the rhythmic pattern so exactly right, it still
sounded like Erroll.

Erroll was as charming offstage as he was on. He was gregarious,
curious, interested in everything. Having put his career completely in
the hands of Martha Glaser, his manager, Erroll relaxed and enjoyed
life. He was happy to let Martha do all the worrying.

Martha was very successful in elevating Erroll from gin mill piano
player to concert artist. She later took him away from Joe Glaser's
booking office and signed him with concert impresario Sol Hurok, as
the only jazz artist Hurok represented.

Martha covered every angle for Erroll. She made sure he had good
pianos to play. She had the lights and sound system carefully adjusted.
And she insisted that Errol's spotlight be trimmed so that it wouldn't
spill onto drummer Kelly Martin. She always kept Kelly and bassist
Eddie Calhoun in the dark, placing all the focus on Erroll.

Martha saw to it that the travel arrangements and hotel amenities on
the tour were comfortable, and she made sure that a Manhattan phone

book always traveled with Erroll. The standard piano bench was lower than he liked to sit, and he had discovered that sitting on the Manhattan directory gave him just the right height.

When our tour left Chicago, Dave Bailey and I entered the railroad terminal with our instruments and met Erroll just inside the door. He said, pointing to a row of shops behind him, "Look at this wristwatch I just bought over here."

We stopped and admired it, then continued toward the platform where the train was loading. Erroll went off to explore the other shops in the terminal. A moment later we met Martha, who demanded, "Where's Erroll?"

We pointed in the direction he had disappeared, and she hurried off in search of him. Then Erroll breezed up from a different direction, saying, "Look at this beautiful pair of cufflinks I found!"

We told him Martha was looking for him. He smiled and waved and headed in the opposite direction.

After locating our coach and strapping the bass and drums safely in a corner of the vestibule, Dave and I settled into a seat, and just before the train pulled out, Erroll climbed aboard with Martha right behind him, making shooing noises. Erroll came over to show us the rest of his shopping acquisitions.

As the train got under way, Erroll began to tell us a story. He talked with great animation while peering into our faces to make sure we were getting the whole picture. Passengers nearby began to listen as he continued his lively tale, and whenever Erroll saw a pair of eyes turned his way, he included that person in the telling.

Erroll's audience gradually got so large that he had to stand in the aisle and raise his voice to include everyone. By the time he got to the climax of his story, he was addressing most of the car. His transition from tête-à-tête to performer-and-audience was smooth and natural. He just included everyone who looked interested.

On our final concert in Philadelphia there was some trouble. Ticket sales had failed to meet the expectations of the local promoter. At intermission, he hadn't produced the money required by the contract, and the tour manager told him that there would be no more music until he did. After a long wait, someone came backstage with the box-office receipts, a cardboard carton filled with cash. The manager began paying off the musicians and told Gerry to go ahead and start the second half. After we played our set and went backstage again, the manager told us, "Sorry. There was just enough money to pay everybody else. There's nothing left for you guys."

I didn't see Erroll again until I dropped in at the Plaza Hotel one night to hear Lionel Hampton's band. The hotel was trying a jazz policy in one of its restaurants, but had provided the band with a disgracefully out-of-tune spinet piano that had several broken keys. Hamp's pianist had pushed it aside and set up a little Wurlitzer electric piano that he carried with him on the road as a practice instrument. Electric pianos were fairly primitive in those days, and this one sounded like a toy.

Erroll lived just up the street at the Carnegie Hall apartments. He and some friends came in and took a table in front of the bandstand. Hampton motioned for him to come up and play, and Hamp's pianist got up from the Wurlitzer to make room for him. Erroll sat down at the spinet instead, indicating his preference for a "real" piano. As he played one measure on the crippled spinet, his eyebrows shot up and his mouth made an O of surprise. He leaped up without missing a beat and continued his solo on the Wurlitzer. Even with its limitations, he made it sound wonderful.

During one of Gerry's New York jobs, the quartet made an appearance on Art Ford's Jazz Party, a television show originating at a studio in Newark, New Jersey. Whenever out-of-town musicians appeared on the show, the Newark musicians' union required the station to hire an equal number of its members, even if they weren't given anything to play. Vinnie Burke and Lou Carter and several other Jersey residents were in that house band. Gerry thought it was ridiculous to have good musicians just standing around, so he organized a jam session that would include them for the last number.

Josh White was scheduled to appear on the show, but wasn't feeling well. He sent his son and daughter as substitutes. During the rehearsal they sang nicely to the accompaniment of Josh Jr.'s guitar. On the camera rehearsal for the jam session, a blues, Gerry invited young Josh to join us. As soon as he began to play, Gerry stopped the music and told him, "Your guitar isn't in tune with the band."

Josh, Jr. said with disappointment, "Aw, what a drag! I really wanted to play with you guys!"

He was greatly relieved when we explained that the situation could be corrected. He tuned up and joined the fun.

Feeling that our quartet needed some fresh ideas, Gerry invited Thelonius Monk to one of our rehearsals. I was intrigued with and somewhat puzzled by Monk's music. With the exception of " 'Round Midnight," and a couple of his blues tunes, I found his compositions difficult from a bass player's point of view. The notes Monk played in his left hand sounded like the only bass notes that fit his tunes. I wasn't sure what variations were appropriate on the blowing choruses.

Monk came to the rehearsal studio and sat down at the piano. When Gerry asked him what he'd like to play, Monk began one of his own tunes. When he got to the end of it he started over again, playing it exactly the same way. We realized that he intended to teach it to us by rote, so we began finding it on our instruments. By the time Monk had played it a third time, Gerry and Brookmeyer were ready to try improvising a few choruses. I memorized the bass notes Monk was playing and tried to identify the chords by ear, but his angular way of playing made them difficult to hear.

When we finished that tune, Monk went right into another of his originals, playing it over and over in the same manner. Again, we played along tentatively until we learned it, and then took a few choruses apiece. By the time we took that one out, my head was beginning to ache from the concentration. I said to Monk, "These tunes are really hard. Before you teach us another one, how about playing something we all know, just for a breather?"

Monk nodded, and without asking what we might like to play, he once again addressed the keyboard. The standard he chose was "Tea for Two." If you've heard his record of that tune, you'll know why we all started laughing. He had found a substitute harmonic cycle that worked wonderfully with the melody, but had nothing whatever to do with the original chord structure. Playing "Tea for Two" with Monk was just as difficult as learning any of his original tunes.

When we took a break, we went around the corner for a beer. Standing at the bar, Monk became more talkative. After we chatted about a number of mundane things, I led the conversation back to his music. I told him I had trouble hearing bass lines on some of his tunes. He said, "Just keep listening, and you'll hear the right thing to play."

He was right. It took me a while, but I did begin to hear what I should be playing.

I told Monk that some of his intervals surprised me. They would sound unusual, but when I checked them out, they were ordinary fifths, sixths, sevenths. It was his touch that made them sound different. He nodded and said, "It can't be any new note. When you look at the keyboard, all the notes are there already. But if you *mean* a note enough, it will sound different. You got to pick the notes you really mean!"

Years later, Monk was asked to do a college clinic for a group of jazz students. He sat and listened carefully as they played for him, and then was asked for his analysis and comments. He stood before the group, lost in thought for a moment. He paced back and forth a bit, rubbing his chin. Then he looked seriously at each of the waiting faces and gathered himself to speak:

"Keep on tryin'! " he said, and sat down again.

chapter 32

Pee Wee Russell

Gerry Mulligan's quartet often played at George Wein's Storyville in the Copley Square Hotel. In the basement of the same hotel, Wein also had a room called Mahogany Hall, where he featured traditional jazz with musicians like Vic Dickenson and Pee Wee Russell. During one year's-end engagement, George wanted to combine both bands in a jam session upstairs at Storyville to welcome the new year. Gerry offered to write an arrangement of "Auld Lang Syne" for the occasion.

Gerry finished the arrangement and called an afternoon rehearsal on the day of New Year's Eve. Pee Wee Russell was worried about reading the music and made suffering noises. He sounded fine, but continued to worry. That night, the musicians from Mahogany Hall came up to jam a few tunes with us before twelve o'clock, and as the hour approached, Gerry called for his chart, but Pee Wee's part was missing. Though we were disappointed, there was nothing we could do. Midnight was upon us. We had to fake a Dixieland version of "Auld Lang Syne." As we left the bandstand afterwards, there on Pee Wee's chair I saw the missing part. The crafty bastard had been sitting on it all the time.

Pee Wee and I were both early risers, so I often met the tall, cadaverous-looking clarinetist for breakfast in the hotel coffee shop. He was talkative at that hour, but it took me a while to catch everything he said. His voice seemed reluctant to leave his throat. It would sometimes get lost in his moustache, or take muffled detours through his long free-form nose.

Pee Wee's playing often had an anguished sound. He screwed his rubbery face into woeful expressions as he simultaneously fought the clarinet, the chord changes, and his imagination. He was respectful of the dangers inherent in the adventure of improvising, and never approached it casually.

Pee Wee's conversational style mirrored the way he played. He would sidle up to a subject, poke at it tentatively, make several disclaimers about the worthlessness of his opinion, inquire if he'd lost my interest, suggest other possible topics of conversation, and then would dart back to his original subject and quickly illuminate it with a few pithy remarks mumbled hastily into his coffee cup. It was always worth the wait. His comments were fascinating, and he had a delightful way with a phrase.

His hesitant and circuitous manner of speaking, combined with his habit of drawing his lanky frame into a concave position that seemed to express a vain hope for invisibility, gave me a first impression of shyness and passivity. I soon discovered that there was a bright intelligence and sense of humor under that façade. Also there was a determined resistance to being pushed in any direction Pee Wee didn't want to go.

I'd heard stories of the many years Pee Wee had spent drinking heavily while playing in the band at Nick's in Greenwich Village. Like many of the musicians of his era, Pee Wee had considered liquor to be an integral part of the jazz life. Over the years, the quantity of booze that he put away eventually wore him down so badly that once or twice he was thought to have died, when in fact he was just sleeping. His diet for years was mainly alcohol, with occasional "meals" that consisted of a can of tomatoes, unheated, washed down with a glass of milk. On the bandstand he always looked emaciated and uncomfortable.

A friend told me that the only time Pee Wee ever came to work sober in those days was once when his wife, Mary, thought she was pregnant. That night Pee Wee arrived at Nick's in good focus, didn't drink all night, and actually held conversations with friends that he recognized. A couple of days later, when Mary found out her pregnancy was a false alarm, Pee Wee returned to his old routine, arriving at work in an alcoholic fog, speaking to no one, alternately playing and drinking all night long.

His health failed him in 1951. Pee Wee was hospitalized in San Francisco with multiple ailments, including acute malnutrition, cirrhosis of the liver, pancreatitis, and internal cysts. The doctors at first gave him no hope for recovery, and word had spread quickly through the jazz world that he was at death's door. It was reported in France that he had already passed through it. Sidney Bechet played a farewell concert for him in Paris.

Eddie Condon described the surgery that saved Pee Wee's life:

"They had him open like a canoe!"

Condon also was quoted as saying, "Pee Wee nearly died from too much living."

At any rate, Pee Wee miraculously rallied, recovered, and limped back to New York. When they heard of his illness and that he was broke, musicians in California, Chicago, and New York gave benefit concerts that raised around $4,500 to help with his medical expenses. Louis Armstrong and Jack Teagarden visited his hospital room in San Francisco and told him about the benefit they were planning. Pee Wee, sure that he was expressing his last wish, whispered, "Tell the newspapers not to write any sad stories about me."

After Pee Wee recovered, he completely changed his life style. He began eating regular meals, with which he drank milk and sometimes a glass of ale, but nothing stronger. He began to relax more and, at the urging of his wife, Mary, tried to diversify his interests.

"I haven't done anything except spend my life with a horn stuck in my face," he told a friend.

He began to turn down jobs that didn't appeal to him musically, staying home much of the time. For a while Mary wasn't sure she knew who he was. She said she had to get used to him all over again.

"He talks a lot now," she told an interviewer. "He never used to. It's as if he were trying to catch up."

After our first sojourn together in Boston, I played with Pee Wee on a couple of jobs with Jimmy McPartland in New York. And, since my apartment in the Village was not far from the building on King Street where Pee Wee and Mary lived, I saw him occasionally around the neighborhood, usually walking his little dog Winky up Seventh Avenue South. We'd stroll along together and chat about this and that while Pee Wee let the dog sniff and mark the tree trunks.

Once in a while Pee Wee would invite me over to the White Horse Tavern for a beer. He'd tell me stories about growing up in Missouri or playing with different bands in Texas or Chicago, but I was never clear about the chronology. I got the impression that he remembered life in the '20s and '30s with much more clarity than he did the '40s.

One summer afternoon I invited Pee Wee to accompany me for a swim at the city pool between Carmine and Leroy streets. He gave me an excruciatingly pained look.

"The world isn't ready for me in swim trunks."

Pee Wee surprised everyone in 1962 when, in collaboration with valve trombonist Marshall Brown, bassist Russell George and drummer Ron Lundberg, he began to use some modern jazz forms. Marshall pushed Pee Wee into learning some John Coltrane tunes and experimenting with musical structures he hadn't tried before. He made the transition with the same fierce effort with which he'd always approached improvisation, and the group made some good records.

Marshall, a so-so soloist who had been a high school music teacher, was tremendously enthusiastic, but was a terrible pedant, though a good-natured one. He couldn't resist taking the role of the instructor, even with accomplished musicians. Pee Wee told an interviewer, "Marshall certainly brought out things in me. It was strange. When he would correct me, I would say to myself, now why did he have to tell me that? I knew that already."

Mary Russell commented, "Pee Wee wants to kill him."

"I haven't taken so many orders since military school," said Pee Wee.

One day Pee Wee told me that he and Mary were moving out of their old apartment. A new development had been built between Eighth and Ninth avenues north of Twenty-third Street where several blocks of old tenements had been torn down. The Russells had bought a co-op apartment there. Around the same time, Aileen and I moved into an apartment building on the corner of Twentieth Street and Ninth Avenue, so I was still in Pee Wee's neighborhood. I would bump into him on the street now and then.

In 1965, Mary came home one day with a set of oil paints and some canvases on stretchers. She dumped it all in Pee Wee's lap and said, "Here, do something with yourself. Paint!"

He did. Holding the canvases in his lap or leaning them on the kitchen table as he painted, he produced nearly a hundred paintings during the ensuing two years, in a strikingly personal, primitive style. With bold brush strokes and solid masses of color he created abstract shapes, some with eccentric, asymmetrical faces. They were quite amazing. Though he enjoyed the praise of his friends and was delighted when some of his works sold at prices that astonished him, he painted primarily for Mary's appreciation. When she died in 1967, he put away his brushes for good.

With Mary gone, Pee Wee went back to drinking, and his health began to slowly deteriorate. In February 1969, during a visit to Washington, D.C., he was feeling so bad that he called a friend and had him check him into Alexandria Hospital. The doctors shut off his booze and did what they could to restore him to health, but this time he failed to respond to treatment. After a few days he just slipped away in his sleep.

The Jersey Jazz Society keeps Pee Wee's memory alive with their annual Pee Wee Russell Memorial Stomp, and there have been occasional showings of his paintings at art galleries. And, of course, there are still the records, reminding us of how wonderfully Pee Wee's playing teetered at the edge of musical disaster, where he struggled mightily, and prevailed.

chapter 33

All Around Town

I left Gerry Mulligan's quartet the first time in early 1957. I found a steady gig in town with Don Elliot's quartet at Cy Coleman's, a club just south of Central Park. We played opposite Cy's trio. Besides me, Don had Dick Katz on piano and Denzil Best on drums. Denzil, the original drummer with George Shearing's quintet, had been in a bad auto accident in Chicago in January 1952. A car he was riding in skidded, hit a light pole, and rolled over, leaving him with multiple leg fractures and head injuries.

On Don's job, Denzil complained that his left leg still tired out rapidly, and he often had to stop playing the hi-hat to rest it. We didn't mind. We loved Denzil's time and the sound he got on the snare drum with brushes. But Denzil's hands began to give him trouble. His palms would swell while he was playing, so that it was hard for him to hold the sticks and brushes. He finally quit, over all our protests, because he felt he wasn't playing well enough. Don hired Al Beldini to take his place.

With Denzil gone, Dick Katz lost interest in the group and left to do something else. Bob Corwin replaced him for a short time, and then Don hired an old chum of his from New Jersey, a scholarly-looking young man named Bill Evans. Bill's playing went straight to my heart. He sounded a little like Lennie Tristano in those days, but with a lighter touch. He played with a wonderful swing and was a sensitive accompanist as well as a brilliant soloist.

That gig ended when the club folded. I got to play with Bill Evans now and then during the following year, but after he joined Miles Davis in 1958, I only ran into him at Newport and when Miles was playing in New York. Then Bill left Miles and began working with his own trio. I went down to the Village Vanguard to hear them, and was astounded by his bass player, Scott LaFaro. I had heard of Scott while he was living in California, but I wasn't prepared for what I heard him do with Evans.

Scott had great speed and control on the bass, but it was his conception of the bass player's role with Bill's trio that interested me. Instead of laying down a steady four-four line, he played counter-figures with Bill, implying the pulse but rarely spelling it out explicitly. It was a wonderful musical game that Bill and Scott played exquisitely.

Bill suffered a terrible setback, and the jazz world was robbed of another of its innovators, when Scott died in an auto accident near his home in Geneva, New York, in 1961. Though his career was short, Scotty inspired a generation of bass players that followed him.

In the spring of 1957, I went to Detroit with Lou Stein's trio, with Dick Scott on drums, and then I rejoined Marian McPartland, who had also hired Dick when Joe Morello left to join Dave Brubeck. Marian had a booking at the Composer, a club on Fifty-eighth Street just off Sixth Avenue owned by Sy Barron and Willie Shore. Sy liked to put groups together for his club. He had good instincts about the music, but he never bothered to find out if the musicians he hired got along together. Sometimes it turned out that they weren't speaking to each other. Fortunately, since Marian had a working trio, he hired us "as is."

It was Sy who came up with the idea of a two-piano trio with Eddie Costa and John Mehegan. Vinnie Burke was hired as the bassist. The absence of a drummer caused some problems; Vinnie often complained that John rushed. One night, after suffering about the tempo for a couple of numbers, Vinnie began furiously playing his bass line way ahead of John and Eddie. John looked around and asked, "What are you doing?"

"I'm rushing!" yelled Vinnie. "How does it feel?"

"Well, stop it!"

"Take me to the union!"

"For rushing?"

Sy's partner, Willie Shore, understood nightclubs but had no ear for music. The partners frequently had heated arguments at the bar. Sy might say, "Get those hookers at the back table out of here!"

"Those are friends of some friends of mine."

"Well, they look like low-class hookers and I want them out of here!"

"Well, what about all those musicians you've got hanging around here? They're taking up space that could be used by customers!"

"Who ever heard of a jazz club without musicians? You're crazy!"

We wondered why they didn't step outside to have their arguments. Everyone in the club could hear them, including all the people they were arguing about.

One afternoon Dave Lambert introduced me to a gorgeous young New York stripper who worked under the name "Sequin." She wanted to develop a club act as a singer, and was getting advice from Dave and several other musicians. We dropped by her midtown apartment one day to listen while she rehearsed. She was trying out some new material with a young jazz pianist who hadn't worked much with singers. He was doing his best to construct an arrangement for her, but she wasn't sure how she wanted it to end.

Oscar Pettiford had dropped by, and was kibitzing. Every time Sequin seemed hesitant about an ending that the pianist suggested, Oscar would loudly interject, "No, man! That ain't it! That ain't it!"

After an hour of this, the pianist swiveled around on the piano stool and glared at Oscar.

"Look, man, you been sitting here all afternoon telling me what it *ain't*. Now, will you please tell me what it *is*?"

Oscar retreated to the kitchen to pour himself a drink. That was the only time I ever saw him with nothing more to say.

Oscar's bass playing was a great ornament to the New York jazz scene in the 1950s. He had a big sound and tremendous technique, especially for those days of unamplified basses and gut strings. The first time I saw him in person, at Le Down Beat on West Fifth-fourth Street, Oscar announced that he would play "Stardust" as an unaccompanied bass solo. He played it in D-flat, a difficult key on the bass because, in the major scale of that key, there are no open strings to make fingering shifts easier.

Halfway through the verse of the tune, Oscar suddenly stopped and grabbed the microphone.

"Quiet!" he bellowed furiously. The noisy conversation in the club stopped as if it had been switched off.

"I've been working on this damn song for three years!" shouted Oscar. "The least you can do is shut up for five minutes while I play it!"

Scowling with menace, he began the tune again and played brilliantly. There wasn't a peep out of the audience until he finished.

Oscar got himself a cello, tuned it like a bass, and featured it as an alternate solo instrument. Around this time he appeared on a television show as the bassist with an all-star jazz group. Also on the bill was Morey Amsterdam, a good-natured comedian who used a cello in his routine. He walked on in front of the band, told a few jokes, and then smiled up at Oscar.

"I understand you play the cello, too?"

"Don't you worry about it!" snapped Oscar.

Morey quickly dropped the subject.

When the Jimmy Giuffre Trio arrived in New York, with Jim Hall on guitar and Jim Atlas on bass, Dave Lambert and I went to hear them at the Village Vanguard. We all became friends right away. I spent a lot of time laughing with Jim Hall, who had a delicious sense of humor. One evening, Hall and Giuffre and Bob Brookmeyer came over to my apartment and we began entertaining each other with stories. Hall was lying on his back in front of my fireplace with his hands behind his head. I said something that struck him funny and he gave a convulsive leap into the air as he burst into laughter. That leap dislocated his left shoulder, leaving him nearly weeping with pain, but still laughing.

Brookmeyer and Giuffre hurried him over to St. Vincent's Hospital where the emergency room staff was able to return Jim's shoulder to its proper location. Giuffre had booked a recording studio for the trio the next day, and was afraid Hall wouldn't be able to play. He managed to get through the date by adroitly shifting his guitar around with his knees to compensate for the soreness and limited movement in his left shoulder. Since then, I've been careful to not be that funny around Jim Hall.

One evening Jim took Dick Scott and me to an Armenian restaurant he had found near the Vanguard. He introduced us to the waitress, Mary Barsamian. When she heard our names, her eyes lit up with interest. She said excitely, "Jim Hall! Dick Scott! Bill Crow! Three guys with one-syllable names!"

In her world of polysyllabic Armenian names, we were exotic.

Dick and I went to Detroit with Marian McPartland to play at Baker's Keyboard Lounge. Whenever we worked in the Detroit area, we always stayed downtown at the Wolverine Hotel. That once grand old hostelry was beginning to show its age, but the price was right.

One morning in the Wolverine coffee shop I looked up from the book I was reading to see Charlie Mingus slipping into the chair across from me. I think he was in town with Ellington. While we were chatting, Marian came in and reminded me that we had promised to join a friend of hers on his boat that afternoon. She asked Mingus if he'd like to come fishing with us.

"Oh, yeah!" he said.

He ran upstairs to get his sun hat while I called Dick Scott to tell him we were ready to leave. The four of us drove out to a pier on the Detroit River where a large powerboat awaited us. Our host provided us with lunch, drinks, fishing poles, and lures. While he showed us how to prepare trolling lines, Mingus kept saying, "Show me them fish! I hear the fish up here are supposed to be bad? Let me at them bad fish! I'm gonna whup me a fish!"

I had rarely seen Mingus in such a jolly mood. He usually agonized a lot about not getting the recognition he deserved. He was often difficult to talk to because of his touchiness, especially about race, but during that entire afternoon he was in high spirits. We laughed and told stories and fished for several hours. None of us caught anything.

After Detroit, Marian took us back into the Hickory House for an eight-month stay. I think it was during that time that they began to tear down the neighborhood. The massive brick moving and storage warehouse that had always faced the Hickory House across Fifty-second Street disappeared within a month. We could see the open sky for a while, until the Americana Hotel (now the Sheraton New York) was built. Before long the Arcadia Ballroom building, next to Roseland, was torn down, and Roseland itself soon followed. Famous places like Lindy's, the Bird in Hand, the B & G, Hansen's Drug Store, the Turf, and Jack Dempsey's, disappeared one after the other. I was amazed at the impermanence of tradition in New York.

I was there on the afternoon that the last wall of the Arcadia, the one adjoining the Roseland building, came down. A crowd of musicians stood on the sidewalk in front of Charlie's Tavern after visiting the union floor, as they did every Wednesday afternoon. A crane operator with a wrecking ball had knocked down the rest of the Arcadia, and we were curious to see how he was going to take down that last wall without damaging Roseland.

The solution was simple. Instead of swinging the wrecking ball at the wall, the crane operator lowered it carefully between the wall and Roseland. Then he turned his crane sideways until the ball and cable pulled the wall inward. As it collapsed, with no damage to the Roseland building, the assembled musicians broke into applause. The crane operator stepped to the door of his cab, removed his hard hat, and took a bow.

When Marian and Dick and I left the Hickory House for another road trip in early 1958, we didn't know it would be the last time we would work there. It took us longer than usual to pack up on our closing night. We were the last ones in the club except the night porter.

We looked around at the familiar, ugly old decor. Marian had often chided John Popkin about the seediness of the place, hoping he would redecorate and get rid of the amateurish paintings that loomed over the bandstand. Popkin had finally agreed to have the walls redone, but he had the workmen carefully repanel around the paintings, leaving everything looking exactly the same, only cleaner.

As we headed for the door, I passed beneath a little oil painting that had always hung there, a horsy tableau with red-coated hunters riding behind a pack of hounds. On an impulse, I borrowed Marian's lipstick and climbed up on a chair under the painting. I intended to make an addition to one of the horses, but I could only reach one of the dogs. I drew a discreet penis on it and climbed back down.

"Let's not tell anyone," I said, "and we'll see how long it stays there without anyone noticing."

The painting of the horses and dogs was still there ten years later, exactly as we had left it, when the Hickory House closed.

chapter 34

Dave Lambert, Last Chorus

That edition of Marian's trio dissolved on the road, when she was canceled out of a summer's bookings at a chain of Indiana hotels. The hotels were sold, and the new owner refused to honor Marian's contracts. The Hickory House was already booked up for the season, so Marian decided to take a vacation. She went to Chicago to visit her stepdaughter, and I returned to New York.

Whenever I came back from a road trip, Dave Lambert was one of the first people I looked up. It was easy to do; he had found an apartment at 24 Cornelia Street in the building next door to mine. Since Dave lived on the top floor of his building, we found it convenient to go across the roofs to visit each other. When Dave moved in, he gutted his apartment in preparation for major renovations, but he ran out of money before he was able to buy the materials with which to rebuild. His apartment looked like a disaster area for a couple of years while he scuffled just to stay alive.

Dave's mellow style of vocal group writing was being used less and less in commercial jingles, so he took any kind of work he could find. He would make a few bucks turning out lead sheets for songwriters who couldn't write music, cleaning up their harmony and scansion in the bargain. In those days the chords in popular music were supposed to resolve logically, and the meter had to be even.

Dave undertook an odd assignment from Jerry Capp, cartoonist Al Capp's brother. Jerry managed Capp Enterprises, which marketed material related to Al's comic strip, *Li'l Abner*. Al liked musical gags. The worst torture that a villain in *Li'l Abner* could threaten was to force his victim to listen repeatedly to a recording of Nelson Eddy singing "Shortnin' Bread."

One of the characters in the comic strip had written the world's worst song, "Lonesome and Disgusted." After several weeks of reference to it, Capp revealed the lyric, which had everyone in Dogpatch throwing up:

I'm lonesome and disgusted
When I think of you
Because you really don't exist
Except in my dreams of blue.

I'm lonesome when I'm away from you
And disgusted when you're near me,
But the thing that makes me oh so blue
Is that you're not real so nat'rally
you can't hear me.

Lonesome every day,
Disgusted every night,
Because you're only in my dreams
And that is far from right, Oh,

Girl of my dreams,
You are sweeter than any,
You won't throw me over for some
Tom or Dick or Benny.

Jerry Capp wanted a record to use for promotion of the strip and the products it generated. He asked Dave to write the world's worst melody to fit Al's lyric, and to think of an appropriately vile way to record it. Dave wrote a repeated four-note melody that seemed pretty banal at the time. He would laugh if he could hear some of the popular songs today.

Dave wrote a constipated-sounding vocal group background and got Leo De Lyon, a comedian he knew from the Paramount Theater, to sing the lyric on the recording. De Lyon had a funny musical act. He sang opera in many voices and could whistle "Humoresque" while humming "Swanee River" at the same time. Leo provided just the right kind of nuttiness to make the record wonderfully awful. There had to be something for the other side of the record, so Dave arranged "For Me and My Gal" with Leo singing in several voices. I still have a 78 rpm acetate copy of that record that Dave made for me at the old Associated Recording Studios on Seventh Avenue.

Dave began to run into the Catch-22 of poverty. He couldn't afford new clothes, and his old ones were so worn that he couldn't make himself presentable enough to apply for the kind of work he did well. At one point he so despaired of the music business that he joined the cement worker's union and took a construction job in order to stay alive. Dave told Gene Lees about a job he was on, using a jackhammer to break up a mass of concrete in the basement of a building that was being wrecked. He said the welders were cutting up reinforcement bars, the place was full of smoke and dust, sparks from the arcs were raining down, and the noise was unimaginable.

"How awful," said Gene.

"I kinda dug it," said Dave.

Dave always made the best of a tough situation. Being the only worker on his crew who didn't speak Italian, Dave began to memorize phrases in that language. When the other workers saw that he had a quick ear, they would teach him Italian insults and laugh with delight when he used them correctly. But concrete work was exhausting. Dave would go home at the end of a day's work, collapse on his bed, and sleep until time to return to the job the next morning. It left him no time to write any music or even look for musical work. When a commission to do a large arranging job finally turned up, Dave thankfully took it and got out of the construction business.

On Sheridan Square was a little hamburger joint where Dave and I sometimes had lunch. One day we found Harry Belafonte behind the counter. We had known Harry as a handsome young singer trying to get something going around the jazz clubs. He had been booked at Birdland as "The Cinderella Gentleman" during its opening months and had made a few records that hadn't done much. Now he occasionally worked club dates with a guitarist and two or three backup singers.

To fill in between his meager bookings, Harry had taken over this lunch counter on Sheridan Square and hired his singers as countermen. Dave and I spent a lot of time there during Harry's short career as a restaurateur. There would be so much laughing and singing at the counter that customers had trouble getting anyone's attention to place an order. I think Harry was barely breaking even on the place.

Dave and Harry decided to try writing songs together. One of them was a calypso called "Mango" that foreshadowed the sort of material that carried Harry to stardom. Another was a Louis Jordan–type song called "Cookin' in the Hall," which identified all the delicious food smells encountered while climbing the stairs of a tenement building. The last line of Harry's lyric went:

"But on my floor, I've got a real sad deal. I'm having old, lumpy, soggy, yesterday's cold . . . corn . . . meal!"

I liked the songs, but when Dave and Harry sang them for publishers and record producers, none of them showed much interest.

Harry thought that the hamburger stand had been too small an operation. He said that what the Village really needed was a Harlem-style rib joint with soul food and jazz. He had the whole thing laid out in his mind and entertained us for hours describing the details. He had his eye on a couple of good locations.

To raise money to get started, Harry threw an old-fashioned rent party at someone's loft in Chelsea, with food and booze and music. A huge crowd turned up, and we were all sure Harry's rib joint would be a great success. The next thing we heard, he was in California, making records. We were happy for Harry when he became a singing star, but Dave and I sure were sorry not to get a good rib joint in our neighborhood.

One afternoon I went over to Dave's apartment and found him talking to a young man whom he introduced as Jon Hendricks. Dave was intrigued with Jon's ability to tailor lyrics to recorded jazz solos. King Pleasure had made the first successful records of that sort of thing, as in his "Moody's Mood For Love." Hendricks took the form a step further than Pleasure, who originally got the idea from the work of Eddie Jefferson.

I met King Pleasure once, at Dave's West Tenth Street basement. He was working on a lyric to Lester Young's solo on "Sometimes I'm Happy." While we were talking, I asked him, "Where did you get your name?"

He laughed and said, "From about a year of hard thinkin'!"

I found out later that his original name was Clarence Beeks.

Jon Hendricks wrote an amusing lyric to Woody Herman's record of "Four Brothers," and Dave re-scored the original Jimmy Giuffre arrangement for a vocal group. They recorded it, but on the playback they found that the lyrics sung at the original tempo were hard to understand. So they did it over at a slower tempo and put it on two sides of a 78 rpm record. Even though the words on the bridge teased Woody for being less modern than his sax section, he loved the record when he heard it.

Dave and Jon decided that their next project would be a vocal album of Count Basie tunes with Jon's lyrics. They sold the idea to Creed Taylor at ABC-Paramount and worked for weeks choosing the tunes, securing the rights to them, and writing the lyrics and arrangements. Whenever I dropped in at Dave's, he and Jon would be working on the material. In 1957 they recorded it for ABC-Paramount with a large vocal group and Basie's rhythm section.

Dave was very disappointed with the result. He hadn't been able to get the singers to phrase the way the Basie band had played on the original records. He'd even called Annie Ross to come and help him teach them the phrasing. Annie had written and sung lyrics to Wardell

Gray's tenor solo on "Twisted," and she understood jazz phrasing. She hadn't been called as one of the singers on this date because she didn't read music, but she knew how to swing. Neither she or Dave were able to get the right feel from the studio singers, though. Dave said unhappily, "It sounds like 'Walter Schumann sings Count Basie.'"

Since Les Paul's pioneer work in multiple-track recording had brought four-track tape machines to many recording studios by then, Dave decided to take advantage of the new technology.

"We'll do the whole thing over," he said. "Just three of us, with the rhythm section. Annie can overdub all the high parts, and Jon and I will do the low ones."

It took many hours of overdubbing, but it paid off. *Sing a Song of Basie* was a hit.

Opportunities for personal appearances followed the success of that record, and Dave had to write arrangements for three voices that would emulate the multi-voice album. Annie's wide vocal range made that job easier than it otherwise might have been, but in order to get the voicings he needed, Dave had to write his own parts uncomfortably high. As a result he didn't enjoy performing with Lambert, Hendricks, and Ross as much as he had enjoyed singing with four- and five-voice groups. But it was good to be making some money again. Dave went around town and payed off all the small debts he had incurred during the lean years.

Several years later, the telephone woke me late one night. It was songwriter Otis Merritt, calling to tell me that Dave was dead. He had been on his way back to New York from a gig in New England. At Westport, Connecticut, he saw a motorist stranded by the highway and stopped to help him. They were standing behind the man's disabled car when a truck wandered off the road and slammed into them, crushing them between the two vehicles and killing them both instantly.

Dave was a dear, sweet friend. It was hard to lose him like that. At his funeral, Zoot Sims played one simple chorus of "Pennies From Heaven," a favorite tune of Dave's. It seemed to perfectly distill his sunny spirit. That chorus still sings sweetly in my memory.

chapter 35

The Gerry Mulligan Quartet

In July 1958 I got a call from Gerry Mulligan to rejoin his quartet. Joe Benjamin had replaced me when I left, and then Henry Grimes had replaced him. Now Henry was leaving to go with Sonny Rollins. Dave Bailey was still Gerry's drummer, and Art Farmer had just joined him on trumpet. I liked Art and admired his playing tremendously. We just had time for one rehearsal before our first appearance at Newport.

That was the year Bert Stern and Al Avakian came to film the Newport Jazz Festival. They got good shots of the performers on stage, but after the sun went down, they couldn't photograph the audience in the dark.

While editing the film, Al found a problem with the lack of closeups of the nighttime audience's reaction to the music. He solved it by throwing a party in New York, at which he showed rough footage of the movie. He filmed the reactions of the partygoers as they watched, and intercut those closeups with the footage from Newport. Aileen and several of our friends who weren't at the festival attended that party and can be seen in the audience shots of the movie, *Jazz on a Summer's Day.*

Willie "the Lion" Smith played at Newport that year, but wasn't included in the film. His afternoon performance was short and sweet. He walked on stage dressed in a beige suit and a white, flat-crowned hat, nodded briefly toward the audience as they welcomed him, sat down at the piano, and addressed the keyboard in a businesslike fashion. He left no doubt in anyone's mind that he was still one of the great two-handed piano "ticklers." He played a second short number, stood up, bowed, and marched offstage, his job done.

"George Wein asked me not to play too long," he told those back-stage who were disappointed he hadn't played more. "I never like to overstay my welcome."

Because of the number of artists and the limited amount of time in which to present them, Wein had asked everyone at Newport not to play long sets, but the Lion was one of the few who were conscientious about it.

During a backstage conversation, the Lion spoke up sharply when someone began complaining about the lack of respect that musicians encountered in the music business.

"Musicians get exactly the amount of respect that they deserve!" he said. "They don't get it because they don't demand it. You got to educate people to give you the treatment you want. I'll give you an example. I was called last month by this club owner up in Connecticut who wanted me to play in his establishment. After we agreed on a price, he started telling me what *bus* to take to get up there! I said, hold it! What I want to know is what time does the *limousine* pick me up at my house? Otherwise, the deal is off! I had to educate him, you see."

On our first afternoon at Newport that year, Dave Bailey and I were sitting by the swimming pool at the Viking Hotel when Sonny Rollins arrived. Sonny was in bathing trunks and sandals, but he kept a white sailor hat pulled down around his ears all afternoon. The reason became evident at the concert that night. He came on stage with his trio (Roy Haynes and Henry Grimes) to reveal for the first time that he had shaved his hair into a Mohawk war-lock. He kept that hairstyle for quite a while.

A couple of years later, when Dave and I were playing at the Half Note with Bob Brookmeyer and Clark Terry, Rollins walked in and sat down at the bar. He was wearing a complete working cowboy's outfit: faded jeans, Levi jacket, sweat-stained Stetson hat, and cowboy boots. With a twinkle in his eye, Dave leaned over to me and whispered, "I guess Sonny found out that the Indians didn't win."

Mulligan had been thinking about band uniforms for the quartet. When Brookmeyer had been with us, we wore sport jackets from the Andover Shop in Boston. For the new group, Gerry sent us to Breidbart's on Sixth Avenue, a men's store favored by stylish dancers like Geoffrey Holder and Sammy Davis, Jr. The gray suits we bought there were sharp, but proved to be too warm for outdoor summer concerts. Gerry decided we needed something lighter and less formal. He took us back to Breidbart's and chose some royal blue linen trousers and short-sleeved gingham shirts with half-inch vertical red and white stripes. He added a touch of formality with black shoestring ties.

Dave and Art both had a little more meat on their bones than Gerry and I did, and their pants fit them very snugly. This was before macho pop singers made tight pants commonplace. When we showed up at the Great South Bay Festival on Long Island wearing our new outfits, Dizzy Gillespie discovered us backstage. He lifted his eyebrows dramatically.

"Will you *look* at these *fools!*" he cried, walking all around us to get a better view. He told Dave and Art, "You better not turn your backs when you get out on stage. You'll freak those little girls in the audience. You cats got some *buns* back there!"

I think Art and Dave were glad when the summer season ended, and we went back to wearing our gray suits.

I enjoyed Art Farmer's company on the road. He had a quiet nature and was very serious about his music, but he also liked to laugh. He sometimes entertained me with stories about the bands of his youth. He told me about working with Johnny Otis's band, and backing up Joe Turner, the great blues singer. At that time Art was infatuated with Dizzy Gillespie's playing, and he thought Joe Turner was old-fashioned. Art said he didn't appreciate Joe until years later.

Joe wasn't too thrilled with Art, either. Art said, after he took a Gillespie-like chorus one night, Joe sang a new blues lyric:

"Play me the boogie, don't play no be-bop for me!"

Turner's influence on Farmer surfaced one night when we were driving home from a gig in Philadelphia. We stopped for coffee at a Howard Johnson's on the New Jersey Turnpike. The restaurant was empty and the counter girl was in the kitchen, chatting with the cook. A microphone for calling orders from counter to kitchen was mounted on a flexible arm near the cash register, and Art pulled it over. I thought he was just going to ask for some service. But Art put his lips to the mike and sang, just like Joe Turner:

"Well, it was early one Monday morning, and I was on my way to school. . . ."

Though it had been years since Gerry and Chet Baker had worked together, many fans of Gerry's early quartet records still expected to see Chet when they came to hear us. While we were playing at Storyville in Boston, two college boys came up to the bandstand. One of them asked Art Farmer for his autograph and Art obliged, but when the guy read his signature, he said, "Oh, aren't you Chet Baker?"

He started to rip up the slip of paper.

"Don't tear it up!" exclaimed his friend, "He may be somebody too, someday!"

In late 1958, we began recording an album for Columbia Records. Gerry complained that he couldn't write anything at home because the telephone and the doorbell were always ringing. I gave him the key to my Cornelia Street apartment and told him, "There's a piano there, and nobody will bother you. I'll be over at Aileen's place tonight. Go write something."

He did, and came to the last session with a lovely treatment of "What Is There to Say?" which became the title song of the album. Gerry had asked the rest of us to bring in tunes, so Art and I each wrote one. Art's was an untitled blues. Since Newport had been our first job together, Gerry suggested the title "Blueport."

Art had told me that "Buckethead" had been his childhood nickname, so I wrote that at the top of my tune, another blues, in three-quarter time. When Art looked at the trumpet part I handed him, he laughed and said, "Oh, no, please don't call it that!"

"How about 'News from Blueport?' " Gerry offered—a spoonerism on "Blues from Newport." That became the title. The liner notes erroneously listed Gerry as the composer of both tunes, but Art and I receive the royalties.

There was also a goof on the liner notes of a recording titled "Spring Is Sprung" that the Mulligan Quartet made later for Philips Records. Willis Conover wrote the notes, but didn't talk about the bass and drums. He assumed that the personnel would be listed elsewhere. Quincy Jones, the producer, thought that Willis would write about all four members of the quartet, and made no separate listing, so Dave Bailey and I weren't mentioned anywhere. Quincy did give a complete rundown of the microphones and recording equipment that were used, so a purchaser of that album might have been under the impression that 2 Altec Lipstiks was on drums and AKG D-24 was on bass.

The quartet worked a week at the Apollo Theater on a bill called "Symphony Sid's Jazz." Sid emceed a show that included Gerry's quartet, Sonny Rollins, Maynard Ferguson's big band, and Dinah Washington, the "Queen of the Blues." Because the star dressing room was being redecorated for Eartha Kitt, who was coming to the Apollo the following week, Dinah found herself assigned to the number two dressing room. Dinah didn't take the insult calmly. She grabbed Symphony Sid after the opening matinee and informed him in a wheezy voice, "All this paint fumes and plaster dust is ruinin' my throat. I'm gonna be sick tonight."

Sid saw that Dinah was serious, but had no power to change the theater's construction schedule. He called Ernestine Anderson, who was appearing that week at Birdland. Ernestine came to the early evening show at the Apollo wearing a stunning gown and carrying several good Quincy Jones arrangements.

Seeing that Ernestine was ready to take her place, Dinah immediately became her sponsor. She brought her on stage and announced in a whisper that her protégée Ernestine was kindly filling in for her while she was indisposed. Then Dinah took a prominent seat in the side box nearest the stage as Ernestine talked over her charts with Maynard's band.

Ernestine tore the house up with her opener, and when the applause ended, one of those loud-voiced guys that always seemed to be in the front row at the Apollo yelled out, "Sing another one, Steen! You can go on home, Dinah!"

We were all pleased to find that Dinah's voice was completely recovered in time for the next show.

The doorman at the Apollo had a small room with a TV set and a few chairs just inside the stage door. I was sitting there between shows one day chatting with Jimmy Rushing, who had dropped in to visit. Symphony Sid came downstairs escorting a stunning redhead in a fox coat, and as they passed us on their way out, we overheard part of their conversation. The lady was upset with Sid, and was letting him know about it with considerable heat. Sid was mostly saying, "Yes, dear."

Jimmy Rushing sat up as straight as his five-by-five frame would allow. His eyebrows shot up to his hairline as he listened to the lady's vituperative monologue.

"Did you *hear* the way she talked to him?" Jimmy howled as they disappeared into the street. "Why, I could *never* let a woman talk to me like that! That's a dis*grace!*" He shook his head and settled pensively back in his chair.

"I remember one time," he said, "on the road with Basie. I had my woman traveling with me. I told her to stay up at the hotel room while we were playing this dance, but about the second set I look over on the side and here she is with her girlfriend, big as life, setting at a table, drinking and carrying on. I couldn't believe my *eyes!*

"I told her to get her ass back up to the room, and she gave me some *mouth* about it. Well! I straightened that out in about one *minute!* I went up-side her head . . . whap!"

He swung his open hand to illustrate the blow. Neither the doorman or I made any comment as Jimmy nodded indignantly to indicate that his point had been made. Then he sat back in his chair and rubbed his chin reflectively. After a moment of consideration, he mused:

"She left me not long after that."

Dinah Washington had her own private numbers runner who came to her dressing room every morning. In those days, before New York State instituted its own lottery, the numbers were very popular in Harlem. I asked Dinah how the game was played, and she said, "You ain't never played the numbers before? Pick out a number, honey, and we'll both bet on it. You probably just ignorant enough to win!"

The three digits of the winning number came out one at a time during the afternoon, and the doorman would chalk them up on the blackboard by the stage door. Dinah and I bet my motor scooter license number, and when the first digit was chalked up, it was the right one. Dinah said, "I knew you'd have beginner's luck, darlin'! Come on in my dressing room and have a taste!"

After the next show the second digit had been posted, also the right one.

"Where's my sweet good-luck boy?" Dinah called, and gave me a big kiss and another shot of brandy.

When the third number came up wrong, Dinah swept by me at the stage door with royal disdain, muttering, "Dummy!"

Dinah was still being billed as the Queen of the Blues when I ran into her again in 1963. The Mulligan quartet was on tour in England, and Dave Bailey and I went to dinner at the home of Max Jones, the British jazz writer. Dinah arrived with Beryl Booker, her pianist.

Dinah had insisted on doing the cooking, and was in Max's kitchen stirring things on the stove while she made a transatlantic call to New York about a wardrobe trunk that had gone astray on the airline.

"Rusty?" she shouted into the phone. "What do you mean, wait a minute? I'm not down at the corner! I'm in London, England! Now I want you to tell Joe Glaser to wire me a thousand dollars! I got nothing to wear over here!"

At the dinner table Max apologized to Dinah for not being able to take her on a tour of the royal palaces.

"Everything is closed this week while the Queen is visiting Canada," he explained.

Dinah snorted and rolled her eyes disdainfully.

"Shit. That bitch *know* there ain't room for but one Queen at a time in this country!"

chapter 36

Europe

The Gerry Mulligan Quartet, with Art Farmer, Dave Bailey, and me, toured Europe for Norman Granz in the spring of 1959, along with the Gene Krupa Quartet and the Jimmy Giuffre Trio. Jim Hall and bassist Buddy Clark were with Giuffre; Krupa's group included tenor man Eddie Wasserman, pianist Ronnie Ball, and bassist Jimmy Gannon. We flew to a different city every day, and Clark, Gannon, and I each had a bass to stow in every plane. At the airports I often had the responsibility of convincing the plane crew that there was space inside for three string basses. There always was, somehow.

In those days it was still possible to talk airlines into accepting basses as hand luggage, and I knew many places inside the various types of commercial airliners where a bass would fit, in coat racks, vestibules, and tail compartments. One plane had bunkbeds for the crew on the flight deck where we stowed two of the basses.

Airplane designers gradually found all those "waste spaces" and either eliminated them or filled them with flying equipment. Then, for a while, the airlines would let us put a bass in a seat at half-fare. We always tried to get food and drinks for the bass, since it had a ticket, but were rarely successful.

Airplane designers have reduced the amount of space between seats until a bass will no longer fit into one. Nowadays the only way to fly with a string bass is to ship it in the cargo hold in a special trunk. Now my solution for traveling is a "stick bass," an electrically amplified bass with a standard neck, fingerboard, and bridge, but no acoustic body. It is much less fragile than the standard bass, and can be unbolted in the middle and packed up in a small, padded fiber case, to be shipped as luggage.

Norman Granz invented the concert jam session in the 1940s and made a lot of money with the idea. He provided a lot of work for many years for the jazz musicians he promoted. When we first arrived in Paris, Granz made a little speech:

"Now, look. I've worked hard to establish the idea here in Europe that American jazz musicians are artists. European audiences pay good ticket prices when my tours come through, so I can pay everyone a nice taste. We have a first-class image here, and I want everyone to go first-class. Eat at good restaurants. Stay at the hotels I've reserved for us; don't be checking into some flea-bag to save a couple of bucks.

"We're all grown-ups, and I'm not your mother. I'll let you know the transportation schedules, but if you miss the bus or the plane, do whatever you have to do to get to the gig. It's your responsibility.

"I expect you to have a ball in Europe. Just don't do anything to screw things up for everyone else who comes over here."

Having established his ground rules, Norman relaxed and enjoyed the tour with us.

After our concert in Munich, I went to a local jazz club and bumped into an old friend from Charlie's Tavern, Jerri Gray. Jerri was a beautiful nightclub dancer who had been married to jazz trombonist Frank Rehak. She was now living in Germany with the Swedish trombonist Aake Persson.

"Do you think you'll ever come back to the Apple?" I asked her. She made a wry face.

"No way. Do you know where I'm going next Saturday night? To a party for the King of Sweden! In New York I couldn't even get invited to a party for Duke Ellington!"

In Frankfurt, I found that Oscar Pettiford, who had moved to Europe, was on the same concert with us, playing with Hans Koller's group. When O.P. came up to our dressing room before the concert to say hello, I noticed that he had the last three fingers of his right hand taped together with a splint.

"Are you still healing up from your accident?" I asked. He had been seriously injured in a car crash in Vienna.

"Naw," said Oscar, "that's all over with. I got this the other night, telling a story at a party at some people's house. I threw my arm out like this while I was talking and knocked over a lamp and broke two fingers!"

Oscar went back down to the stage and played marvelously with the fingers that were still working.

After our concert in Berlin, we were scheduled to fly to Milan. Norman Granz had been driving from city to city on the tour, but had flown with us from Frankfurt to Berlin, which was then inside East Germany. Norman said, "How am I going to get my car to Italy? I have to fly back to New York for Ella Fitzgerald's opening tomorrow night. I want to rejoin you guys in Milan, but my car is at the airport in Frankfurt."

I volunteered immediately. A chance to drive Norman's Mercedes 300SL convertible through Switzerland to Italy seemed a golden opportunity. Norman's road manager, Pete Cavallo, said he'd go with me.

"How long should it take us?" I asked Norman.

"About eight hours."

What we didn't know was that Norman always drove as if bandits were after him. To make that trip in eight hours, we would have had to average better than sixty miles an hour. We didn't do that well on the autobahn, and once we reached the Alps, the winding, unfamiliar roads and the fantastic views slowed us down even more.

We reached Milan late in the afternoon and discovered when we checked in at the Hotel Duomo that the rest of the musicians had already taken the train to Bologna, for the concert that night. We jumped back in the car, sped to Bologna, and arrived just in time. Pete found Norman, apologized for our late arrival, and asked where he wanted us to deliver his car.

"Oh, there's no hurry," he said. "I got back early and needed a car, so I bought a new Maserati."

We made Milan our headquarters for several days, taking a chartered bus to do concerts in other towns. At the first Milan concert, Giuffre received unusually enthusiastic applause when his name was announced. We found out later that a bank robber named Giuffre had recently pulled a big heist in Milan.

Granz always took us to the best restaurants in every city we visited.

Before our concert in Genoa he arranged a banquet at his favorite seafood restaurant there. They had spent the whole day preparing the house specialties. We ate and drank ourselves into a torpor that made it difficult to play the concert.

On the way back to Milan someone asked the bus driver for a pit stop. He pulled to the side of the dark, lonely road and most of the group clambered out and lined up alongside the bus to relieve themselves. Giuffre, looking for a little more privacy, took a step away from the bus into the darkness and disappeared with a cry and a splash. He had stepped off the edge into an irrigation ditch that ran alongside the road.

The guys standing near him pulled him out and wiped as much mud as they could from his tuxedo trousers and dress shirt, and everyone got back on the bus. The laughter at Jimmy's predicament finally subsided and we rode on quietly for several minutes. Then Jimmy's rueful voice broke the silence:

"I didn't even get to pee!"

The next day Giuffre and I awoke feeling queasy. By that afternoon we were both sick in bed. The final concert in Milan that night combined the remainder of both groups. Jimmy and I had the symptoms of food poisoning, and we suspected the milk at the seafood restaurant, since he and I were the only ones who drank any. Pete Cavallo called the hotel doctor, who promptly came to my room. He spoke no English, but seemed to understand my problem. He indicated that I should stay in bed, and prescribed some medicine that calmed my insides and let me get some sleep.

The next morning I felt much better. I went up to Giuffre's room see how he was doing and found that the same doctor had diagnosed him as having mumps! Evidently he had misread Jimmy's natural facial structure, and the language barrier had prevented him from associating Jim's case with mine. When Norman Granz heard that Giuffre had been treated for mumps, he called an English-speaking doctor who came to Jimmy's room, examined him, and called in the hotel doctor for a confrontation. It took place in Italian, but the gestures made the conversation easy to translate:

"This man is suffering with stomachache and diarrhea! How could you diagnose mumps? Any fool can see that he does not have mumps!""

"Did he take this medicine that I prescribed yesterday?"

"Yes, of course he took it."

"Then, of course, he does not have mumps, *now!*"

Dave Bailey and I stayed with friends in Milan for a few days after the rest of the tour returned to New York. Since Lars Gullin, the Swedish baritone saxophonist, was in Milan, promoter Mario Fattori set up a record date with Lars, Dave, and me. Mario asked who we liked on piano, and we recommended George Grunz, whom Dave and I had met at a jam session in Zurich. George flew down for the day and we recorded eight tunes with Lars, but I don't know if that record was ever released.

Dave and I routed our return tickets through London in order to visit the jazz clubs there. Then we caught a flight back to the States on a BOAC Comet Four. As we landed in Boston before continuing on to Idlewild Airport, the pilot told us on the intercom that a strong tail wind had helped us to set a new east–west transatlantic record.

When we came in over Idlewild, I watched out the window as the wide wing flap lowered smoothly. Suddenly the plane jolted sharply and the edge of the flap burst apart and twisted back toward me. We had hit something hard. We landed and rolled to a quick stop, and the flight crew began an emergency evacuation of the plane. The rear door was opened and a ladder put up for us to climb down.

My bass was in the coat rack by the door, so I quickly unlashed it and started down the ladder carrying it. The airlines official at the foot of the ladder tried to make me leave the bass behind.

"No luggage . . . leave your luggage in the plane!" he commanded.

"This isn't my luggage," I yelled, "it's my living!"

I continued down the ladder with my bass. The pilot had climbed out the front and was standing there as Dave and I reached the ground. We looked back and saw that the metal jet-blast fence at the edge of the airfield had two huge bites missing where our landing gear had hit it. Someone said a downdraft had caused the accident. Both landing gear were badly damaged, and it was a wonder that they hadn't collapsed when we landed. The British pilot simply said, "My, my!"

chapter 37

Good Gigs

After playing at Birdland with Gerry one summer night, I came home to my apartment on Cornelia Street to discover I'd been robbed. The burglar had come in through a window I had left unlocked. He must have known I was at work; he took the time to sort through my record collection. He only stole the modern jazz. He also took my tux and a suit, my overcoat, a collection of cufflinks that I had made from foreign coins, my camera, a couple of sweaters, and two suitcases, which he used to carry the boodle.

I didn't feel so bad about losing the stuff. Most of it could be replaced. But I hated losing the feeling of safety and privacy in my home. Even with better locks on the windows, I felt nervous when I went to sleep and anxious when I left the place.

The night after the robbery, during a long intermission at Birdland, I jumped on my motor scooter and ran downtown to make sure everything was all right at home. The apartment was just the way I had left it, but as I stood at the refrigerator pouring myself a glass of milk, the door suddenly flew open and Jim Hall came rushing in, yelling, "All right, you bastard!"

I had told Jim about the robbery. When he saw it was me, he began laughing. He said, "I was in the neighborhood, and I thought I'd make sure your apartment was okay while you were at work. When I saw the light under your door, I was sure the burglar had come back. But as I rushed in, I thought, 'What am I doing? What if he's got a gun?' So I'm really glad that it's you!"

I was equally relieved that it was only Jim bursting through my door.

In the summer of 1959, Gerry Mulligan went to Hollywood to appear in a movie based on Jack Kerouac's novel *The Subterraneans*. Dave Bailey called a week or two later to tell me that Gerry had talked the producers into using the quartet, and they were offering us $300 a week for a couple of weeks' shooting. Dave said, "That's not much bread. I think that's the same as saying they don't really want us. What do you think?"

I agreed that it seemed like a low price for a movie, but I wasn't sure. I wasn't interested in going anyway, since being on the road was interfering with my personal life. I had found a job in New York, and I wanted to stay where I could be with Aileen. Dave said he and Art were going to ask for more money.

A week later Dave called and said, "Pack your bag. They raised the offer to five hundred."

I still turned the movie down, and it was just as well that I did, since the shooting of it ran far behind schedule. Dave and Art sat around Hollywood for three months waiting for their scenes to be filmed. When that movie was finished, Gerry stayed in California to make another one, *The Ratrace,* and Art and Dave came back to New York with Benny Golson to form the Jazztet. That was the end of that edition of the Mulligan quartet.

I had joined Gene Di Novi's trio at Willie Shore's new Arpeggio Club on East Fifty-second Street, with Johnny Cresci on drums. During our first two weeks there, we were the only attraction. Then Shore hired Meg Myles, an ex-stripper turned chanteuse. We had to spend half of each set accompanying her. Next, Shore brought in a comedian who didn't need much music, but who took up most of the remaining time. We were only playing one trio number at the beginning of each show. Gene began to look around for a job where we could play more of our own music.

Eileen Barton came in one night, liked our trio and hired us to open her new East River Club, on Fifty-second Street at the river. She had spared no expense. The decor was elegant, the two Steinway grand pianos were brand-new, the sound system was excellent, the chef was cordon bleu.

Mel Tormé had agreed to open the room. We were to accompany Mel for his show, and the rest of the evening we would play whatever we liked. To make sure we would leave the Arpeggio, Eileen offered us more money than Shore was paying us and signed us for forty weeks. Gene gave Shore our notice and we bought new tuxedos for the opening of Eileen's new club.

As the hostess, Barton wasn't part of the show, but since she intended to sing now and then, she came to an afternoon rehearsal with Mel to set her sound balance. Gene played an introduction for her, but

when she began to sing, her mike was dead. Eileen called to her manager, "Tell the sound man to turn on the mikes."

"He says they are on."

"Well, this one's not working. Maybe it's no good."

"It's a brand new Telefunken."

"Well, then, Telefunken sound man to turn the damned thing on!"

They found the problem, got the balance, and we were all set for the
gala opening. Eileen had booked a private party that night for Jane
Fonda, who I think was appearing on Broadway, and reports filtered
out from the private dining room that the theatrical contingent was
happy. In the main room, Tormé gave a good performance to a packed
house, and everyone predicted that the club would be a tremendous
success. Then, at midnight Eileen came to the bandstand looking positively ill. She asked us to stop playing while she made an announcement.

"I'm terribly sorry to throw a wet blanket on this wonderful party,
but I have to announce that we're unable to serve any more liquor after
twelve o'clock! Our temporary license expired at midnight, and the
permanent one we were promised hasn't arrived yet. So please bear
with us. Everything will be straightened out tomorrow. Meanwhile,
everything else is on the house for the rest of the night."

Eileen's backers had greased the necessary palms at the State Liquor
Authority and had been assured that the permanent license was on its
way, but then the same palms had evidently been greased a little more
generously by competitors who did not want Eileen's club to cut into
their territory. We heard that Jules Podell, the owner of the Copaca-
bana, had used his considerable influence against her.

The club began to empty out as the thirsty customers headed for
licensed premises, so Eileen sent us home early. We hung on for two
more days, playing to small groups of sober diners and waiting for a
liquor license that never materialized. Then New York was hit by one
of the heaviest snowstorms it had suffered in several years, and Gene
Di Novi phoned to tell me the club would be closed that night. It never
reopened. On some technicality the liquor license application was permanently denied, and the club was dead. The musicians' union had
secured a bond for our first week's wages, so we just about broke even
on our new tuxedos.

I picked up a brief trio gig at Birdland with Bobby Scott, and on a
long intermission I ran over to Basin Street West, a block away, to hear
Woody Herman. One of Woody's ex-sidemen, trumpeter Doug Met-

tome, had also come in to hear the band. Doug had just finished playing a club date, and looked elegant in his tuxedo, but he had taken on
a lot of liquid cargo and was feeling pretty limp. He collapsed into a
chair beside the bandstand, hung his head back, and closed his eyes as
he listened to the music.

The guys in the trumpet section noticed Doug, and when the band
finished its number, Al Porcino leaned over the railing to greet him.

"Hello—Doug—Met-TOME" he intoned in the slow, metallic vocal cadence that his friends love to mimic. "What—would—you—like—to—
hear—the—band—play?"

Doug couldn't even raise his head to reply. His lips barely moved as
he sighed a faint request:

"High notes."

George Wein, the owner of Storyville in Boston, put together a sextet
to work at the Embers in New York, and at his own club afterwards. I
was the bass player and Mickey Sheen was the drummer. I had never
played with either George or Mickey before. I knew that George, busy
running his nightclubs and the Newport Jazz Festival, didn't play the
piano regularly. But I jumped at the chance to play with the front line
George had hired: Harold "Shorty" Baker, Lawrence Brown, and Pee
Wee Russell. Shorty had played the trumpet beautifully with Duke Ellington, and Lawrence's trombone work with that band had entranced
me since I was a teen-age record collector. And I knew that my old
friend Pee Wee would be fun.

When George's "Storyville Stompers" got together to rehearse, I was
pleasantly surprised with his piano playing. George's style had been
formed before the modern era, but he accompanied well and played
straightforward solos. His respect for Shorty, Lawrence, and Pee Wee
brought out the best in him. I also got along well with Mickey Sheen,
though he was more interested in drum solos than I was.

The front line was a treat. They were all fine soloists, and their ensemble work was outstanding. On the first and last choruses of each
tune, Lawrence would harmonize Shorty's full-toned lead, leaving Pee
Wee free to decorate however he chose. Pee Wee rose to the occasion
and played wonderful ensemble parts.

Lawrence Brown, not given to effusiveness, was clearly enjoying himself on that group. He said to Wein, "For God's sake, George, get some
more work for this band, or I'm going to have to go back with Duke.
He's got me playing those damned plunger parts!"

Lawrence had always played open horn during his early years with Ellington, but Duke had talked him into returning and taking over the plunger solos when Quentin Jackson left the band.

Shorty told me that he liked the way I played behind him, and then spoke indignantly of a job he had recently worked with a young rhythm section.

"I couldn't believe my ears!" he cried. "I played a phrase, and when I took a breath, the *bass* player answered me! He *answered* me!" Shorty shook his head with disbelief. I was relieved that I had not yet committed that sin, and I was careful never to play anything that might sound like an answer to Shorty.

We played our last job in the garden of the Museum of Modern Art. When George announced the first tune, he dedicated it to a huge Henry Moore statue that loomed over the bandstand, a nude with enormous breasts. The tune was "That's a Plenty."

The *Herald-Tribune*'s review of that concert was amusing. Written by Diane de Bonneval, who may have been more comfortable covering the art beat than the jazz world, it cited "the nervous clarinet of Pee Wee Russell, the easy trombone of Lawrence Brown, the excited trumpet of Shorty Baker, the obstinate bass of Bill Crow and the insistent drums of Mickey Sheen." I imagined getting some club owner or concert promoter to quote that review in his advertising:

"Obstinate" —*New York Herald-Tribune.*

Ms. de Bonneval must have been distracted, or absent, when George Wein announced the names of the musicians at the museum concert. Tyree Glenn was our trombonist. Lawrence Brown had already gone back with Ellington, playing those damned plunger parts.

chapter 38

The Concert Jazz Band

I spent the rest of the Spring of 1960 involved in the production of three one-act plays at the Jazz Gallery, a short-lived club in the East Village. In one of my few outings as a band leader, I put together a small jazz group, featuring saxophonist Hal McKusick, to provide incidental music. One of the plays was the premiere of Edward Albee's *The Sandbox,* with my friend Sudie Bond playing Grandma.

Then Zoot Sims called me for a month at the Atlantic House in Provincetown, Massachusetts, at the tip of Cape Cod. He said the owner would provide us with rooms, so I could bring Aileen with me. Zoot took my bass up in his car, and Aileen and I made the trip on my motor scooter.

Zoot's joyful playing and his good natured directness quickly made him the darling of the P-town summer crowd. Occasionally we were visited by friends from New York. Gerry Mulligan, Allen Eager, and Nick Travis came up and sat in with us. The place was packed every evening and the music was very satisfying.

The band (Paul Motian on drums and Nico Bunink on piano) always sounded best during Zoot's solos. His great swinging time made him the strongest member of the rhythm section. Sometimes the audience felt the urge to participate. One night Zoot stopped playing and listened as customers ineptly rapped on glasses and bottles, thumped on the tables, and clapped along with us. He stepped to the microphone and surveyed the audience disapprovingly.

"None of you know where it is!" he said.

When Paul Motian took that job, he told Zoot that he had to leave in July to do some work with the Bill Evans trio, starting at the Newport Jazz Festival. Paul went to Newport with Bill, but they never got to play. That was the year of the uninvited-audience riots outside the festival grounds, and the final Sunday evening concert on which Bill's trio was to appear was canceled.

Before Paul left, he reminded Zoot several times about getting a replacement, but Zoot kept putting it off. Suddenly it was Paul's last night, and Zoot still hadn't hired anyone. He made a panicked call to a friend in New York:

"Find me a drummer and get him up here in time for the gig tomorrow! I don't care who it is!"

The friend made a lot of phone calls and finally found a fine drummer who brought a lot of experience with him. Unfortunately, he also brought some drugs. He played all night with his eyes half closed and a big smile on his face, and he gradually slowed down every tempo Zoot set.

The drummer's time problem wasn't so noticeable on Zoot's choruses. Zoot's rhythm was strong, and between us we could keep the tempo from slowing down. But on Nico's choruses the drummer would pull it down no matter how much I leaned into the wind. If Zoot gave me a solo, the tempo dropped even further as soon as I stopped playing four beats to the measure.

For the last tune of the evening, Zoot called "Indiana" and kicked it off at a bright tempo. The smiling, somnambulistic drummer slowed the tempo down a little during Zoot's solo, quite a bit more during Nico's, and by the end of my bass solo had gotten so slow that Zoot shrugged and came back in playing "These Foolish Things" as a ballad. Fortunately, the drummer used up his supply of drugs quickly, and in a day or two the band was sounding good again.

When we returned to New York I picked up a couple of weeks at the Embers with Ralph Flanagan's band, and then joined Zoot and Al Cohn at the Half Note, with Mose Allison on piano and Gus Johnson on drums. That was the first of many happy gigs that I worked there. I also spent a lot of my free evenings at the Half Note, listening to other bands.

At the bar there one night I found Roy Eldridge standing beside me. He and Coleman Hawkins had been making concert appearances together. I said, "You and Hawk have a nice thing going, there, Roy."

He nodded and then frowned.

"Yeah, but that man's done me out of a lot of work," he said indignantly. "If Hawk don't like the bread, he won't take the gig. And he don't know no word but *thousand dollars!*"

Eddie Costa's older brother, Billy, called me to play an Off-Broadway revue called *Greenwich Village, U.S.A.* at a theater at One Sheridan Square, just two blocks from my apartment on Cornelia Street. While that show

was running, I got a call from Gerry Mulligan. He had put together a
big band and taken it to Europe for a three week tour. After the tour,
two of the three West Coast members of the band, Conte Candoli and
Buddy Clark, had gone home to California. The third, Mel Lewis, decided to stay in New York. Clark Terry was taking Conte's chair, and
Gerry asked me to replace Buddy, starting the following Tuesday night
at the Village Vanguard. I sent in a sub to finish out *Greenwich Village,
U.S.A.*, and took my bass over to the Vanguard to rehearse.

To make it clear that we weren't a dance band, Gerry called us the
Concert Jazz Band, and put together a book of arrangements designed
primarily for listening. It was a great band: Gene Quill, Bobby Dono-
van, Jim Reider, and Gene Allen in the reed section; Willie Dennis,
Bob Brookmeyer, and Alan Raph on trombones; Nick Travis, Don Ferrara, and Clark on trumpets, and Mel on drums.

The money Gerry had earned in the movies had made it possible for
him to pay for arrangements and equipment to get the band started.
By the time Clark and I joined, Norman Granz had become involved
as a backer. I'm not sure what sort of deal he and Gerry had made, but
with Granz's support, it looked like we would be working steady for a
while. The music was first-class, and we were all excited at the prospect.
Our esprit de corps was very high; nobody sent in subs unless they
were dying.

Besides having good soloists, one of that band's assets was having a
good riff-maker in each section: Gerry, Clark, and Bob. On most arrangements, we didn't go to the next written section after someone's
solo unless Gerry gave the signal. Gerry would improvise a background
riff on a soloist's second or third chorus and the reeds would join him,
in unison or in harmony. Bob or Clark would make up counter-riffs in
the brass section, and soon we'd have developed something strong and
new to lead into the next written section.

Gerry's music library included arrangements by Bill Holman, John
Mandel, Brookmeyer, Al Cohn, Thad Jones, and Wayne Shorter, as
well as his own charts. Gary McFarland, new in town, showed up at a
rehearsal one day with a couple of compositions that had a strong fla-
vor of Duke Ellington's writing. Gerry made a number of excisions and
repositionings to make them more Mulliganesque. Gary saw what Gerry
wanted and came in with several new pieces that were just right. We
recorded them all. Gary's exposure with our band launched him into a
successful arranging career in New York.

Gerry did another kind of editing when Al Cohn brought in an original he had titled "Mother's Day." Gerry retitled it "Lady Chatterley's
Mother." After rehearsing it a couple of times, Gerry said, "Al, it's a

wonderful chart, but I wish there was more of it. It just gets rolling and it's over. Could you add a few more choruses?"

Al nodded and gathered up the parts, and at the next rehearsal he passed them out again. The ending had been turned into a lead-in to another solo chorus for Gerry, and then Al's great shout chorus began. The first time we played it, the whole band cheered. If Gerry hadn't asked for more, we'd have had a good Al Cohn chart, but without that wonderful climax.

One Sunday afternoon at the Vanguard, Nick Travis brought in a movie projector, set it up in the kitchen, and showed us a reel of 8mm film that he had taken on the band's tour of Europe. Zoot had gone along as guest soloist. While the musicians were waiting on a railroad platform somewhere in Germany, Nick had started his camera rolling, and Zoot and Gerry had begun to do a soft-shoe dance. Zoot's dad was a vaudeville hoofer and had taught his sons the steps. As soon as Gerry realized that Zoot really knew how to dance, he stepped aside and let Zoot go by himself.

While Zoot continued a lovely, funny solo dance, the camera also recorded the approach behind him of a stolid German couple wearing very stern expressions. As they loomed directly behind Zoot, he did a spin that brought him face to face with them. Zoot registered their disapproving looks for a split second and then simply continued his spin for another quarter turn and stopped, facing Gerry, where he managed to look as if he'd been standing there talking all the while. Chaplin couldn't have done it better.

After a weekend in Fort Lauderdale, Florida, concerts at Freedomland in the Bronx, a week at Birdland, and another week at the Vanguard, Gerry broke the sad news. He and Norman Granz had terminated their business arrangement. When Norman sold his record label, Verve, to MGM Records, Gerry's recording contract, along with all the other Verve artists', was part of the deal. With no more Granz-sponsored European tours for the band, Gerry couldn't afford to keep us together. He had only one concert in Boston booked for the rest of the summer. He canceled that engagement, broke up the band, and told us he'd call us if he found anything in the fall.

The band re-formed now and then during the next three years for record dates and an occasional week at Birdland, but the spirit wasn't the same. We weren't the family we had been; we had lost the continuity and the feeling of commitment. Gigs with the Concert Jazz Band were still fun, but the band wasn't the center of our lives any more.

Gerry continued to work with his quartet: Brookmeyer, Mel Lewis, and me. We appeared on Mike Wallace's television show during the time that Wallace was in the process of building a reputation as an investigative reporter. Wallace's TV interviews were popular partly because of his prosecutorial style.

At the rehearsal Wallace was courteous and low-key. He asked questions that had been prepared by his staff, and Gerry answered frankly about his career, his experiences with drugs and the law, and other aspects of his life. On the air, Wallace's tone became more contentious, and instead of asking the questions he had asked at rehearsal, he said accusingly, "I understand that you were involved with drugs, and did some time because of it!"

This left Gerry with little more to say than "yes." Though Wallace was using the information Gerry had given him at the rehearsal, he gave his audience the impression that he was confronting Gerry with the results of his own private investigations. Gerry managed to field Wallace's questions with his usual aplomb, but he found himself at a loss when Wallace asked him, "I notice there are no black musicians in your group. Is this accidental, or by design?"

Actually, it was the first time in many years that, by happenstance, there were no black musicians in Gerry's quartet, but any short answer to that question would have sounded lame. As Gerry considered how best to respond, Bob Brookmeyer glared at Wallace, jerked a thumb at Mel Lewis, and said frostily, "We've got a Jewish drummer. Will that help?"

Wallace dropped the subject.

chapter 39

Judy Holliday

Some time after Gerry and Arlene Mulligan's marriage came to an end, Gerry began seeing a lot of Judy Holliday. She liked his music and quickly made friends with the quartet. We were working in Los Angeles when Judy was touring there with her musical, *The Bells Are Ringing*. We went to her show and she came to hear us play.

Judy had spent a lot of time in Hollywood, but none of the tinsel had rubbed off on her. She had self-respect as an actress, but success hadn't inflated her ego. She examined her own work with the clear eye of reality, and was probably her own best critic.

While Aileen and I were visiting her one day, Judy talked about her experiences with Hollywood studio politics. After a stunning success on Broadway in the role of Billie Dawn in *Born Yesterday,* Judy had found herself completely out of the running for the movie version. MGM wanted the part to be played by an established movie star. If Katharine Hepburn hadn't been in her corner, Judy would never have had a chance to even audition for the part.

Hepburn got her a small but crucial role in *Adam's Rib,* a film she was making with Spencer Tracy, which proved that Judy belonged in the movies. But even when MGM gave her a screen test for *Born Yesterday,* they just used it as a benchmark against which to evaluate the stars they were considering for the part.

Thanks to Hepburn's considerable influence and a lot of luck, Judy finally did get to play Billie Dawn in the film version of *Born Yesterday,* but before giving her the part, MGM insisted she sign a seven-year contract with them. The movie established her as a star, and then for the next seven years MGM wasted her on lightweight scripts. She had to go back to Broadway to find another good role.

Judy enjoyed jokes and word play. She helped Gerry invent titles for some of his tunes. "Butterfly with Hiccups" was her name for a jazz waltz that he wrote, and Gerry made it the title of one of our albums. Then Judy began writing lyrics to some of Gerry's songs, and a project developed between them. Judy thought Anita Loos's play *Happy Birthday,* would make a good musical, and got her consent to work on a treatment of it.

Within a very short time Gerry and Judy had finished a number of attractive songs. Aileen and I visited them at Judy's country house in Washingtonville, New York, where she sang them for us, with Gerry at the piano. A few weeks later Judy told me that *Happy Birthday* had hit a dead end. Anita Loos wasn't willing to work on the book with them.

Evidently Loos had thought that making a musical of her play would just be a matter of adding songs to it. Judy knew the sort of rewriting that would be needed to make it into a successful musical, and didn't think she could do the job by herself. The project was shelved, never to be completed.

While Gerry and Judy were at work on the songs for *Happy Birthday,* Al Cohn hired me to play in a big band he had put together to accompany Mel Tormé for a month at the Roundtable, an East Side jazz club that had opened where the old Club Versailles used to be. Dave Lambert's daughter, Dee, a teen-ager at the time, was interested when I told her about the job.

"Mel Tormé!" she said. "I love the way he sings!"

"Why don't you come and hear him some night as my guest?"

She picked a date, and I stopped at the captain's desk on the way into the club that night to make a reservation for her.

"Can't do it," said the captain.

"What do you mean?"

"No unescorted women allowed in the club."

"She won't be unescorted. She'll be with me."

"Not while you're on the bandstand."

I took my problem to Morris Garelick, the owner, thinking it could be reasonably resolved.

"She's the daughter of a good friend of mine," I told him. "How can I arrange for her to hear the music?"

"No dice. I don't let no unescorted broads in here."

"What do you do when your wife wants to come to see the show?" I asked with rising irritation.

"I wouldn't let my wife into a place like this."

"What kind of a place are you running here?"

"Look, get lost, will ya? No single dames!"

I had to retract my invitation to Dee, with apologies.

A few nights later, Gerry and Judy came in and ordered drinks at the bar. When the show ended and the band headed for the bandroom, Gerry came back to say hello. The hellos turned into storytelling, and Judy was left alone longer than Gerry had intended. Then one of the musicians who had gone to the bar rushed into the bandroom.

"Gerry, come right away! They're trying to throw Judy out!"

Gerry rushed out and raised hell.

"What's the matter with you people?" he yelled. "This isn't some trollop off the street. She's a famous actress!"

Garelick was adamant about his rule.

"I don't care if she's the Queen of England! No unescorted broads in my club!"

In the spring of 1961, Gerry and Judy began working on a record album. She chose four of the songs that they had written together and seven of her favorites by other songwriters. Gerry did some of the arrangements himself and assigned the others to Ralph Burns, Bill Finegan, Al Cohn, and Bob Brookmeyer.

Judy was a skilled musical comedy singer, but she was very nervous on those record dates. She was intimidated by the jazz world represented by the arrangers and musicians in the studio. She didn't want to prerecord the band and then sing her part later; she felt it was more musical to sing with live accompaniment. But I could see that she didn't like the way she sounded on the playbacks.

"Relax," I told her. "You're on a separate track. If you want to fix something later, you'll be able to."

Judy still looked distressed. Gerry spent most of the studio time discussing the music with the arrangers. Judy muttered from the vocalist's enclosure behind me,

"Gerry knows how scared I am of this band. Why isn't he over here helping me through this? When he came to Hollywood and made his first movie, I took him by the hand! He doesn't know how tough Hollywood can be. Wait 'til I get him out there again!"

She never got the chance. She was already suffering from the cancer that took her life four years later, though none of the rest of us knew about it until nearer the end.

Judy hated her singing on that album and wouldn't allow it to be released. I think she intended to redo her tracks some day, but she never found the right combination of time and desire. In 1980, Gerry remastered those dates and the album came out as *Holliday with Mulligan* on the DRG label. I love having that sweet souvenir of Judy's voice. But she'd be furious if she knew about it.

I went back to the Atlantic House in Provincetown in the summer of 1961 to work with Mose Allison's trio, and that autumn I joined a sextet that Ruby Braff and Marshall Brown had put together for the Town Tavern in Toronto, with Tommy Newsom on tenor, Howie Collins on guitar, and Buzzy Drootin on drums.

I had first met Marshall a few years earlier, when he was leading a high school jazz band in Farmingdale, Long Island. The Farmingdale band and Mulligan's quartet had appeared together at a concert for refugees of the Hungarian revolution who were being temporarily housed at Fort Dix, New Jersey. Marshall's kids also played at Newport that summer, and the following year George Wein sent Brown to Europe to assemble a similar band of European kids for Newport.

Marshall loaded his International Youth Band with talented young professionals and then drove them crazy by treating them like mentally deficient schoolchildren. At Newport the entire Youth Band was ripe for revolt. Several of them came to Gerry, asking him to save them from Brown. Gerry calmed them down, gave them some of the professional respect they had been missing, and advised them to ignore Marshall, who really didn't understand what he was doing to upset them.

My teacher, Fred Zimmerman, asked me during my lesson one day if I knew a man named Marshall Brown. He told me, "He called and made an appointment for a lesson, but when he came here, he spent the whole hour showing me how to play the bass! He never came back, but now I hear he's telling people that he has studied with me."

When Ruby called me for the Toronto job, he didn't mention that Marshall was part of the band. He just told me the rehearsal was at Marshall's place. Marshall had a large music studio that he sometimes rented out to rehearsal groups. When I arrived and saw him getting out a valve trombone, I assumed he was filling in for the regular trombonist, but Buzzy Drootin told me that Marshall was not only going to play the gig, he was the co-leader of the group!

Marshall wasn't a good enough trombone player to play with Ruby, so I assumed he was making some other contribution to the group. Whatever the reason for his presence, he was ecstatic to be playing in a good jazz band. He absolutely wagged his tail with happiness. On the job, at the end of some numbers, he would go down on one knee while holding the last note, in the manner of Al Jolson.

Ruby, a very conservative man, was obviously pained by Marshall's playing and embarrassed by his bandstand deportment. He would say out of the corner of his mouth, "Marshall, for God's sake, get up off the floor!"

Marshall was impervious to insult. When Ruby would castigate his playing, Marshall would clap him on the shoulder and laugh as if he appreciated Ruby's wit. He persisted on the valve trombone, and over the years his playing did improve considerably.

In Toronto, most of the Braff-Brown group checked in at the Warwick, a seedy but reasonably priced hotel where traveling musicians from the States usually stayed. Dizzy Gillespie had nicknamed it "The Airwick," after a popular brand of room deodorizer.

Ruby was the only one who resisted.

"I don't care what it costs," he said. "I'm not staying in that flea-bag."

He checked into a pricey new apartment-hotel farther up Yonge Street.

Ruby developed a cold one night, and I dropped by his apartment the next day to see how he was feeling. He had a beautiful room on a high floor, with a balcony outside a glass wall open to the sky. I found Ruby huddled in the bed against the opposite wall.

"Nice view," I said.

"Yeah, but I can't go near all that damned glass. I can't stand heights."

Ruby's vertigo kept him from setting foot in most of that expensive apartment; he lived in the two or three square feet of floor space near the inner wall.

When I got back to New York, I played a month at the Village Vanguard with Jimmy Raney and Lee Konitz. Then Dave Frishberg got me a gig at the Metropole with Sol Yaged's quartet when Sol's regular bass player had to take off. We played opposite Henry "Red" Allen's group. Red was a powerful trumpet player, a member of the old New Orleans school of combative jazzmen. He challenged all comers, not content until he had established his supremacy.

The two groups played alternate sets, but twice during the night we had to play a "jam session" set combining both bands, with a double rhythm section. On these, Red threw down the gauntlet.

"What is that you got on, Sol?" he signified loudly, peering at Sol's tuxedo with exaggerated disdain. "You look like a waiter!" He broadly demonstrated laughing up his sleeve.

"Now, this is what a bandleader should look like!" Red strutted around the microphone in a tiny circle, modeling the burgundy cut-velvet jacket and white lace shirtfront that adorned his barrel-like torso. Sol smiled affably as he wetted a clarinet reed.

"What you want to play?" Red demanded. Sol suggested "After You've Gone."

"Okay, 'After You've Gone,' in B!" Red snapped, calling a key he hoped Sol would find uncomfortable. He stomped it off quickly before anyone could demur. After an ensemble led by Red's exuberant melody line, we all played choruses, feeling our way through the unusual key. Red waited to solo last, and he was ready. Standing with his shoulder blades pressed against the back wall of the narrow bandstand, he pumped a continuous stream of aggressive, swinging jazz through his horn.

While he played, Red began marching in place. As he continued shifting his weight from one foot to the other, his large feet began to carry him forward, an inch at a time, so that by the end of his last chorus the toes of his shoes, still marching, protruded over the edge of the stage. For the listeners at the bar in front him it must have been like facing an oncoming army.

With his mouthpiece jammed against his leathery embouchure, Red pointed his trumpet over the customers' heads and bounced the last notes of his chorus off the mirrors on the opposite wall of the Metropole, winding up on a screaming high B. Dripping with sweat, he accepted his applause like a fighter who had just kayoed his opponent. He was the only one who had entered the contest, but he was clearly the winner.

chapter 40

The Sherwood Inn

Gerry Mulligan reassembled the Concert Jazz Band to record an album in 1961. Clark Terry couldn't make it, but he sent in Doc Severinsen, his section mate in Skitch Henderson's band on the Tonight Show. Johnny Carson and the gang were still broadcasting from New York then. Doc played as if he'd been on Gerry's band all along.

About a month later, Doc and I found ourselves playing together on a jazz concert on Long Island. Marty Napoleon, the leader, asked each of us to be ready with a feature number. On such occasions I usually played "I Can't Get Started with You." It hadn't been used much as a bass solo and was a safe selection. Trumpet players had done it so much that they usually chose something else.

To my surprise, the tenor saxophonist played "I Can't Get Started." When he finished, Marty announced me and asked what I was going to play. I just called the first tune that popped into my head:

" 'Margie,' in C!"

I played the melody and a couple of choruses and took it out. During the applause Marty laughed and said, " 'Margie'! What made you pick that old chestnut?"

I said, "The tenor player took my tune, and 'Margie' was the only other song I could think of. It was okay."

Severinsen made a wry face. "Yeah, okay for you," he said. "But now what am *I* going to play?"

I was on the road too much in the '50s and early '60s to get into the busiest part of the recording industry, but so much recording was going on that whenever I was in town, a few dates would come my way. Like everyone else, I learned about playing for record dates by trial and error. Most recording engineers seemed unable to function without setting up artificial playing situations, with the musicians separated from each other by sound-absorbent barriers. I had to learn to play while wearing headphones. It was often the only way the musicians could hear each other.

It should go without saying that musicians need to hear well in order to play well, but it is surprising how far down on the list that requirement can be in recording studios, as well as in many other places where musicians play.

I remember a big band date at the WOR studios with Jackie Cain and Roy Kral, where we had a lot of trouble with the sound. Lucky Thompson was the tenor sax soloist. The engineer had set the band up in a long semicircle in a single row, with Jackie standing behind Roy at the piano at one end, Ed Shaugnessy's drums next, then me, Barry Galbraith on guitar, then the trumpet section, the trombones and the saxophones, with Lucky at the very end of the line. There were acoustic barriers between the sections, and a cabinet of acoustical paneling had been constructed around the piano keyboard, large enough for Jackie and Roy to inhabit. This not only isolated the two singers from the band, it kept Roy from hearing the full sound of the piano he was playing.

On the first take Lucky had a solo, but he was so far away from the rhythm section that we sounded late to each other. We tried to adjust to the situation by wearing headphones and ignoring the live sound, but the playbacks still sounded stodgy to us. The swing was missing. After a few takes, Roy said:

"This setup isn't working. Let's move that riser over here by the piano and set up like we were on a stage, with the brass on the riser and the saxes on the floor in front of them. Get rid of this box we're singing in and put the piano over with the rhythm section, right beside the horns. Then we'll be able to hear each other. Whoever has a solo, come down and play into the front mike, just like you'd do in a theater."

The engineer rushed out of the booth in full cry:

"The mikes will all be too close together! There'll be leakage! I can't be responsible for the sound if you do this."

"Oh, yes you are!" said Roy. "My responsibility is to get this sounding like music, and then yours is to record it. Just pretend you're recording at a live concert."

For once, the musicians' ability to hear each other was the first consideration in the recording studio, not the last.

There were many large holes in Gerry Mulligan's work schedule. To fill some of them, I played several weekend gigs with Billy Bauer, who had been the guitarist on the early Lennie Tristano records. Billy had found a neighborhood bar in New Hyde Park, Long Island, not far from his home, that was willing to try jazz on weekends. The Sherwood Inn was a small roadhouse with a bar, a few tables, and a kitchen.

Billy had proposed a jam session format to the proprietor, and having sold him the idea, he felt obligated to make the job seem like a real jam session. He tried to hire guys who didn't usually play together and did his best to keep things spontaneous, but unlike most jam sessions, Billy's were by invitation only. He absolutely prohibited sitting in.

I think he made that rule to keep out the neighborhood amateurs, but having made it, he abided by it religiously. He wouldn't even let stars play if they hadn't been hired. Some great players who lived on Long Island dropped by with their horns and were surprised to discover that they weren't welcome to join the fun. Billy even wrote a theme song titled "No Sittin' In at the Sherwood Inn."

Among my souvenirs is an old menu from the Sherwood Inn, complete with prices:

"Hamburger .50; Cheeseburger .60; Shrimp cocktail .75; Chicken in a Basket 1.50."

It also lists some of the musicians who played there:

"Bob Alexander, Mousey Alexander, Ruby Braff, Ted Brown, Don Butterfield, Buck Clayton, John Cresci, Bill Crow, Sonny Dallas, Hank D'Amico, Willie Dennis, Rusty Dedrick, John Drew, Morey Feld, Arnold Fishkin, Urbie Green, Henry Goodwin, Bobby Hackett, Bob Haggart, Peanuts Hucko, Milt Hinton, Peter Ind, Budd Johnson, Buddy Jones, Max Kaminsky, Al Klink, Lee Konitz, Don Lamond, John La Porta, Cliff Leeman, Clyde Lombardi, Warne Marsh, Dante Martucci, Whitey Mitchell, Miff Mole, Paul Motian, Jimmy Nottingham, Pat Merola, Tony Parenti, Charlie Perry, Bernie Privin, Pee Wee Russell, Dick Scott, Mickey Sheen, Doc Severinsen, Rex Stewart, Nick Travis, Johnny Varro, Johnny Windhurst, Phil Woods."

It was at the Sherwood that I discovered Al Klink's versatility. I knew he had played tenor with Glenn Miller, but since Tex Beneke got all the solos on that band, I wasn't familiar with Al's jazz playing. On our first set, I could hear his admiration for Stan Getz. Though a dozen years older than Stan, Al understood his sound and the kind of musical ideas he used. He could play just like him.

While chatting with Al at the bar during intermission, I mentioned my admiration for Ben Webster, and on the next set Al played all his solos with Ben's tone and phrasing, sounding exactly like *him*. I discovered that Al was a musical chameleon. He could play in dozens of different styles.

Many years later I participated in a mild deception involving Al. We were on a radio jingle date for George Roumanis. I forget the product being advertised, but George had planned to use Astrud Gilberto and Stan Getz, unidentified, emulating their hit bossa-nova album. Astrud was there, but Stan never showed up. After waiting around for half an hour, George came out of the control booth, where he'd been unsuccessfully trying to locate Stan by phone.

"Well," said George calmly, "I could reschedule, but I don't know if Stan will show up next time, either. My other option is to have Al Klink play Stan's solo, and who'll know the difference?"

Al imitated Stan perfectly, and when the jingle was aired, nobody knew the difference.

The Sherwood Inn was too far from my apartment in the Village to travel there by motor scooter with a bass strapped to my back, especially in the winter. If I couldn't get a ride with another musician coming from Manhattan, I'd take my bass on the F train from Washington Square to the end of the line at Jamaica. There I'd catch a bus on out to New Hyde Park. One winter night I was the only one Billy Bauer had hired who didn't live on Long Island, so I took the subway and bus.

It was snowing lightly when I left Manhattan, but when I left the train in Jamaica I found myself in the middle of a blizzard. I waited a long time for the bus, and when it finally came it crept slowly along its snow-covered route. I arrived at the Sherwood Inn an hour late, went in, and found no one there but the bartender. I called Billy at his home.

"Gee," he said, "everybody else called to cancel because they didn't want to drive in such a snowstorm. I tried to reach you, but you'd already left."

I had a brandy with the bartender, said goodnight, and headed back

out into the snow with my bass, where I waited another forty minutes
for the bus back to Jamaica. I never did find out what interesting combination of musicians I had missed playing with that night.

Billy's desire to keep his jam sessions sounding spontaneous gave him
an aversion to riffs and organized endings. If he heard any organization beginning to take place, he would call out in his high-pitched voice,

"No arrangements! No arrangements!"

Charlie Shavers didn't know about Billy's rules. On the night he played
there, the first tune Billy called was "The Man I Love," at a medium
tempo. Charlie played the melody and then let Billy have the first solo.
After everyone else had played, Charlie took a chorus and started to
develop his climax on a second. He built up his volume, played some
spectacular figures on his last bridge, and on the final eight bars went
into a bravura restatement of the melody an octave higher, leading to
what he clearly intended to be a strong ending with a ritard and a hold.

As Charlie hit his last high note, we all held a chord with him. All
except Billy Bauer. Billy dashed off into another chorus of the tune, a
double-time guitar solo. As the startled rhythm section caught up with
Billy, Charlie's eyes popped open with surprise. He listened as Billy
took his chorus and then passed the tune all around the band again.
When it came Charlie's turn, he marched energetically into a new chorus,
doing his best to build even stronger effects than he had on his earlier
solo. As he approached the natural place for an ending, he looked
around at me.

"Is this out?" he asked, between phrases.

"I think so," I said with a shrug, "but I could be wrong."

Charlie hit a final high note and conducted a hold with his left hand.
The rest of us again played a chord with him, and as we all released it
together, Billy played four or five additional descending chords at the
end.

"No arrangements," he muttered.

chapter 41

Benny Goodman

In the spring of 1962 I got a call from Benny Goodman's manager, Jay Finegold. Benny wanted me to join his new band for a six-week tour of the Soviet Union, with a few concerts across the United States and a week at the Seattle World's Fair beforehand. I had been warned by many of Benny's ex-sidemen that he was a tough bandleader to work for, but I was seduced by the adventure of the trip, and by the fact that John Bunch had put together a great band for him. Teddy Wilson, Zoot Sims, Phil Woods, Joe Newman, Joe Wilder, Willie Dennis, and Victor Feldman were the main soloists, and my old section mate Mel Lewis was the drummer.

Though Benny drove a hard bargain on my salary, my feelings toward him during the rehearsal period were positive. He was a little patronizing, and would get on different guys about inconsequential things, like trying to get Joe Newman to sit up straighter. But I loved the band, and was glad to be part of it.

We were all proud of the band, and we couldn't understand why Benny didn't feel that way, too. If he had just let us play and taken his solos and his bows, the tour would have been a piece of cake for him. Instead, he seemed to be always on his guard against us, as if we had been shanghaied and had to be watched for signs of mutiny. He rarely expressed approval, undermined everyone's musical confidence, and rarely seemed to appreciate his best soloists.

Benny eventually made us all unhappy, but we still played a lot of good music. Jerry Dodgion said later, "No matter what went down with Benny, I had the best seat in the house, right between Zoot and Phil. I was in heaven."

Jim Maxwell was making a good salary at NBC playing trumpet on the Perry Como Show, and didn't want to go to Russia with Benny, even though their personal relationship had been a long one, and Jim was grateful to Benny for establishing him in the music business. Their families were friendly and Benny was fond of Jimmy's son, David. Benny told Jim that it was essential that he be his lead trumpeter on this tour.

He kept raising his salary offer, but when Jim said no to $1,000 a week, Benny tried pressure. Jimmy got a call from one of the head men at NBC telling him that he could have the time off, and was to go. Then someone from the State Department called, telling Jim it was his patriotic duty to make the trip. Jim said, "I take care of my patriotic duty by paying my income tax."

The man from State said, "Yes, and we can look into that, too."

When Benny called again, Jim was still reluctant.

"I don't like to leave my family," he said.

"Bring them along," said Benny.

"My wife works, and my daughter has already planned her summer," said Jim.

"Well, bring David along. He can be the band boy. It will be a great experience for him."

David, just out of high school, was eager to go. So Jim, deciding it might be his last chance to do something with his son before sending him off to college, finally agreed to make the tour for $1,000 a week, and to bring David along as band boy. At one of the first rehearsals, Benny showed David how he wanted the band set up, and Mel showed him how to assemble the drum set.

In Seattle Benny changed his mind. He had a talk with Maxwell, telling him that he was getting too old to play lead. He said, "Why don't you take it easy, play fourth, play a little jazz, and enjoy the trip?"

He divided most of the first trumpet parts between John Frosk and Joe Wilder. Maxwell was surely the most expensive fourth trumpet player Benny ever had.

In Leningrad, after the fifth week of the Russian tour, Benny's secretary, Muriel Zuckerman, presented Maxwell with a bill for subsistence for David, at $32 a day. Jimmy couldn't believe it. He confronted Benny and reminded him of the deal they had made. Benny denied ever having said that David was to be the band boy.

"And I never said anything about feeding him, Pops."

Jimmy reminded Benny that he had shown David how to set up the band, but Benny denied having done that.

When he realized that Benny wasn't going to back down, Jimmy told him, "Have the Russians give me a bill. I'll pay them, not you."

Intourist, the Soviet travel agency, billed Jimmy for David's food, lodging and transportation. They charged him $10 a day, not $32.

Benny had commissioned new music from several well-known jazz composers, but by the time we reached Moscow, we weren't playing much of it. John Carisi wrote one new chart that Benny liked, called "The Bulgar, and Other Balkan Type Inventions." John had structured it like Benny's old hit, "Sing, Sing, Sing." He took a Bulgarian folk theme, wrote the first chorus fairly straight, then put in a tom-tom figure over which Benny could play a solo in a minor mode before the full band took it out. Benny played well on "The Bulgar," and at the Seattle fair, he called it every night right after the opening theme.

Benny would sometimes have Zoot Sims or Phil Woods play before his long clarinet duet with Mel Lewis's tom-toms. One night in Moscow, when Benny pointed to Phil during "The Bulgar," Phil stood up and played an absolutely spectacular solo, filled with singing and dancing and fireworks. It was one of those rare, inspired performances that takes your breath away. When he finished, the whole band joined the audience in a roar of approval.

As Mel continued the tom-tom beat, Benny made several false starts on his own solo. He usually played well on that section, but he was obviously stunned by Phil's solo, and couldn't seem to concentrate. He fumbled through a perfunctory solo, but he probably should have skipped it and gone straight to the out chorus. Anything else was bound to be an anticlimax.

Benny never gave Phil a chance to do that again. In that spot the next night, he called his old arrangement of "Bugle Call Rag," and we never played Carisi's chart again. The concerts were recorded, but Benny didn't include "The Bulgar" on the album, *Benny Goodman in Moscow.*

Benny gave us a hard time during the Moscow concerts, but after the first concert in Sochi, he invited the band to a champagne party in the hotel dining room. He apologized for being rough on us, blaming the tensions involved in putting the tour together.

"But it might happen again," he joked. Then he proposed a toast "to a great band."

On the concert the next night he seemed to have forgotten his toast. He snapped at Mel Lewis and Jimmy Knepper about their playing, glared at us, and generally made us all feel miserable onstage. He tried to give Zoot one of Phil Woods's solos, but Phil jumped up before Zoot could get his horn in his mouth and took his solo anyway.

Our hotel in Sochi, the Primorskaya, faced the Black Sea. Each room had a small balcony. On our second night there, a party developed after the concert in the room occupied by Jimmy Knepper and Jerry Dodgion. The door to their balcony stood open to the warm night air.

Phil Woods began holding forth on the deficiencies he perceived in Benny's character and personality. He improvised freely on his theme, with a supporting response of amens from the chorus.

Phil, a confident musician with great ears, a daring imagination, and complete command of his instrument, was not a man to mince words. At the climax of his diatribe, he stepped out onto the balcony, stretched his arms toward the sea, and in a voice made stentorian with vodka, declaimed,

"FUCK YOU, KING!"

On the floor below, Benny had stepped out on his own balcony for a breath of air. He heard everything.

We had planned to spend the next day at the beach, but at breakfast Jay Finegold announced that Benny had called a twelve o'clock rehearsal. We set up in the open-air concert hall in the bright sun. Benny spent several hours going over everything in the book that we weren't using. He said nothing about Phil's outburst from the balcony, but he gave us many significant looks. We hadn't all been at the party, but we were all being punished.

Benny rode Phil a lot during that rehearsal, until Zoot told him to lay off.

"What's it got to do with you?" Benny asked.

"You're pickin' on my roomie!" said Zoot.

As we were packing up after the rehearsal, Jay Finegold told Jimmy Knepper that Benny had "demoted" him. He'd been playing the first trombone book, and Benny wanted Wayne Andre to take his chair.

"What's wrong?" asked Jimmy.

"Benny says you're making faces at him."

Benny didn't realize that's just the way Jimmy plays.

One afternoon in Tblisi we were given a private performance by the Georgian National Dance Company at their theater. They did their whole show for us. Since Jay had told us that Benny wanted to play a little jazz for them afterwards, several of us had brought our instruments.

When the dancing was over, the rhythm section set up center-stage and Benny, Joe Newman, and Jimmy Knepper got out their horns. The dancers, who had changed into their street clothes, crowded around to listen. Benny looked disturbed.

"No, no," he said. "We wanted to get pictures. Can't they put their costumes and makeup back on?"

"Benny," we urged, "don't ask them to do that! Don't you realize how much time and work that involves?" We wanted them to be able to relax and enjoy themselves.

Benny reluctantly agreed, and we began playing *Caravan*. Joe Newman lit a fire under the melody as Benny and Jimmy played a background riff. As Jimmy Knepper began his chorus, playing with his eyes closed, Benny saw the photographers coming down the aisle. He nearly knocked Jimmy down as he shouldered him aside and stepped to the front of the stage to strike a pose for the cameras.

When we finished that tune, Benny began urging "just one or two of the dancers" to get back into their costumes and makeup for some pictures. He spent the next half hour posing for pictures instead of playing.

Mel and John Bunch and I refused to continue with this discourtesy. We packed up and went back to the hotel. We felt, after having been given such a wholehearted performance by the dance company, that Benny had treated them shabbily. Rather than giving them our best music in return, he only seemed interested in getting publicity shots.

Benny played a last tune with Joe, Jimmy, and Turk Van Lake before he left. He complained of the "unprofessional behavior" of those of us who had abandoned him.

In Leningrad, when our cultural attaché, Terry Catherman, told Benny that Mr. Moiseyev of the famous ballet company wanted to come backstage to pay his respects, Benny said, "Get the photographers." When Terry couldn't find them, Benny told him, "Then just forget it."

The main event in Leningrad was to be our performance of the *Rhapsody in Blue* with Byron Janis. Benny cancelled one of our two scheduled rehearsals with Janis to go on a fishing trip, leaving us only half prepared. At the concert, Benny didn't want Janis to be farther downstage than he was. He wouldn't let the stagehands move the piano where Janis could see him. It wouldn't have helped much if they had, since Benny failed to do any conducting.

Janis got through the performance somehow, but it wasn't a night for any of us to be proud of. By default, Byron had to conduct us with his left hand while playing. It didn't work out too well. We were all embarrassed, and sorry to have been a part of what must have been a humiliating experience for him.

Time magazine, in its June 29 issue, gave a report of the event that correctly identified Benny's failure to conduct as the cause of the fiasco. After describing the success of the rest of the concert, the article concluded:

"The only unhappy man in the hall was pianist Janis. Said he, still brooding over Goodman's insistence on remaining at stage center, 'Incredible vanity.' "

The letters column in the June 29 issue of *Time* brought a comment from Janis:

Sir:

I read with interest your perceptive article on Mr. Goodman's Leningrad performance of the *Rhapsody in Blue,* in which I was soloist. I would like to say that unfortunately I had no time to "brood" at the auditorium as I was Milan bound for my next engagement well before the second half of the program got under way.

I must take exception to the remark that I was "the only unhappy man in the hall." Members of the American embassy, press and band to whom I spoke shared my anger at Mr. Goodman's obvious lack of interest in making this performance of the *Rhapsody* a success. Indeed, after our rehearsal I would have canceled the performance outright had it not been for the very special circumstances. . . .

. . . Maybe Mr. Goodman does not feel, as I do, that vanity certainly has no place in the cultural exchange where one is playing for one's country as well as one's art. . . .

Benny received an invitation for the band to play a week of concerts in Warsaw on the way home from Moscow. We were curious about Poland, and could have used the work, but nobody wanted to go with Benny. Jim Maxwell phoned his wife and told her to send him a telegram saying there was an emergency at home and he was needed. The telegram she sent said:

"COME HOME AT ONCE. THE DOG DIED. THE CAT DIED. EVERYBODY DIED."

I'm not sorry I made the tour. It was fascinating to visit the U.S.S.R. But we were all happy to be home again, away from Benny's leadership. Reports about our adventures with him got home before we did, and all our New York friends were eager to hear the details. At Jim and Andy's bar, Gene Lees was one of those several of us entertained with stories about the trip.

Many years later, Gene started publishing his *Jazzletter* in California, and when I ran across it, we began a correspondence. After I wrote a couple of short articles for *Jazzletter,* Gene suggested that I write the story of the Russian tour. I agreed, but called him a month later to tell him that the piece was getting pretty long. He said, "Make it as long as you like."

To reinforce my recollections, I interviewed most of the other musicians who had been on the tour, and I checked names, dates, and sequences with an unpublished manuscript that our guitarist Turk Van

Lake had prepared right after we returned from Russia. When I finished the first draft, Gene gave me some helpful suggestions and I began to rewrite. The whole project took me about six months.

I sent the finished article off to Gene in the first week of June, 1986. When I heard the news of Benny's death on June 13, I called Gene and said, "What do we do now?"

"I think we should go ahead and publish it," said Gene. "It's the truth."

"Okay, let me send you another printout. I need to put a few things into the past tense."

Those were the only changes I made.

Gene spread my article, "To Russia Without Love: The Benny Goodman Tour," over four issues of *Jazzletter*. It created a furor I hadn't expected. I had only reported what had happened. My story was just a longer version of the sort of Benny Goodman stories that for years had been exchanged by all the musicians who ever worked for him. But many Goodman fans didn't want to hear about their idol's feet of clay.

The letters columns of *Jazzletter* exploded with comment about my Goodman article for several months after it was published. Some people wrote to cancel their subscriptions, and some wrote to cry shame on me and on Gene for telling the truth about Benny so soon after his death. One correspondent called me "UnChristian." But many others expressed approval. Margaret Whiting wrote, "Thank God the truth is out." There was such a flood of comment that Gene finally put a note in the July 1987 issue of *Jazzletter* that said, "Enough already. This correspondence must now cease."

The complete story of the Russian tour is too long for this book, but Gene plans to include my original article in a collection of writings by contributors to *Jazzletter,* to be published by Oxford University Press.

When I came home from Russia, I did a little work with Al Cohn and Zoot Sims and then rejoined Gerry Mulligan's quartet for a Norman Granz–sponsored tour of Europe, with Horace Silver's quintet. Horace had Blue Mitchell on trumpet, Junior Cook on tenor, Roy Brooks on drums, and Gene Taylor on bass. Blue nearly missed the tour. He discovered at Idlewild that he had left his passport at home, and had to jump in a cab and dash back to the city to get it. He just barely made the plane.

We all missed our concert in Berlin. The Cold War was at its height, the Berlin Wall had gone up, and often the city was cut off from West

Germany. On the day we were scheduled to fly to Berlin, all planes were delayed because Russian MIGs were buzzing all flights and turning them back. We sat for hours in the Frankfurt Airport until it was safe for our plane to take off, and we arrived in Berlin too late to play the concert. Though he lost money because of it, Granz shrugged off the situation philosophically.

"When there's nothing you can do, you might as well accept it and forget about it."

I brought Aileen along on that trip. We had traveled to a different city every day for two weeks, and had enjoyed glimpses of France, Germany, Denmark, Sweden, Finland, and Holland, but we wanted to spend a week in Paris when the tour was over. When we mentioned this to Norman, he told us we were on special-rate airline tickets that expired on the day we were scheduled to return to New York.

"But let me call the airline for you," he said. "What the hell, I give them a lot of business. They owe me a favor."

That night after the concert he told us everything was arranged. He took our old return tickets and gave us new ones that routed us home to New York via Paris, with a week's layover there, at no extra charge. It was a lovely gift. We stayed in a little pension on the Left Bank and spent a week exploring that beautiful city before returning home.

In those days Aileen sometimes worked as assistant to Ruth Morley, the theatrical costume designer. Ruth was costuming two shows that were opening at the same time, one in New York and another in San Francisco, so she sent Aileen to California to take care of last-minute problems there. The show was called *The Tender Heel*, and starred Kay Medford and Chester Morris. Gerry had a booking coming up at San Francisco's Jazz Workshop, so I flew out a week early with Aileen.

We stayed at Buck Wheat's houseboat in Sausalito while Buck was on the road playing bass with the Four Freshmen. I commuted every night in a rented Volkswagen between North Beach and the houseboat in Sausalito. It was an idyllic time. During the day we watched the birds on the bay with Buck's field glasses as we floated gently at our moorage, the breeze bringing us the aroma of the wild anise that grew by the dock.

"The Tender Heel" wasn't a very good play, but Kay Medford was wonderful. She understood subtle comedy both on and off stage. She was philosophical about the insanities of show business, telling Aileen, "Success in the theater isn't about talent. It's about matching neuroses."

Rehearsals for the show were in a North Beach warehouse, not far from a cable car stop. Kay rode the cable cars every day, and was charmed by them.

"And the nice thing," she said, "is that they never ask you for any money!"

Since we knew that wasn't true, we surmised that when the conductor made his rounds, Kay was successfully acting the part of someone who had already paid her fare.

When our San Francisco job ended, Aileen stayed in California for a week while our quartet flew back to New York to tape a Danny Kaye TV special. Then I returned to San Francisco, picked up Aileen, and met the rest of the quartet in Los Angeles for two weeks at Shelly Manne's club, the Manne Hole. I enjoyed hanging out with Shelly, still a New Yorker at heart, though he'd been living in California for years.

"It's the horses that keep me here," he told me. "Out here I can have horses, and I'm crazy about them."

We arrived in Los Angeles on the morning after a fierce coastal storm that had cleared the air, giving us a glimpse of how beautiful it must have been there before the age of the automobile. We were staying at the Montecito Hotel in Hollywood, which sat on a little hill. I looked out our window on the second morning and said to Aileen, "It looks like they've put up some sort of wall across the street down in the next block." It wasn't a wall, it was the smog coming back.

That night at Shelly's, the air in the club was filled with cigarette smoke. On our break, I pushed open the back door and walked outside to get some fresh air, but it was worse outside! You could have cut the smog with a knife. I decided to stay out of Los Angeles. The air gets bad in New York, too, but the region is blessed by vigorous weather systems that move the pollution out to sea and disperse it.

Whenever Mulligan's work thinned out, I would make a few phone calls to spread the word around New York that I was available, and then would drop by the union floor and the musicians' bars to see what was happening. One of the leaders who occasionally came up with something was Sol Yaged. Sol was Benny Goodman's number-one fan. He had perfected Benny's clarinet sound, style, appearance, and physical mannerisms. He was so good at being Benny that they hired him to coach Steve Allen on his portrayal of Goodman in the Hollywood fantasy, *The Benny Goodman Story*.

Dave Frishberg told me that while he was working at the Metropole,

Sol got away from his Goodman imitations one night and played several choruses that sounded quite original. Dave told Sol, "You should play like that all the time!"

Sol seemed a little embarrassed.

"Aw, nobody wants to hear that."

Until the day Benny died, Sol stood in awe in the presence of the King of Swing. When we were preparing for Goodman's Russian tour, Sol attended all our rehearsals, a TV taping in Brooklyn, and a press conference before we left. He sat on the sidelines smiling happily, his eyes rarely leaving Benny. He whispered to me as we left the taping, "You sure can see why they call him the King!"

Sol hired me to play a New Year's Eve party with him at John Hammond's penthouse in the East Sixties the year after the Russian tour. He met me at the elevator and beckoned for me to follow him. I assumed we were headed for the bandstand. Carrying my bass, I followed him through several rooms full of people and out onto a cold, windy terrace. Sol pointed across the rooftops to another penthouse and confided with delight, "That's Benny's apartment!"

Then he led me back inside to the bandstand.

Frishberg told me a similar story. Sol was driving him to a gig in New York, but took a long detour through a dingy commercial area downtown, and stopped in front of a darkened building. Pointing to an upper floor, Sol told Dave, "That's where Benny buys his suits!"

chapter 42

The Half Note

Composer Edgar Varese had someone assemble a group of jazz musicians at Greenwich House one afternoon to experiment with a new form of composition he had devised. There was one of each instrument: me on bass, Ed Shaugnessy on drums, Don Butterfield on tuba, Teddy Charles on vibes, Art Farmer on trumpet, Eddie Bert on trombone, Teo Macero on tenor sax, and one or two others that I can't remember. Varese explained that as the composer, his only control of the music would be choosing who was to play when, and for how long. He wanted us to improvise freely within the time parameters he would give us. He said he had chosen jazz musicians because he felt that classically trained musicians weren't "free enough."

Varese pulled out a stopwatch and a notepad that contained his composition. He announced something like this:

"First, the string bass and the trombone will play together for eighteen seconds. Then the trumpet and the tuba play for fifteen seconds. Then the saxophone and the percussion for twenty-one seconds. Then the vibraphone, saxophone, and tuba for eleven seconds. Then everyone together for twenty-five seconds. I want you to play whatever you like, but be free. Let your imaginations run wild."

With Varese keeping track of the seconds, the various combinations of instrumentalists he had chosen began to improvise tentatively. We listened to each other and invented phrases that related to what we heard each other playing. Varese looked disappointed.

"You're being too careful," he said. "Let's try it again, and this time, take more chances. Play wilder. Play high, low, loud, soft. Use the entire capability of your instruments."

Art Farmer muttered, "I haven't used the entire capability of this trumpet in fifteen years of playing it! And this cat wants me to do it in fifteen seconds!"

Al Cohn and Zoot Sims sometimes hired me to work with them at the Half Note when Major Holley, their regular bassist, wasn't available. The two tenor players had great empathy and appreciation for each other. They had the most popular group at the club.

They were both drinking a lot in those days. Liquor put Zoot into a partying mood. His playing made everyone feel like they were dancing. Al swung, too, but his forte was the instant invention of original melodic phrases. He was also a more dignified drinker. Even though he downed as many doubles as Zoot did, instead of dancing and singing, he just planted himself stolidly on the bandstand and made his saxophone moan most wonderfully.

When either of them got thirsty on the bandstand, he would signal to Mike Canterino, standing below them behind the bar. Mike would hand up a double shot and stand waiting. The saxophonist would hold the glass to his lips, down the contents in one gulp and release the glass, which would drop straight down into Mike's waiting hand. Mike always made the catch without looking up.

One night both men had been drinking steadily. Zoot bounced around in the tiny space allotted him on the Half Note bandstand while playing lively choruses. Al played vigorously but moved nothing but his diaphragm and his fingers. When the set ended, Zoot jumped down and caromed from table to table, laughing and carrying on, losing his balance and deftly regaining it again in the same moment. Going up the two steps to the upper table level, he tripped and then turned what was nearly a fall into a vaudeville time step.

Al climbed carefully down the bandstand stairs and stood next to me at the bar, quietly contemplating some inner space. A man standing on the other side of him watched Zoot's amazing progress around the room and said, "Boy, that Zoot can really drink a lot of booze!"

Al slowly focused on Zoot for a moment. Then he looked at me with a bleary twinkle in his good eye.

"Yes," he said carefully, "but he doesn't drink *well.*"

I also spent a lot of time at the Half Note with Bob Brookmeyer and Clark Terry. Whenever Mulligan wasn't working, Bob would call the Canterino brothers to book a week or two for the quintet that he and Clark co-led, with me on bass and Dave Bailey on drums. Hank Jones was supposed to be our piano player, but he was one of the busiest pianists in New York, and something always came up that forced Hank to cancel. The first two times I played with Bob and Clark, Tommy Flanagan substituted for Hank. Then, when Tommy couldn't make it, Bob hired Herbie Hancock.

When Clark ran into Hank in a recording studio one day, Hank asked, "How come you don't call me for the Half Note any more?"

"You always cancel out!"

"I'll make it next time. I promise."

So Clark booked Hank the next time. Bob called a rehearsal for an hour before the job started, to run down a couple of new tunes. At rehearsal time there was no sign of Hank, but a few minutes later a pianist none of us knew came in and told us Hank had sent him to sub for him. Clark, who had spoken to Hank that morning about the rehearsal, asked, "When did he call you?"

"He passed me about ten minutes ago on the West Side Highway and flagged me down!"

Clark and Bob had a conference and decided they'd rather hire someone whose playing they knew. They sent Hank's sub home, and

Bob called Roger Kellaway. From then on, Roger was our regular pianist.

Bob and Clark had developed a good repertoire for us. Each number had some unique quality in its treatment that made it interesting to play. Our arrangement of "Battle Hymn of the Republic" was the favorite of Frank Canterino, Mike and Sonny's father, who presided over the club's kitchen, making spaghetti, meatball sandwiches and eggplant parmigiana. Whenever we began to play the "Battle Hymn," Frank would appear at the kitchen door and stand just outside it until we finished, wearing his white cook's apron and a broad smile. Clark never called that tune by its title. He'd just say, "Let's get Frank out of the kitchen!"

Clark was expecting a call from Nick Travis at the Half Note one night. Clark and Nick had become friends in the trumpet section of Mulligan's big band, where they started calling each other "Kasavubu" and "Lumumba." (African leaders Joseph Kasavubu and Patrice Lumumba were in the news in those days.) When Sonny Canterino told Clark there was a phone call for him, he grabbed the receiver and shouted, "Hey, Kasavubu?"

A puzzled voice on the line replied, "No, Olantunji!"

It was drummer Michael Olantunji, the only real African Clark knew, calling him about a job. Clark couldn't think of how to explain that he wasn't putting him on.

Our quintet was very popular at the Half Note, but we couldn't seem to get a record date. Every time Bob or Clark would approach a record producer, they would be told, "I'll be down to hear you this week. Don't make any other commitments." But none of them ever showed up.

In December 1964, Bob Shad at Mercury Records (who never came down to hear us) agreed to have us do an album for the Mainstream label. By that time we had developed a large and varied book, and were confident about recording. We were disappointed when Shad wouldn't book the date at the A & R recording studios, since Phil Ramone was our favorite engineer. Shad always used the Capitol studios on Forty-sixth Street, and that was where we made the album.

When our album, *Tonight,* was released, the local jazz disc jockeys gave it a lot of air play, and the record stores in New York quickly sold out the first distribution. When friends began to complain that they couldn't find our record, Bob and Clark called Shad to ask when he was going to press more copies.

"Let's do another album," said Shad.

We thought it was a dumb idea to make another album before satisfying the demand for the first one, but the distribution of the record was out of our hands.

Bob and Clark did insist that the new one be recorded at A & R studios, and Shad consented. But when we took our instruments to A & R on the appointed day, we found another band in the studio. Phil Ramone came out and checked his calendar. We weren't listed anywhere. Shad was out of his office when Clark called, but his secretary told Clark, "You're booked at the Capitol studios." So we trooped disgustedly over to Capitol and made the second album. It sounded fine, but Ramone would have done it better.

Derek Smith replaced Roger Kellaway for three weeks at the Half Note in April 1964, and during that time we also did a television show for WNDT. Gene Bertoncini was added on guitar, and Ben Webster was the guest soloist. When the taping began, we played a couple of tunes with the full ensemble, and then Bob and Clark left the stage in opposite directions while Ben played a ballad alone with the rhythm section.

During Ben's first chorus, I glanced over at Dave Bailey and saw that he was laughing. He nodded in the direction Clark had exited. I looked over and saw Clark crouched down behind some scenery, only visible to Dave and me, with his trousers down around his knees. He was mooning us on television.

Aside from his brilliance as a jazz improviser, Clark has a flawless brass player's technique, and he is a master of rotary breathing, a method of continuing a tone on his horn by pushing air into the mouthpiece with his cheeks while momentarily closing the back of his mouth with palate and tongue and quickly sniffing more air into his lungs through his nose. The trick is to switch support of the air column from diaphragm to cheeks and back again without any break in the sound. Using this method, Clark played unusually long phrases, and could hold a note as long as he wanted to with no audible interruption for breathing.

At the Half Note, Clark would sometimes return to the bandstand after an intermission, grab his flugelhorn, and play a nice fat G, holding the note while the rest of us climbed back up on the stand and got ready to play. We always took our time, knowing that the longer Clark held the note, the more effective it would be. When we were all ready,

Clark, still holding the G, would nod, and we'd all hit a C together to begin "Lullaby of the Leaves."

Aileen's mother Mae was in town one night and had come down with her to hear the band. Mae watched with interest as Clark held his note for two or three minutes while we all got back on the bandstand. When the tune finally began, Mae said to Aileen, "Must be an ear breather."

I noticed that Clark spent generous amounts of time giving playing tips to young trumpeters who came to hear him. When I made an approving comment about this, he told me:

"I always try to help as much as I can because I got so little help when I was starting out. There was one guy in St. Louis that I idolized. I asked him how he got such a big sound in the upper register, and he told me, 'Always keep your teeth clenched tight together when you're playing high.' I tried to play that way for a long time before I found out that son of a bitch was putting me on!"

Bob and Clark were fun to play with, but there weren't enough bookings to keep the quintet together regularly. Mulligan was doing a little better. His quartet was even invited to play for President Lyndon Johnson. We participated in a concert at an awards ceremony for young scholars on the White House lawn in the summer of 1964.

When Dizzy Gillespie "ran" for president against Johnson and Goldwater, I supported him. He added an element of delight to an otherwise grim campaign. For our appearance at the White House, I got out my "Dizzy Gillespie for President" button. It was prominently displayed on my lapel when Lyndon Johnson and his Attorney General, Robert Kennedy, came through the crowd, shaking hands. I happened to be in the swath they cut through the crowd, so my hand was clasped in assembly-line fashion by both luminaries.

Kennedy's momentary grip was light and cool. Then Johnson towered over me briefly and engulfed my hand in both of his, giving it a strong, professional squeeze. His hands were huge, and rough as those of a farm worker. I felt like a cow being milked, or a cornstalk being stripped.

Surrounded by Secret Service agents, the two handshakers pressed quickly on through the crowd, harvesting good will. The scene had a cockeyed aura of overkill, all that power being exerted on a simple exercise of courtesy at a party. I don't think Johnson's eyes came far enough into focus to see my "Dizzy Gillespie for President" button, but I got very stern looks from the pair of Secret Service agents that were covering his back.

chapter 43

Japan

Bob Brookmeyer, Dave Bailey, and I toured Japan with Mulligan in the spring of 1964. Judy Holliday came with us. By this time we all knew that Judy had cancer. She had been fighting it for over three years, but I hadn't known anything about it during the early stages. She was so beautiful and full of life that I was stunned when I heard about her illness. She never talked about it, but on the way to Tokyo I could see that she was beginning to have a rough time, often looking tired and dispirited. Her condition worsened after we returned to New York, and her long ordeal finally came to an end in June 1965. She was only forty-one when she passed away.

Reggie Ichinose, the man who brought us to Japan, met us at the Tokyo Airport with a group of newspaper and television reporters and a bevy of young girls bearing bouquets of flowers for us. Reggie told us he was a boxing promoter. He hoped that handling Gerry's first Japanese tour would establish him as a musical entrepreneur. He only set up brief publicity appearances for us during the three days before our first concert in Tokyo, so we had plenty of free time to explore the city. We chose to stay in Frank Lloyd Wright's famous Imperial Hotel, to have the experience of living in one of Wright's creations.

Reggie was an Okinawan. Since Japan only allowed its corporations to be headed by native Japanese, he had made the young man who carried our luggage president of his company. When we found this out, we started calling him "Pres."

I had agreed to come without my bass, saving Reggie an extra plane fare. I had been assured that he would rent me an instrument in Japan that would meet my specifications. To be on the safe side, I brought my tool kit, a bass bridge, and a new set of strings. On our second morning in Tokyo, Pres drove me to a small music store that had one bass in stock, a shiny new plywood one with a warped bridge. I told him, "No, you don't understand. Somewhere in Tokyo there must be a place that has old basses. With stringed instruments, old is better."

Pres told me not to worry now that he knew what to look for, and the next morning he came to the hotel and proudly opened the back of his panel truck for me. Inside were four of the most beat-up old plywood basses I had ever seen. He must have raided some school orchestra's music room. The instruments were covered with scrapes and scratches, and chips of wood were missing from the edges. I began to despair. I realized that a boxing promoter's assistant wouldn't even know whom to ask about locating a decent bass.

Out of courtesy, I tried out the ones he had brought, and was surprised to find that one of them had a fairly decent sound, even though it looked terrible. Since time was getting short, I decided to use it.

"I'll take this one," I told Pres. "But I'll need a bottle of brown liquid shoe polish and a soft cloth. And see if you can find a cover for it."

I took the miserable-looking instrument to my room, and Pres got me the polish and a canvas cover. I darkened the nicks and scratches with the shoe polish and rubbed down the finish until it looked a little better. Then I put on new strings and adjusted the bridge and soundpost. With an hour of practice, the bass settled in and played fairly well.

Since it was made of plywood, it needed no pampering. For the first time in my career, I was able to forget about my instrument. Pres took good care of it for me. When I walked on stage at each concert, I'd find the bass lying beside Dave's drum set. I'd tune it up, play it, lay it back down, and forget about it until the next concert.

There were other jazz tours in Japan while we were there. Duke Ellington's band came through with a heavy schedule. They played every day, with two concerts on some days. They passed us several times as we leisurely toured the country during our second and third week. There was also a three-part tour that came to Japan that summer. One part was a pop show headed by Sam Donahue and the Tommy Dorsey band, with Frank Sinatra, Jr. The second part, traditional jazz, had Gene Krupa's quartet, Dakota Staton, Red Nichols and his Five Pennies, and the Dukes of Dixieland with Edmond Hall. The third part of that tour, modern jazz, featured the Miles Davis quintet, the Wynton Kelly trio, Carmen McRae and her trio, the J.J. Johnson All-stars, and the Sleepy Matsumoto quartet.

Miles and some of the others came over to our hotel to hang out with us one day. Dave Bailey, who had been in Tokyo before, took Tony Williams, Wynton Kelly, and me to a jazz coffee shop he knew. It was run by a smiling lady called Mama-San. Tea and cakes were served there, but the main course was jazz records played on a good sound system.

A waitress brought us the looseleaf book of record album covers from which patrons could choose the music they wanted to hear. Tony leafed through it and found a new release by Cecil Taylor that interested him. Wynton had heard of Cecil, but hadn't heard him play. Tony requested the album, and the waitress went to put it on the turntable.

While we sipped our tea and waited, Dave said he'd heard that in May, Cecil had been in a fight with some drunks on the street near his home in New York's East Village, and in the scuffle his left hand had been broken. Wynton winced, and we all agreed that it was a terrible thing to happen to a piano player. Then Cecil's record began to play.

Wynton's eyes opened with dismay as he listened to Cecil's uninhibited disregard of traditional pianistic parameters. He looked at each of us, registering first disbelief, then mock outrage. He growled, "They should have broke *both* of his hands!"

After one of Ellington's Tokyo concerts, some of his musicians came over to our hotel. After dinner, Harry Carney and Dave and I settled down for a chat in comfortable old leather easy chairs in the quiet lobby of the Imperial. Harry was exhausted. Duke's heavy schedule had worn him down. He kept sinking deeper into his chair as the effects of the dinner and the wine crept over him. He roused himself once and murmured, "Oh, Crow, take me to my room."

"Harry, you don't live here. Your hotel is across town."

After a moment's consideration of this information, he sank back into his chair and went to sleep.

It would have been difficult to get him back to his own hotel. When we explained the situation to the manager of the Imperial, he quickly produced a pillow and a blanket, tucked Harry up in his chair, and left him there for the night. In the morning, I checked the lobby. Harry was gone, back on the road again.

I spent every free minute during the day exploring Tokyo, and Dave Bailey and I spent many evenings at Mama-San's. Gerry and Judy went their own way most of the time, but it took me a few days to realize that Bob Brookmeyer had been staying in his hotel room when we weren't playing. He had become overwhelmed by the crowds and the language barrier in Tokyo. He retreated to his room and ordered martinis from room service.

I called Bob one evening and told him that I had found some interesting places quite near the hotel, and he accepted my invitation to come for a walk. I took him to a nearby plaza where vendors were selling everything from barbecued eels to plastic pinwheels and live goldfish. Calligraphers had set up booths where they would inscribe mottos beautifully on scrolls. A million fascinating facets of Japanese culture were all around us, but the farther we got from the hotel, the more uncomfortable Bob became. Finally he said, "Do you mind if we go back? I really can't make all this chaos, and all these little people running around."

I gave up and took him back to the Imperial. He didn't even enjoy living in that unique old hotel. It had been designed to the scale of the average Japanese.

"I keep bumping my head," he complained.

Japan just wasn't the right place for a tall young fogy like Bob. He had been much happier on our trip to England, touring stately pubs with Ed Harvey.

During our last week in Japan, Gerry told us he'd been approached about going on to Singapore, Thailand, and Australia, but Brookmeyer absolutely refused. He couldn't wait to put Asia behind him. Without him Gerry didn't have a quartet, so he had to turn down the offer. I was terribly disappointed. I would have loved to have seen those places and met those people.

We played concerts in Nagoya, Kobe, and Hiroshima, and finished our tour in Osaka. In Kobe we were met at the train by a sharply dressed young Japanese man who spoke a sort of 1940s hep talk. He was the proprietor of a restaurant, and insisted that we have dinner there as his guests. We sat at a low table where the food was prepared in metal basins heated with spirit lamps. While it was cooking, our host passed around various appetizers. One was a lacquer box of dried and salted sardines shaped in little S curves.

"Now, dig," said our host. "Any shmuck can salt a sardine. But to salt them so they look like they're swimming . . . baby, that's art!"

Back in the States, Gerry's quartet continued to work around the East Coast, and we made a runout to Chicago; Seattle; Vancouver, B.C., and San Francisco in early 1965. In Chicago, a pretty young woman in a Playboy "bunny" costume showed up one night at the London House, where we were playing. Gerry and Bob had won the *Playboy* jazz poll in their categories, and the bunny had come to present their awards.

Bob felt that a girlie magazine had no business running a jazz poll.

"I don't care how many intellectual articles Hefner prints," he said. "It's still just a stroke book."

When the bunny handed Bob his silver medal, he took it brusquely and laid it inside the open piano. It was still there when we left town.

chapter 44

Al the Waiter

During another week at Chicago's London House in the summer of 1965, Gerry Mulligan and I had a disagreement, which I resolved by resigning from the quartet. I went back to New York and worked a variety of gigs around town, and I continued to play frequently with the Brookmeyer-Terry Quintet at the Half Note.

That legendary jazz club had developed gradually from a small Hudson Street restaurant. Mike and Sonny Canterino had convinced their father Frank that his business could be expanded by putting music in the back room. The boys liked jazz, and the groups they booked began to attract other jazz lovers. As business improved, they opened up the wall between the bar and the back room, built a bandstand behind the bar and put in more tables and chairs.

They needed a waiter to serve the tables, so they called an agency. The next day Al the Waiter showed up for work in his tuxedo, with two small children in tow. He explained that his wife had just abandoned him, leaving him to care for the kids. Frank put them at a table in the corner and fixed them something to eat, and Al went to work. Not long after that, Al's wife came back, took the children, and disappeared again. From then on he lived alone.

Al's last name was Berg, but not many people knew it. Everyone called him Al the Waiter. As a youth he had been known as Al the Goniff in the neighborhood where he lived. His New York City cabaret cards bore various names. Some early difficulty involving the police had permanently stained his record as far as the licensing department was concerned. The city's cabaret law provided for no legal means of clearing one's record once a cabaret card had been denied or withdrawn, but there were other ways. Al worked at the Half Note for over twenty years on temporary cards, which he got by going downtown every so often to pay somebody off.

Al looked cadaverously thin, the effect exaggerated by the absence of several molars. He kept up a constant stream of patter in his New York street dialect as he rushed from tables to bar to kitchen. When Al took an order, he repeated the names of the drinks loudly, but he often came back with something that hadn't been ordered.

When Al saw a customer take out a cigarette, he would dash over while pulling a match, lit, from the book of matches he kept hooked over his waistband. He could reach under his jacket with one hand, pull a match loose and strike it with the same motion, the effect being the sudden extraction of flame from somewhere inside his clothes. He worked in a tuxedo that was not new when he bought it, and he gave it many years of hard wear. The constant ignition of matches at close quarters had created a large singed area at the top of his trousers near the spot where he hung the matchbook.

As Al arrived at a table to take an order he would cry, "My greatest pleasure is to serve you!"

When he returned with drinks or food he would shout, "Sorry to keep you waiting!"

His ministrations were a little overwhelming, and sometimes competed with the music. Though manic and loud, he really was eager to please his customers, and made Half Note regulars feel they were part of the family.

Al's existence away from the club was a lonely one; he lived by himself in a small room on West Twentieth Street. He was as brassy as a carnival pitchman, but he had a sentimental side that was easily evoked by musicians' wives and girlfriends. When a musician brought a female guest to the Half Note, Al became super-solicitous. He would select the best table in the house and establish the couple there with every amenity available: clean ashtray, napkins, silverware, salt and pepper shakers, coasters for their drinks.

Al would hover at the table, suggesting possible food and drink selections, lighting cigarettes, tidying the ashtray. Wives and girlfriends who came regularly would receive candy and greeting cards from Al when they arrived. If anyone turned up with a child, Al would be beside himself trying to think of special treats that he could invent from ordinary bar and restaurant supplies.

Al's favorite was Margo Guryan, an attractive and talented young woman who became Mrs. Bob Brookmeyer for a few years. Whenever Margo came down to hear Bob and Clark, Al would produce all sorts of goodies and trinkets to please her. Margo felt a little embarrassed by Al's ministrations. The simplest polite "thank you" would cause him to double his efforts the next time she came in. When she once tried to tell him he was overdoing it, he began to look so crushed that she couldn't go through with it.

At every holiday season, Al chose Bob and Margo as the objects of his affection. If the band wasn't working at the Half Note, the Brookmeyers would receive greeting cards and letters at their Greenwich Village apartment. An Easter card from Al, decorated with gold foil and glitter-covered flowers, carried this printed message:

> You're mighty nice to think of
> When Easter Day is here,
> But then you're nice to think of
> Just any day all year . . .
> And at this Happy Easter time
> Good wishes go to you
> For just a world of gladness
> Today and all year through.

Al wasn't content with this sentiment; it didn't go far enough. After writing "Mr. and Mrs. Bobby Brookmeyer" at the top, he inked in, before the printed message:

> From My Heart To You Both Always The
> VERY BEST OF EVERYTHING

Then he added extra words to the text, so it read:

> You're mighty nice to think of ALWAY'S
> When Easter Day is here, AND EVERY DAY
> But then you're nice to think of ALWAY'S
> Just any day all year AND FOREVER
> And at this Happy Easter time AND EVERY TIME
> Good wishes go to you BOTH
> For just a world of gladness HEALTH SUCCESS HAPPINESS
> AND HEALTH
> Today and all year through. AND FOREVER
>
> MAY YOUR BOTH LIFE'S ALWAY'S AND ALWAY'S BE AS HAPPY
> BRIGHT SUCCESSFULL AND VERY HEALTHY AS THIS MOST BEAUTIFULL
> LOVELY BRIGHT HOILDAY WHICH IS CALLED EASTER IS
>
> Alway's and Alway's
> Your Sincere Faithfull
> Pal and Waiter
> Al

(The spellings and punctuation in the above and following examples are Al's own.)

To add even more emphasis, every word Al had added to the card was surrounded with closely spaced little penstrokes to indicate radiance, and the entire message was surrounded with larger radiance marks.

. When Al's generous feelings seized him he expressed them in letters, always scrupulously addressed to both Bob and Margo. He didn't wish to be misunderstood. He thought they were the ideal couple, and treated them as his adopted family. Al's letters were written in a large hand on blue-lined foolscap writing paper, the pages carefully numbered with Roman numerals. One said:

Mr and Mrs Bobby BrookMeyer.

Hope that my letter to you Both Finds you Both in the Very Best of Health Happiness and also Very successfull in everything that you both do. and Plan to do always.

I hope that you both had a very wonderful Summer.

And I also Wish you both a Very Happy Successfull and Very Happy Winter. and Healthy One. Please let me know What you both Want for Christmas. Please. Thank you very much.

Please Always let me know If You both ever need Anything As it's my greatest Pleasure and Honor to Always give You both the Very best of every thing that you may need or Want always.

And Please never ever Thank me for anything As its my great Pleasure Always to give you both everything.

As soon as I get tickets for the Football Giants Games I will and with the greatest Pleasure Mail them to you. Or if I see you I will give them to you.

Thanking you Both for always being so very nice to me I always Wish to be your both Very Best sincere Friend And always your Both Very Sincere and Very Faithful Waiter

Al

In late December 1964, Al played Father Christmas, sending the Brookmeyers extravagant greeting cards and delivering gifts to their apartment house. After Christmas another letter arrived, repeating the offer to get them tickets to shows and sports events. In it, he added:

When my oil Well strike oil Which I own, plenty of acres of Oil Land I will buy you your own Night Club and make you both Very Very Rich As you both Have alway been Very kind and good to Me which I alway appreciate it very much. from my Heart.

Did the Door Man of you Apartment House give you both 3 Big Shopping Bags Thursday Night Dec 24

Please let me know if he did. Thank you both.

Use and Wear evrything Alway in the Very Best of Health and Happiness Always. I hope, that you both like and enjoy everything . . .

Thank You. I alway wish to be and remain

Your Very Sincere

Faithfull Friend and Waiter

                                                                              Al

At the bottom of the last page, surrounded with radiance marks, Al printed:

1965   MAY THE NEW YEAR   1965
       JUST BRING TO YOU BOTH
       ALWAY'S LOTS OF
       HEALTH SUCCESS
       WEALTH HAPPINESS
       AND ALWAY'S
       THE VERY BEST OF
       EVERTHING TO YOU BOTH

New Year's Eve brought the Brookmeyers a telegram from Al:

MR AND MRS BOBBY BROOKMEYER

FROM MY HEART TO YOU BOTH AS THE CHIMES BRINGING IN THIS NEW YEARS MAY IT BRING TO YOU BOTH ALL THE HEALTH HAPPINESS WEALTH SUCCESS AND THE BEST OF EVERYTHING FOR YOU BOTH ALWAYS YOUR SINCERE AND FAITHFUL FRIEND AND WAITER

                                                                              AL

In early 1965, when our quintet made its first record, Bob gave Al the Waiter a copy. Al's thank you letter said:

Mr and Mrs Bobby Brook Meyer

I want to thank you both from my Heart For the beautifull Stero Record that you both gave me I will always Play it on my Stero Player

Bobby:

I want to wish you all the Happiness Success and Good Luck on your first Record "called" TO NIGHT [radiance marks]

With Clark Terry Roger Kellaway Bill Crow and Dave Baily.

May and I will pray to "God" That it should and will become a Big Smash Hit And over Two Million People Should and Will buy Your Smash

Hit Record called TONIGHT [radiance marks] and I Will Personely tell everybody to buy it. Thanking you both for this wonderfull Gift which I thank you both Very much for.

I alway wish to be your sincere Fathfull Friend and Waiter

Al

In April, Bob received a card depicting roses and ferns entwined around a white satin ribbon, with the legend: "To Congratulate You." Bob had just joined the staff orchestra on the Merv Griffin Show, so he assumed that was what had occasioned the congratulations. Added to the printed "best wishes on your success," and thoroughly high-lighted with radiance marks, was Al's block-lettered message:

FROM MY HEART TO YOU ALWAY'S THE VERY BEST OF EVERYTHING FOR YOU AND MRS BROOKMEYER AND ALL THE HEALTH SCCESS AND HAPPINESS ALWAYS TO YOU BOTH FROM MY HEART TO YOU

Always your Very Sincere Best Pal and Waiter

Al

Al the Waiter's final note in Margo's collection covered a single page:

Mr and Mrs Bobby Brookmeyer
   I am Very sorry that
   I couldn't get you both Better Seat for the Ball Game
   Please forgive me
   Have a Very Enjoyable Time Watching the Ball Game
   It always and always Will be my greatest Pleasure to be your Both
Very Sincere Pal Friend and Waiter always

Al

How do you like the ZOOM LENSE

Bob and Margo's marriage came to an end without a great deal of turmoil. Margo said the hardest part was disillusioning Al the Waiter, who had supported their union so avidly. When she remarried, Margo gave me Al's letters and cards in case I should ever want to write about him.

Al called the Half Note one night to say he wasn't feeling well, and wouldn't be coming in. When Mike and Sonny heard no more from him for a couple of days, they decided they'd better go and see how he was. They went to his rooming house but got no response when they knocked. Fearing the worst, they broke down the door and found Al had died in his bed. In his tiny cell a giant air-conditioner was going full blast. Mike said it was so cold in the room that if they hadn't found him, his body would have been preserved forever.

Al's only possessions were the air-conditioner, a large-screen television, a well-stocked liquor shelf, a few clothes, and three thousand dollars in one-dollar bills, each bill wadded into a tight little ball and tossed into a drawer.

When Mike and Sonny moved the Half Note to Fifty-fourth Street in 1972, it lost the ambiance that had endeared it to musicians and customers alike. Higher rent in the new location forced them to raise their prices, and business suffered as a result. Before long the new Half Note closed, and the Canterinos went their various ways, as did the groups that had made so much music for them. But, for those of us who were part of the family, the memories are poignant.

We remember the old club, aglow with light among the surrounding industrial buildings (closed for the night), the cobblestones of Hudson Street empty of daytime truck traffic. We remember the musicians who played there and the friends and fans who crowded the bar and tables. And hurrying among the throng, bringing drinks, serving food, lighting cigarettes, we remember Al the Waiter, insisting loudly to one and all:

"Sorry to keep you waiting! My greatest pleasure is to serve you!"

chapter 45

Condon's, The Playboy Club

When Aileen and I got married, we found an apartment in a building in Chelsea that adjoined the one where Dave McKenna lived. Dave was playing piano with the house band at Eddie Condon's club on East Fifty-sixth Street, and he gave them my name when they needed a bass player. Eddie hired me to play one weekend, and it turned into a steady gig.

Condon's only used a bass three nights a week. The band did without me Tuesdays through Thursdays. I couldn't understand the economic priorities of Condon's manager. He could have had a full-time bass player for another $75 a week, but felt the club couldn't stand the financial strain. Yet he'd often grab $200 out of the till and throw it away at the track the next day without giving it a thought. I guess he considered that an investment.

Having played for three nights without a bass, the band always made me feel welcome when I came to work on Fridays. McKenna played better walking bass lines on the piano with his left hand than most bass players played with both hands, but he preferred the sound of the string bass in that role.

We had Peanuts Hucko on clarinet, Yank Lawson on trumpet, Cutty Cutshall on trombone, and Morey Feld on drums. Condon played guitar whenever he wasn't out working the house. He was a great conversationalist, much appreciated by his steady customers. The music was wonderful, but sometimes there was friction on the stand. When Yank had one too many to play his best, Peanuts couldn't resist mentioning it, though he knew that Yank only took offense when he'd had one too many.

When Eddie joined us on the bandstand with the old four-string guitar he called his "pork chop," he played so confidentially that I often couldn't tell what chords he was using, but his pulse felt good, and he got the band in the mood to play. He had a nice way of eyeing you appreciatively when you got off a good solo.

Eddie drank a lot, but rarely looked stoned. He looked like he'd been drinking, all right; you can't put away as much alcohol as he did every day without having it affect your complexion and add a special determination to the way you walk. But I never saw Eddie sloppy drunk. At worst, he lost his elegant grace and staggered a little. He did become an easy mark for muggers at the end of a long night of drinking, and was ripped off several times on his way home. He accepted this as part of the price he had to pay for feeling the way he wanted to feel.

I saw Eddie one night near Roseland, trying to cross Fifty-second Street. His face was flushed and his legs didn't seem to be working exactly right. A friend had him by the arm, trying to steady him and steer him. Condon indignantly tried to pull away, lurching toward the opposite curb. The friend pulled him back and yelled, "Eddie, the cars are coming! You'll be killed!"

Condon pulled away again and chided, "Well, let me do it on my own!"

McKenna moved on to another gig and Dick Hyman replaced him

at Condon's. Around the same time, Cliff Leeman took Morey Feld's place on drums. Hyman knew all the traditional tunes we played, but he sometimes modernized their chord structures. Condon was impressed with his technique, and sometimes featured him on a number with just Cliff and me. He played a jazz waltz one night, with a lot of cross rhythms and altered harmonies. When it was over, Condon fixed Dick with a look of amazement.

"And you don't drink at all, do you?" he asked.

One night Peanuts asked me if I could play a Fender bass. He and a record producer had cooked up a gimmick to record a tune he had written called "Peanuts, Popcorn and Crackerjazz," with a Dixieland front line and a rock rhythm section. I told him I'd rent a Fender for the date.

At the recording studio I found Gary Chester setting up. We had played together on *Greenwich Village, U.S.A.* Gary had since become one of the hottest drummers in the recording field. He had learned all the rock beats, and he could read music better than most rock drummers, so he was the king of rock-oriented commercial jingles.

"I didn't know you played the Fender bass!" said Gary.

"I rented this one for the date. I used to own one, but I sold it years ago."

"Well, get another one! I can get you a lot of work!"

As soon as the date was over I returned the Fender I'd rented and went shopping for one of my own, but there wasn't a Fender bass in stock anywhere in New York. It was just before Christmas, and there had been a run on them for presents to aspiring teen-age rock musicians. The clerk at Manny's music store said they were back-ordered until February.

Attila Zoller had some instruments that the Framus guitar company had sent him in lieu of cash payment for an advertising deal he had made with them. Rather than let Gary's offer get cold, I bought a Framus electric bass from Attilla and started practicing. When I had it pretty well under my fingers, I called Gary.

"I got the electric bass, like you said."

"Great. Nothing much is happening right now, but I'll let you know if I hear of anything."

I felt considerably let down. It was less than a week since he had told me he could get me a lot of work. About a month later, on my way to a recording studio on Fifty-seventh Street, I saw Gary walking in the opposite direction. I pointed to my electric bass and said, "Remember, I've got one of these now."

"Are you on your way to a date?"

"Yeah."

"See, I told you you'd get a lot of work if you got one!"

I enjoyed playing at Condon's, and probably would have stayed there if they had given me a full week's work. But Aileen and I found a little house that we wanted to buy in Rockland County, New York, and I was looking for a more reliable income in order to be able to afford the move. Kai Winding called with an offer I couldn't refuse, a steady job at the New York Playboy Club.

The club, on Fifty-ninth Street near Fifth Avenue, had been open for a year or so with only a state liquor license. For some reason, the New York Department of Licenses had disapproved the club's application for a New York City cabaret license. In those days, any establishment without a cabaret license could only use small string groups. Playboy had been making do with piano-bass duos.

When an investigation revealed that Hugh Hefner had been forced to pay off state officials to get his New York liquor license, he provided the evidence that convicted the culprits. The city licensing department then became cooperative, and on appeal, Hefner finally got his cabaret license. The club installed a full line of entertainment the week after Christmas, in 1965.

The opulently decorated club was an adolescent male fantasyland, filled with beautiful young girls wearing bunny ears and tails. Their corsetlike costumes showed a lot of leg, shoulder and poitrine, but were uncomfortable and impractical to work in. Most of the poor girls thought of themselves as models or showgirls, but they were really waitresses, and they walked many uncomfortable miles every night in their impossibly high heels and tightly laced costumes, serving food and drinks while the customers ogled.

Between the ground floor Playmate Bar and a mezzanine cocktail lounge called the Living Room, there was a bandstand shaped like a giant champagne glass. Kai Winding, the club's musical director, led a jazz quintet there, with pianist Monty Alexander, bassist Earl May, drummer Al Foster, and guitarist Les Spann. Nat Jones played solo piano during their intermissions. Al Gafa took over on guitar when Les Spann left, and later Larry Willis replaced Monty Alexander.

Kai hired me to play with Walter Norris's quartet in the Party Room on the fifth floor, with Bobby Donaldson on drums and Jerome Richardson on tenor. We also played in the Living Room on Sundays when Kai's band was off. On the second floor Harold Francis played solo piano in the gourmet dining room, and in the third floor Playroom,

Frank Owens played with a trio, with Paul West on bass and Ralph Jones on drums. In the fourth floor Penthouse, Marlena Shaw sang with a trio.

I was impressed with Marlena. She was a good singer and an appealing entertainer, funny and charming and beautiful. I wondered why she wasn't better known. A few years later I noticed that Marlena had finally made a record album. Since she was still unknown to the general public, she titled it *Who Is This Bitch, Anyway?*

The manager of the New York Playboy Club was always being second-guessed by Playboy Enterprises, the parent company in Chicago. Within a month of our opening, Walter's quartet was put on notice. We were told that Chicago had decided to put a rock band in the Party Room. Jerome Richardson and Bobby Donaldson immediately found other things to do and sent in Joe Farrell and Ray Mosca to finish out the two weeks. But our room director, Joe Palazzo, hit the ceiling when he heard about the policy change.

"Half of the business in this room is private parties for middle-aged New York businessmen!" he said. "What the hell am I going to do with a rock band?"

Evidently he screamed loud enough to be heard in Chicago. Our notice was canceled and Joe Farrell and Ray Mosca stayed on the job with Walter and me for about a year. We played jazz for dancing, and Farrell played whatever he liked. Sometimes he would entertain us with impressions of all the modern "freedom" tenor players. He could imitate each one's style and physical attitude perfectly. He also sent in interesting subs, like Joe Henderson and Harold Ousley. Farrell eventually left when the club cut our group down to a trio.

Ray Mosca's dad, a dapper barber who loved ballroom dancing, came to the club one night as Ray's guest. Dressed in his best black suit, he sat beside the Party Room bandstand watching the dancers. There were never any single women at the club; most of the members were men, and the women were all escorted. But one guy left his lady sitting at a table by herself for a long time while he hung over the piano, trying to impress Walter with his hipness.

Ray nudged me and pointed to his dad, who was heading across the dance floor toward the woman sitting alone. He bowed formally and asked her to dance. As she stood up, took his hand, and stepped out onto the floor, Ray and I quickly realized from her movement that she was completely blotto, barely able to stand. Ray's dad was concentrating on his dancing and didn't seem to notice. When he stepped back and spun the lady gently away from him, she let go of his hand and kept right on going, falling flat on her back with a loud thud. She lay there on the dance floor without moving, breathing but unconscious.

Ray's dad knelt solicitously beside the woman, fanning her with his handkerchief as Joe Palazzo rushed over to help. Her escort, intent on his one-way conversation with Walter, hadn't even looked up. I tapped him on the arm and said, "The lady you came in with is lying on the floor over there! She's out cold!"

He looked over his shoulder, nodded, and turned back to Walter: ". . . so I told Bud Powell. . . ."

Attila Zoller subbed for Al Gafa in Kai Winding's band one night, and when we both finished work, we were chatting as we walked to our cars, which we had parked a couple of blocks north on Fifth Avenue. Just as we rounded the corner of the posh Sherry Netherland Hotel, two dazzling women emerged from its revolving door. They were blonde beauties, subtly coiffed and made up, wearing high-fashion evening dresses that whispered of money and good breeding.

Attila and I stopped and stared in wonder as we beheld their radiance. The fabulous women accepted our awe as the normal state of affairs, appraised us with a glance that summed up our net worth as less than the cost of a trip to the beauty salon, and dismissed us simply by refocusing their eyes beyond us.

On an impulse I dashed into the revolving door, which was still moving from the exit of the gorgeous pair. Coming full circle onto the sidewalk behind them as they walked toward the curb, I shook my fist like an outraged house detective and shouted, "And *stay* out!"

Attila laughed so hard I was afraid he might hurt himself. The two beautiful ladies glided obliviously into a waiting limousine and vanished down Fifth Avenue.

Attila shared my enthusiasm for Oscar Pettiford. He had played with him in Austria in Hans Koller's group. Attila had followed opportunities to play jazz from his native Hungary all over Europe before coming to the United States in 1959. I met him that summer when I played at the School of Jazz in Lenox, Massachusetts, with Mulligan's quartet. Attila's wonderful mangling of the English language, his readiness to laugh, and his eagerness to play charmed everyone there.

Attila encountered Ornette Coleman's music at Lenox that year, but wasn't captivated by it. In later years, he took a dim view of the direction some of the modernists were taking jazz. If required to, he could play "free," but he preferred the sort of improvisation that was based on standard chords and harmony.

Attila subbed one night on a job I was working at Jimmy Weston's in a quartet led by pianist Jimmy Lyons, with Steve Little on drums. Attila walked in and waved hello as he climbed onto the bandstand, plugged in his guitar, adjusted his shoulder strap, and quickly tuned up. Then he turned around and looked cheerfully at Jimmy, whom he hadn't met before.

"Vell?" he inquired. "You vant to play jazz, or freedom shit?"

Joe Puma, the guitarist Attila was subbing for at Weston's that night, has an acerbic sense of humor that is prized by his friends. Joe's delivery adds a special spin to his remarks; he speaks in a low, slightly husky voice. Louise Sims called him one day around noon, and when she heard his voice she said, "Oh, I'm sorry, Joe. Did I wake you?"

"No, that's okay," wheezed Joe. "This is as good as I get."

Joe was the originator of a quip that has been attributed to many different musicians. When a club date leader who was considering Joe for a job asked, "Do you know all the tunes?" Joe decided to tease him a little.

"Actually," said Joe, "I only know two tunes. 'The Star Spangled Banner' and 'Lush Life.' "

Joe worked a steady job in Las Vegas for a while. One night he recognized some New York musicians in the audience who were traveling with a singer. Joe invited the two horn players to sit in, and had just begun to enjoy playing with them when their guitar player jumped onto the bandstand in the middle of the tune and said eagerly, "Hey, Joe, can I play?"

Joe looked up stonily and asked, "Do you want my permission, or my opinion?"

Joe told me that the owner of that Vegas club was asking for suggestions for a singer to book in his showroom. When an agent asked, "How about Tommy Leonetti?" the owner said, "No, I don't want a trio. Just one guy."

Like many of our over-sixty generation of jazz musicians, Puma feels further removed every year from the bygone era when the music he plays so skillfully was appreciated by a larger segment of the general public. In a restaurant where Joe was working, a member of the audience asked conversationally, "Where are you from, Joe?"

Joe replied sadly, "From the past."

chapter 46

Comedians

At the Playboy Club, the shows changed frequently in the showrooms on the third and fourth floors. Between shows, the comics would go down to the bandstand in the Living Room to do a few jokes and drum up business for their rooms. One Sunday, when our quartet was playing in the Living Room, a young comedian from the Penthouse came down to plug his show. He had an easygoing delivery that was completely different from the brash style of Jackie Gayle, the circuit's top banana, who was appearing in the Playroom. Gayle was a bargain-basement Don Rickles who specialized in tough insult humor.

When Gayle finished his first show and came down the stairway that passed our bandstand, he began heckling the young comic, bellowing standard nightclub insults. The youngster waited until the laughter died down and then spoke softly into the microphone:

"Jackie, my agent warned me that you'd heckle me. Since I don't do that kind of material, he wrote down something for me to say in case you did this. Wait a minute."

He fumbled in his jacket pocket and pulled out a slip of paper. From it he read aloud:

"Fuck you, Jackie."

Our favorite comedian on the circuit was Pete Barbutti. We always caught his shows when he worked the Playroom. Pete, a musician himself, made wonderful musical jokes. One of our favorites was his portrayal of a third trumpet player who wants to be a bandleader. When he gets his own band, he features himself playing third trumpet parts and counting rests.

Pete came down to the Living Room to sit in with us on piano one Sunday night. After taking a few choruses that got more and more physically demonstrative, Pete stood up, flailed wildly at the keys and played the last eight bars with his nose. As we hit the final chord, Pete gave a wild yell and dove head-first over the edge of the bandstand railing. He landed beside the bar, eight feet below us.

We rushed down the staircase to see if he was still alive. As he sat up and tested himself for broken bones, we asked him what possessed him to do such a thing.

"It seemed like the only thing left!" said Pete.

Walter Norris always let me take off so I could continue to play with Clark Terry and Bob Brookmeyer whenever they picked up a job for their quintet. Bob and Clark had television staff jobs at that time, Clark on the *Tonight Show* and Bob on the *Merv Griffin Show*. Both programs were taped during the day, so they were free to play jazz gigs at night. In March 1966 they booked a week in Philadelphia at the Show Boat Lounge, but because of their television shows, they had to be late for the job every night.

Barry Harris was our pianist that week. He and Dave Bailey and I stayed in Philadelphia that week and played the first set each night as a trio while Bob and Clark raced down the Jersey Turnpike in Clark's car after taping their shows, arriving in time for the second set. They drove back to New York after the job every night. At the end of the week they were both exhausted.

When we finished our last night at the Show Boat, the club owner gave Clark our money. Clark handed Bob his share and paid the rhythm section, and then he gave a ten-dollar tip to each of the three regular bartenders. As an afterthought he slipped a five to an extra bartender who had only been there on Saturday night. The payroll had included a $500 bill, which Clark kept for himself. On the way out of town, Clark pulled out his wallet to pay the bridge toll and saw that the $500 was missing.

Remembering the five-dollar tip to the extra bartender, Clark realized the mistake he'd made and raced back to the club, but the guy was long gone. When they found him he had already been to a crap game and lost all his money, but he never admitted having seen more than a five-dollar bill. Everyone knew what had happened, but there was nothing to be done. Clark had worked all week for nothing.

When Bob and Clark played the Half Note later that year, we were visited one night by Roland Kirk. I don't think he was using the name "Rahsaan" yet. The blind saxophonist had come with his instruments, to sit in. He had a tenor saxophone case and a cylindrical black fiber case packed with his manzello and stritch. He unpacked it all and hung everything around his neck, and then felt his way up onto the narrow, precarious bandstand. There he planted his feet and didn't move them again until the set was over.

Roland's ability to play two and three instruments at once was amazing. When he heard Bob and Clark playing background figures behind each other's last choruses, he chimed in with three more parts, making us sound like a big band. On his own solo he played several choruses on the tenor sax, then played a multi-horn chorus and finished off with a blast from a referee's whistle. Brookmeyer, who had the next chorus, shook his head and laughed.

"How the hell am I supposed to follow that?" he asked.

Bob moved to California in 1966 and the group broke up. I was terribly sorry to see the end of it. We played a lot of good music together. I stayed at the Playboy Club and continued to work in the recording field during the day.

The large pool of New York recording musicians were accurate sight-readers, but that was only part of their skill. They specialized in quickly getting the close ensemble feeling that it sometimes took a permanent organization months or years to achieve. They created an easygoing atmosphere filled with storytelling and laughter in which they performed their difficult musical tasks. It was always a pleasure to walk into a studio and be a part of such a fine group of professionals.

Some of those musicians had come up through the big band era, and others were classically trained musicians with an ear for jazz. John Barrows was one of the latter. One of the world's finest French horn players, he combined great control of the instrument with a sensitivity and flexibility that made him a joy to play with.

While Gunther Schuller was still playing French horn in New York, he was already exploring the blend of jazz and classical music that, in his writings, he called "Third Stream Music." On a record date at Manhattan Center, the orchestra took a break and the French horn section headed for the men's room. Schuller stopped to chat with someone while Barrows and Ray Alonge went in and took their places in front of a row of urinals. When Gunther joined them a moment later, Barrows quipped, "Here comes the third stream."

I got a call one day for the *Merv Griffin Show,* which at that time was an afternoon game show on NBC. Sonny Igoe and Gene Bertoncini were on staff there, accompanying Merv when he sang and filling in occasionally when music was needed elsewhere during the show. I'd never been called by NBC before. They needed a bass player and half a dozen violinists that day for a musical question that required the playing of a tune called "Fiddle Faddle."

Aaron Levine, the house contractor, came to the rehearsal. After we played, he came over to me and said, "You're a very good bass player. Come up to my office tomorrow. I'm going to give you a lot of work."

I went home and told my wife the good news. The next day I put on a suit and went up to Levine's office, but his secretary told me he wasn't in that day. Surprised, I explained my visit, but she knew nothing about it. She had me fill out a standard employment application. A few days later I stopped by Levine's office again to remind him of his offer. He was in, but he didn't seem to remember me. He had certainly forgotten his enthusiasm for my playing. He said, "The network is cutting back a lot on live shows, so I'm afraid there isn't much I can offer you."

I never heard from him again.

Musicians who work in nightclubs often find the daytime hours in the broadcasting and recording field difficult to get used to. On one early morning date, when Luther Rix was being encouraged by the producer to "really get down" on the drums, Luther complained, "I can't get down. I just got up!"

Some guys who worked late just stayed up for any date that started before noon. Frank Rehak shambled onto one morning call at ABC looking like he'd been up all night. He was unshaven, rumpled, and his nose was several shades rosier than the rest of his face. As Frank unpacked his horn, Maestro Alfredo Antonini decided to give him a little special attention.

"Tune up, orchestra. Trombone, give me an A."

"Okay, Maes," said Frank.

He slipped his mouthpiece into his horn, raised it to his lips, and blasted a loud double high A, perfectly in tune. Maestro Antonini made no further comments to Frank.

My nights at the Playboy Club were musical and pleasant, though we were getting farther away from the jazz we had originally been hired to play. Walter Norris and myself and Ronnie Bedford, who had replaced Ray Mosca on drums, were assigned to the fourth-floor Penthouse to provide music for revues. The first was a Second City–type show featuring three young improvisational comedians from Hollywood. Two of them were sons of the famous: Joey Bishop, Jr., and Rob Reiner. The third was a talented young unknown, Richard Dreyfuss.

The best revue we played was a show called "Floor of Fun." The shining light of the cast was Lily Tomlin, who was just beginning to make her mark in New York. Lily opened the show on a pogo stick. Later she sang a song while toe-dancing in army combat boots. She also portrayed several of her original characters in sketches. Her "Lupe, the Makeup Expert" and her "Life of the Party Lady at a Funeral" were our favorites. Our trio was on stage with the actors, so we had the best seats in the house.

One of Lily's throwaways tickled me. She would preface one of her songs with a genteel announcement that she had originally studied ballet. She would say, wistfully, "Mother wanted me to be a dancer, but an unfortunate accident cut my career short. Mother and I were having a little breakfast one Sunday morning, and she dropped a six-pack on my foot."

Between shows the cast and the musicians sat in the sixth floor employees' cafeteria, laughing together. A couple of times, when a line of mine appealed to her, Lily wrote me a check for ten dollars, insisting I take it as a writer's fee. Lily said she hated comedians who cribbed their material from others.

One day she told me she was scheduled to appear as a guest on the Arlene Francis radio show.

"And the other guest that day is Jacqueline Susanne! I've been trying to read her latest book, but it's such trash, I can't take it seriously. How am I going to sit there and make conversation about it?"

I had an idea.

"Why don't you tell her you've read her book and think it's wonderful, but then keep making allusions to passages and characters from some other novel. You can pour on the compliments, and be talking about a completely different book."

Lily's eyes began to shine with the special light that indicated she was savoring a good piece of devilment.

"Oh, it will work! I'll never have to admit that I don't like her book!"

I missed hearing the program, but Lily evidently worked on the idea and turned it into a marvelously bizarre interview.

"Every time I'd describe a part of the book that I just adored, she'd give me the most bewildered look. It was perfect!"

Another of our Playboy Club shows was put together by Lewis and Christie, a pair of harmonica players from Chicago. They enlisted a hometown friend, John Thompson, to write them a revue for Playboy. John was a sleight-of-hand magician who produced red silk handkerchieves out of thin air and then extracted live white doves from them. I watched backstage as he prepared his gaffs, and was impressed with his skill even after I knew the secret of his illusions. John concocted the sketches and blackouts for the show. Some of them were chestnuts from vaudeville, but John breathed new life into them.

Sonny Mars, a standup comedian and the father of Hollywood actor Kenneth Mars, was another of Lewis and Christie's Chicago friends. Sonny, a regular on the Playboy circuit, was booked into the Playroom for a week while the Lewis and Christie show was running in the Penthouse. Lewis and Christie weren't on very good terms that week because of some personal problems. Sonny worried and mother-henned them while he was there, cajoling each of them separately to make up. By the time he was booked for a return engagement, Lewis and Christie were friends again, but they decided to put Sonny on. They enlisted John Thompson to help set him up.

They pretended to be even more on the outs with each other and told Sonny they were going to break up the act. Sonny tried desperately to patch things up, but it looked bad. Christie told Sonny that Lewis was such a rat he didn't deserve to live. Then Lewis showed Sonny a gun he was carrying for protection. One night as Sonny finished his last show in the Playroom, John Thompson ran in and said that Lewis and Christie were up in their dressing room fighting, and that he was afraid something serious might happen. They rushed upstairs to intervene.

As they opened the door, the partners were screaming at each other. Lewis pulled out his pistol. Thompson tried to prevent him from using it. The gun went off, John fell to the floor and blood began to spread across his shirtfront and dribble from the corner of his mouth. Christie picked up the gun from where it had fallen and pressed it into Sonny's hands, saying, "Get rid of this!" Just then the house security man rushed in. He took the gun away from Sonny and put him in handcuffs. Sonny, in shock, began to babble that he was innocent. Then, to his amazement, the "corpse" stood up and began to do a soft shoe with the two comedians as they all sang a chorus of "Friendship."

When Sonny realized he'd been conned with a blank cartridge and fake blood, he joined the laughter, but could barely contain his craving for revenge. He cornered me when I came in the next evening and told me the whole story. I think he was flattered at being the focus of such a complex plan, but he couldn't let them get away with it.

"How can I get even with them?" he asked. "How much would it cost to have their kids stolen?"

"Sonny," I said, "the best thing is to do nothing."

"What do you mean?"

"They'll be expecting you to cook up something elaborate, and they'll be watching out for you. Act like you have a plan, but don't do anything. They'll be looking over their shoulders for the next six months."

I never saw Sonny again after that engagement, so I don't know if he ever got his revenge.

Another policy change at Playboy put traveling package shows with their own musicians into the Penthouse. Our trio was moved downstairs to the Playroom, where we played for a different singer and comedian each week. The Playboy Club was considered a good showcase for talent. "Showcase" is often synonymous with "low salary" in the entertainment world. Playboy was getting good performers for very little money. No big names, but many of them later became famous: Flip

Wilson, Pat Morita, Stu Gilliam, Linda Hopkins, Al Jarreau, Charlie Callas, George Carlin. Of course, there were many others who remained unknown.

One of those was a tall, muscular young man who was pleasant and willing, but who had just an ordinary singing voice and no stage presence. He was being shepherded by a pair of tough-looking "men of influence" who had an interest in his career. At the end of the week, they asked Walter Norris for his opinion of their boy. Walter didn't want to offend such dangerous-looking people, but he had to tell them the truth.

"I hate to give you bad news," he told them, "but he really isn't a very good singer. I don't think he has any chance at a career in show business."

One of them patted Walter on the arm.

"Don't worry about it, kid," he growled. "I think we make a fighter out of him."

chapter 47

The Studios

Radio Registry called me one day: "A double date tomorrow at Columbia Records, Fifty-second Street, Studio B, seven P.M. Fender and acoustic bass." I sent in a sub for the night at Playboy. When I arrived at Columbia, half an hour early, I found the studio dark and empty. I checked Studio A and found a rock group there that had its own bass player. After calling Registry to made sure I was in the right place, I went back to Studio B to wait.

Around 7:15 an engineer showed up.

"Yeah, you're in the right place. This is for Simon and Garfunkel. I never come on time for them any more. They're always at least half an hour late."

"Who else is on the date?" I asked. He shrugged.

"Nobody tells me nothin'."

Ten minutes later John Simon wandered in. No relation to Paul, he was his recording producer and arranger. I was all set up, tuned up, plugged in, bow rosined, pencil sharpened, ready to go.

"Where are the other musicians?" I asked John.

"You're it," he said. "They only asked for a bass player tonight."

Just before eight, in came Paul Simon and Art Garfunkel.

"I'm still having trouble writing the bridge to this tune," said Paul as he shook off his duffel coat. "I'm not sure it's finished."

"How do you want to do it?" asked John.

"I don't know. Let me play it for you."

He got out his guitar and sang the tune. He had nothing written down, and the form was a little hard to remember because of extra beats in certain bars and a couple of chords that resolved in unusual directions. I had Paul go back over it, a few measures at a time, while I made a quick sketch for myself.

"What sort of a feeling do you want from the bass?" I asked him.

"Just play something and we'll see."

Paul was very clear about what he didn't want, so I kept trying different things until I found an accompaniment he liked. Then we recorded a test track. It was now about nine o'clock.

"I'm getting hungry," said Paul. "Let's go over to the Gaiety."

At the delicatessen we leisurely feasted on pastrami sandwiches while telling stories and getting acquainted. Finally, around eleven, Paul led us back to the studio. He had the engineer play back the track we had made.

"I don't know," he said. "I don't feel like working on this song any more tonight. I need to think about it. Have you got that one we did with the toy piano last week? Why don't you make Bill a cassette of that so he can take it home and learn it, and we can work on it next time."

They made me the tape, said goodnight, and I was out of there by eleven-thirty.

A couple of days later I got a last minute call from John Simon. It was Simon and Garfunkel at Columbia again, but this time I had company. There were several jazz players there, including Don Lamond and Phil Woods. John had made some jazz arrangements of Paul's tunes, and we recorded them with jazz solos all around. There was no mention made of the toy piano tune I'd been learning.

The following week brought a call to Columbia's big studio on East Thirtieth Street. This time Paul had a full orchestra and a Moog synthesizer. We didn't record much music that night. Paul, fascinated with the Moog, spent most of the session having the synthesist demonstrate the various sounds it could produce. Then he spent some time recording the tuba's low notes and playing them back at half speed to make them sound an octave lower. The rest of us drank a lot of coffee and read, or worked crossword puzzles.

In the recording booth, the engineer muttered darkly, "They call this a composer? Fuckin' Mozart didn't have any synthesizer or eight-track tape to play with!"

As I left that night, I told Paul, "I'm sorry we didn't get more music on tape for you."

"Don't worry about it," he said. "When I brought our first album in for union scale, Columbia just put out enough copies to get their money back, and that was the last anybody heard of it. I decided they'd never get a cheap album out of me again. Now, when they see a bill for hundreds of hours of studio time for one album, they panic and crank up the promotion department full blast, and we've got another hit!"

When the next Simon and Garfunkel album came out, none of the music that we had recorded was used. Most of their songs were accompanied just by Paul's guitar. It was a hit.

John Simon called me again to play on a soundtrack for a movie Peter Yarrow had made with Paul Butterfield and Tiny Tim, called "You Are What You Eat." During the date, Yarrow came out of the control booth and said to John, "I need a really disgusting sound for the national anthem. What instrument do you suggest?"

I dug a humanatone out of my bass case and showed it to him. A humanatone is a whistle that fits over the nose and mouth. You play it by blowing air through your nose into a cone that directs the air across a whistle-hole in a little plate that fits over your open mouth. The pitch can be altered by changing the size of your mouth cavity.

When I was a kid, the humanatone, along with the Jew's harp and the harmonica, was a standard folk music instrument. My dad taught me to play one when I was six or seven years old. I had forgotten all about humanatones until I saw one in a music store in Harrisburg, Pennsylvania. They were originally made of folded tin, but this Gretsch model was made of molded plastic. I bought one, figuring I could have some laughs with it on jobs.

I gave Yarrow a quick demonstration of the slippery, eerie sound of the humanatone. He put me in a booth with a mike and headphones while the band faked a brash accompaniment for me. A couple of takes gave him what he wanted. It was certainly a disgusting rendition of the national anthem. I never saw the movie, so I don't know how it was used. My check for the date included an extra payment for doubling on humanatone.

The recording studios in New York were taping day and night during those years. Busy arrangers often hired other arrangers to help them meet their deadlines. Sometimes the credit for the writing got misapplied. On one jingle date, after playing through a first reading of an arrangement, I said to the young arranger who was conducting, "That's beautiful writing."

From the brass section behind me I heard trombonist-arranger Hale Rood say softly, "Thank you."

Hale was a much-sought-after ghost writer in those days.

The jingle business was a lucrative field, especially for the advertising agencies. But some of the agency people couldn't be content with just handling the business end of things. Since there was a creative process involved, they wanted to be creative too.

"Let's try it again, this time with just the strings."

"What if we play it a little faster? A little slower?"

"Let's try it in three-quarter time."

"What if the trombone plays the melody?"

This sort of second-guessing of the arranger would sometimes go on for hours, wasting everyone's time and patience and the agency's money on what was often just a few measures of rum-tum, most of which would be covered by the voice-over announcement anyway.

After many years of studio work, Trigger Alpert got tired of that sort of thing. He put away his bass one day and began to occupy himself full-time with his hobby, photography. To illustrate his reason for leaving the music business, Trigger told me about playing on a date with guitarist Barry Galbraith, doing a jingle for Stouffer's frozen foods. When the agency representative asked for soft, unobtrusive music behind the announcer, Barry and Trigger played some blues. The agency rep came out of the booth and said, "It's nice music; I like it a lot. But it sounds too much like Beef Stroganoff. Can you make it sound more like Standing Rib Roast?"

chapter 48

Lainie Kazan

In October 1970, the New York Playboy Club and Local 802 negotiated a new contract that for the first time included a two-week paid vacation for the musicians. My working life had been liberally sprinkled with unpaid vacations, but I had never had a paid one before. The following April, Aileen and I and our four-year-old son, Daniel, flew to Florida with our camping equipment, rented a car, and lived for two weeks in campgrounds on the Keys, in the Everglades, and on Sanibel Island. We had a perfectly lovely time.

An hour after we got home, Walter Norris called.

"I knew this was coming before you left," he said, "but I didn't want to spoil your vacation. We're fired, and our two-week notice starts today."

Walter had run afoul of the Playboy hierarchy in Chicago. A woman who had begun booking the entertainment for Playboy Clubs International had sent the New York club a cut-down version of a Las Vegas show that had originally featured a stage full of singers and dancers accompanied by a busy rock band with two keyboard players, two guitarists, a drummer, a Fender bassist and a full brass section. The show had been trimmed to fit the tiny stage in the Playboy Club's Penthouse. There were four young women who paraded about in extravagant costumes with tall headdresses, four scantily clad female dancers, and one male singer.

The Chicago booker told Walter to hire four musicians to play the arrangements: a lead trumpet player, a trombone player, a drummer, and an organist. She said, "Rent him a Hammond Organ, and he can play the bass parts with his feet."

Walter consulted Stan Rubenstein, the pianist who had played the previous show in the Penthouse. Stan looked at the music and groaned. He was expected to supply all the missing parts on the organ. He told Walter, "I'll take the job because I need the work, but please, don't rent a Hammond organ. These Fender bass parts are much too busy to be played on a Hammond. Get me a Farfisa electric organ, and I'll try to play them with my left hand."

Walter also hired Count Basie's former lead trumpet player, Renauld Jones, a trombone player whose name I've forgotten who had Broadway show experience, and drummer Al Beldini. At the rehearsal, Walter could see that the arrangements didn't work. Instead of having them rewritten for the smaller band, they had just sent the original first trumpet and trombone parts. A high lead trumpet part without the rest of the section under it sounds thin and is difficult to play. Stan, working from the conductor's score, filled in some parts on the organ, but the music sounded terribly unprofessional.

Walter consulted with the lead dancer:

"Why don't we forget about these charts and just have the quartet improvise some music at the same tempos?"

"Oh, no! We've memorized our entire routine to these arrangements. It would take weeks of rehearsal to change anything."

Walter sighed and told the four musicians to do the best they could.

The band got through the first night without any train wrecks, but the music sounded pitiful. Walter expected complaints about it from the lady booker, who had flown in from Chicago for the opening, but she said nothing about the way the music sounded. Her only comment to Walter was, "Why did you hire such old-looking musicians?"

"With music this difficult, I thought I'd better get guys who had some experience," said Walter.

"There are hundreds of good-looking young musicians who can play anything you put in front of them," she sniffed.

Walter whipped out a pencil and notebook.

"Give me their names!"

She ignored his irony.

"These musicians won't do at all. Fire them."

"Lady, I couldn't fire them if I wanted to. They're hired under a union contract. I can't even give them two weeks' notice. I was so afraid they would give me *their* notice when they saw this music that I signed them for the whole month that the show will be here."

The union representative met with the booker the next day and told her that if she fired the musicians, she would still have to pay them a month's salary. She went home, and a week later the manager of our club got instructions from Playboy Enterprises in Chicago to fire Walter.

The manager was furious. He liked Walter's work, and didn't think the Chicago office had any business telling him whom to fire. He flew to Chicago to see about it personally. When he returned, he called Walter into his office.

"I'm sorry," he said. "Hefner owes this woman a favor. Before she came to work for him she used to book acts for a couple of other Chicago nightclubs, and she got Hefner some name talent at low prices for his television show. He owes her one, and she's decided to collect. I can't save your job. This comes straight from the top."

Harold Jones and I got the axe along with Walter. Harold had replaced Ronnie Bedford on drums with Walter's trio. We were sorry to lose the steady job, but nothing in the music business lasts forever. The club itself only lasted another year.

When I began working "the outside" again, Harold Lieberman, a New Jersey trumpet player and educator, hired me to play a jazz concert with him at a small Southern college. We had the name of the school but no other information about it. When we arrived we found that it had an entirely black student body and faculty. Chatting with the lady who was showing us where to set up, Harold said, "This is kind of unusual, an all white jazz band playing for an all black audience."

The lady gave Harold an amused look and said, "Well, you better be good!"

After our opening number, Harold announced the names of the musicians. When he got to me he drew a blank for a moment. I saw he needed help.

"Jim," I whispered.

The term "Jim Crow" has a special significance for African Americans. Whenever I'm introduced to a black person, there is the chance that he will get my first name wrong because of the power of the images associated with Jim Crow. After I first met Milt Hinton, he mentioned to a friend of mine that he had met a bass player named Jim Crow, and added:

". . . and that really *is* his name!"

I first played for Maxine Sullivan on a jazz concert at the library in New Brunswick, New Jersey. I wasn't surprised when Maxine announced me to the audience as "Jim Crow," but when we came offstage during the intermission she confided, "You know, I had to be careful out there not to say Jim Crow when I introduced you." I didn't tell her that she had said the word she'd been trying so hard not to say.

Marvin Kutcher, who was doing the booking for Ray Bloch's office, put me into the Americana Hotel with Hal Turner's band. We played in a room called the Royal Box, for shows and dancing. At the first rehearsal I found that Lainie Kazan was the featured singer for the first week. When I heard her arrangements, I began to look forward to a pleasant week's work. The music was well written, her conductor knew his business, and she sang beautifully.

Marvin had told me to bring both my acoustic and my fender bass. On one number my part began with a bowed note on the acoustic bass for four measures, and then had a quick switch to the Fender bass for a busy pop-rock figure.

"Miss Kazan," I said, "It's going to take me a minute to switch instruments. I could play that long note on the Fender if you'd like, and eliminate the instrument change. I have a way to make it sound pretty much like bowing."

"No," she said, "I want the real bow sound. Don't worry, I'll wait for you."

That night on the first show, she waited all right, but she turned around and frowned impatiently at me while she was doing it. Then, when I began to play the Fender bass pattern, she told her conductor that I was too loud. At his signal, I played softer.

Before the second show, I got a note from him that Lainie thought the Fender bass was still too loud. I was surprised, since I had barely been able to hear it on the first show, but I turned my volume down a bit more. In the morning I got a call from Marvin Kutcher.

"What's going on over at the Royal Box?"

"What do you mean?"

"Lainie's manager called to complain that she's got an uncooperative bass player over there."

"I have no idea what he means. I'll find out tonight and let you know."

When I walked into the hotel that evening, Hal Turner gave me a message that Miss Kazan wanted to see me. I went up to her room and asked her about the complaint to the Bloch office.

"Didn't my conductor tell you to turn the Fender bass down last night?"

"Yes, just before the second show. I turned it down."

"No, I mean during the show."

"No, he didn't say anything to me during the show."

"That sonofabitch! I told him to tell you it was still too loud!"

"Maybe he thought it was okay. I was playing pretty soft. Do you think it could have been your guitar player that you were hearing?"

"Really, I think I know the difference between a bass and a guitar!"

"Look, Miss Kazan, it's the easiest thing in the world to make an electric bass softer. There's a volume control knob on it. Any time you think it's too loud, just give me a signal, and I'll be happy to turn it down."

She seemed relieved and thanked me for my cooperation. On the first show, she turned around and gestured "softer" twice during her first number. My volume was already so low that I couldn't hear a note I was playing, so I switched the amplifier off. A Fender bass without an amplifier makes no sound at all. Even so, she again gave me the signal to play softer. I don't know what she was hearing, but it certainly wasn't me. For the rest of the week I played all the Fender bass parts silently.

Miss Kazan had a tough time at the Royal Box. Her conductor quit after she put him through a stormy post-mortem of the show on the third night. She hired Sy Mann and then Hank Jones to fill in on piano for the rest of the week and left the conducting responsibilities to her drummer and guitar player, who had come with her from California. The drummer showed up on the fifth night in no condition to be of any help, having fallen off the wagon. The rest of us did as professional a job as we could under the circumstances, but the music had lost much of its charm for us.

I had accepted the job with the understanding that I had to be off on the first Saturday night because I had already booked a gig with Al Cohn. Marvin Kutcher hired a substitute for me, so I missed Lainie's closing night. When I came in on the following Monday afternoon to rehearse the next show, one of the guys in the band said, "Oh, you didn't get the gift Lainie gave everyone in the band on closing night."

They had saved mine for me. It was an unsigned eight by ten publicity photo of herself.

chapter 49

Peter Duchin

When the Americana Hotel abandoned their entertainment policy, the Royal Box became a restaurant with Muzak, and Hal Turner's house band was disbanded. With less jazz work turning up, I turned to the New York club date offices to make a living. Before long I was doing all of Peter Duchin's society jobs, which often meant flying out of town with him to the mansions and country clubs of the wealthy.

Since outrageous prices are often taken by rich people as a symbol of quality, or at least of privilege, Otto Schmidt, Peter's manager, charged outrageous prices for Peter's music. His musicians were just paid union scale plus a small premium for being in his "first band," but I understood. Peter's overhead was high; he and his wife lived in the world of Peter's affluent clients, and spent a lot of money keeping up appearances.

Once, at the airport, Denny LeRoux asked Peter to refund a ten-spot with which he had tipped the skycap who checked all our equipment onto a flight. As Peter reached for his billfold, his wife, Cheray, said,

"You guys throw Peter's money around like it's water. I wish you'd stop thinking Peter is rich. He's not rich!"

Even as she spoke, workmen were building the Duchins a new luxury home in Bedford Hills, New York.

"Cheray," I said, "you'll never feel rich if you keep hanging around with the Harrimans and Kennedys and Rockefellers. Come across the Hudson and hang out at my house for a day or two, and I guarantee you'll feel rich."

Mrs. Duchin was not amused.

Peter's mother had died soon after he was born, and his father, bandleader Eddy Duchin, died when Peter was thirteen. Peter was then raised by the W. Averill Harrimans. He hobnobbed with wealth and power as a young man, and stepped easily into his father's role of society bandleader. He had charm and good looks, and had learned his way around the piano keyboard well enough to get by. He always had a good band; he hired musicians who were skilled at playing dance music for parties.

Like most club date bands, Peter's musicians worked without arrangements, relying on their encyclopedic knowledge of songs and chord structures. At times they found their leader's musical limitations a bit trying. One night in the middle of a job, guitarist Tony Gottuso turned up his volume and began playing a very loud accompaniment with the band. Peter looked around from the piano keyboard and frowned.

"What are you playing?"

"The right chords!" snapped Tony.

The elementary bass notes Peter pounded out with his left hand restricted my ability to construct interesting bass lines. One morning in the VIP lounge at LaGuardia Airport I overheard a bit of the conversation Peter was having with Nels Laakso, our trumpet player. Apropos of some aspiration or other, Peter said, "Oh, man, I'd give my right arm to do that."

"Peter," I interrupted, "would you mind making that your left?"

Peter flew the band to Florida one evening to play at a country club in Fort Lauderdale. It was built on an inlet where a dozen "gold-plater" yachts were moored, one of which belonged to Ralph Evinrude, the outboard-motor magnate, and his wife, Frances Langford. Evinrude invited the band aboard and showed us around, pointing with great pride to all the yacht's luxury features. When we arrived in the lounge, he waved toward a little piano in one corner.

"Do you know who the last person was who played that piano?" he asked. "President Richard Nixon! And he played very well, too."

"Well," I scoffed, "he's no Harry Truman!"

If you wonder why I thought that was funny, you're too young to have heard radio broadcasts in the late 1940s of Truman playing the "Missouri Waltz."

Ray Cohen substituted for Peter Duchin on a job at the Plaza Hotel, where we were providing music for an affair at which the Thomas A. Dooley Foundation was presenting "Splendid American" awards to Spiro Agnew and Frank Sinatra. (I'm not making this up.) Since Agnew was Vice President of the United States at the time, there were Secret Service agents all over the place.

The affair was black tie; the only sartorial color was provided by the red bandanna, fringed leather shirt, blue jeans, black motorcycle boots, and grizzled beard of Denny LeRoux, our rock singer.

Halfway through the evening a Secret Service man with a pronounced stutter stopped to chat with the band.

"You kn-n-ow," he said haltingly, "I heard S-Sinatra say that your p-piano player is one of the b-best in the c-country!"

We congratulated Ray and asked if Sinatra had said anything about the rest of the band.

"N-n-no," said the agent, "but A-Agnew said he l-liked the d-d-dirty b-bum that sang *B-Bojangles.*"

I liked Peter Duchin personally and was grateful to him for keeping my bills paid for a couple of years, but a steady diet of society music was beginning to wear me down, and I was ready for a change. Milt Hinton was responsible for pointing me in a new direction in the music business. I bumped into Milt on Seventh Avenue one day, and he put his arm around my shoulder and said, "Now, here's what I want you to do for me. I'm playing this show at City Center, and it runs for another week. I've got to open at Michael's Pub Monday night, so I want you to go over there and do the last week for me."

The show was called *Music, Music.* Milt took me to City Center, introduced me to Johnny Lesko, the conductor, and showed me what to do. That was my introduction to the pool of musicians who play Broadway shows. When I was called later to do *Rodgers and Hart* at the Helen Hayes Theater, I resigned from Duchin's band and for the next fifteen years made my principal living playing Broadway musicals. It was pleasant work, and I could send in a sub whenever any jazz gigs turned up.

Milt is the last remaining master of the slapped bass solo. His double and triple slapping sounds like tuneful tap dancing. I asked him, "Where did you learn to solo that way?"

He said, "When I was coming up, if they gave you a bass solo and you *didn't* play that way, they didn't give you another one!"

In 1990 at the Church of the Heavenly Rest, Milt and some friends gave a concert in honor of his eightieth year on earth, and his sixty-second as a professional musician. As "The Judge" announced one number, he looked out at the audience and said, "You know, I've been doing this for a long time. I've got *shoes* that are older than most of you!"

My last job with Peter Duchin was a private party in Rochester, New York. On the way back, we ran into Dizzy Gillespie's quintet at the airport, going back to the Apple after a week at a Rochester jazz club.

We all took the same plane. Dizzy wore a matching jacket and trousers made of bleached, fringed denim and a wide brimmed leather hat, and he carried his "rhythm stick," a long walking stick covered with little tambourine conchas that jingled merrily whenever it was moved. In Dizzy's hands it became a musical instrument.

On an interview show some years later Dizzy was asked why he carried such a stick, and he answered, "For the musicians. When I'm in an airport or someplace, all the musicians hear this and know it's me. They hear it all the way across the lobby, and know I'm there."

I chatted with Dizzy during the flight, but lost track of him when we landed at LaGuardia. When I didn't see him at the baggage claim area, I assumed he'd already left the airport. Then the baggage conveyor started up, and out of the portal came Dizzy, lying on his back on the moving belt. His hands, clutching his hat and jingle stick, were folded on his chest, and the corner of a baggage check was clamped firmly between his lips. As the conveyor belt trundled him past me, Dizzy cried piteously, "Somebody claim me! Somebody claim me!"

I claimed him immediately.

chapter 50

Doubling in Brass

Between jobs with Duchin I often played at the new Eddie Condon's. Eddie had closed his East Fifty-sixth Street club in 1967 and gone into retirement, and he died in 1973. Later, bassist Red Balaban arranged with Eddie's widow to use his name. Red opened a new Eddie Condon's on West Fifty-fourth Street, a few doors from the relocated Jimmy Ryan's. He had Ed Polcer on cornet, Vic Dickenson on trombone, Herb Hall on clarinet, Ronnie Coles on drums, and Jim Andrews on piano, with Red Richards playing solo piano between the band's sets. Balaban often called me to sub for him.

Connie Kay later replaced Coles as the house drummer. Connie is one of my favorite drummers. He knows how to swing hard without getting loud, and his broad understanding of jazz drumming goes back to his work with Coleman Hawkins, Lester Young, and Charlie Parker, as well as his many years of brilliant playing with the Modern Jazz Quartet. At Condon's, we always hit a good groove together.

The aging Roy Eldridge was playing at Jimmy Ryan's next door. He came over to Condon's one night with a young musician in tow. Connie and I stood near the crowded bar, chatting with them before we went back on the bandstand. There was an attractive young woman sitting alone at the bar, and Roy's young friend gave him a significant look, raising his eyebrows and cutting his eyes at her. Roy wouldn't play that game.

"You like that?" he asked loudly. "Well, *hit* on her!" He pushed the young man over toward her. "Ain't *nothin'* gonna happen unless you *hit!*"

When the young man, embarrassed, backed away from the unsuspecting object of their attention, Roy gave him another shove in her direction.

"Go on and hit on her, man! If you don't, I will!"

Having gotten his laugh, Roy went back to his conversation and the relieved youngster eased back out of Roy's range.

Eddie Condon's remained on West Fifty-fourth Street for ten years, and became a midtown hangout for musicians of all persuasions. It was forced to close when the building was sold and razed to make room for yet another skyscraper. Red Balaban and Ed Polcer scoured the neighborhood for another site, but couldn't find anything in their price range. Another jazz club has opened on East Fifteenth Street with the name "Condon's," but it has nothing to do with Eddie Condon or Red Balaban. It is owned by a different Condon altogether.

Polcer continued to book jobs around New York. He put together a band one winter to play for the Christmas tree lighting ceremony at Lincoln Center Plaza. The enthusiastic audience that gathered around knew the words to all the carols and eagerly sang along with Ed. When someone requested "Good King Wenceslas," Ed found it in his book of carols and began singing. The light wasn't very good, and as Ed concentrated on the words, he mistakenly sang "Good King Wenceslas looked out" to the tune of "Old MacDonald Had a Farm." The crowd joyfully responded,

"E-I-E-I-O!"

A Broadway show contractor told me that theater bass players were sometimes asked to double on tuba. Having spent my youth playing the baritone horn, I knew I could learn to play the tuba, and I also knew, from listening to Bill Barbour, Bill Stanley, Bob Stewart, and Harvey Phillips, that the tuba could be a beautiful instrument. Jack Gale, the trombonist on *Rodgers and Hart,* loaned me a tuba that he wasn't using at the moment, and I began working on an embouchure between shows. It was nice to be playing a horn again. Twenty years had passed since I had sold my valve trombone.

When I was ready to find a tuba of my own, Sam Pilafian, a fine tuba player, was kind enough to go shopping with me. He found me a horn at Giardinelli's on Forty-sixth Street. I arranged to exchange lessons with Sam, who wanted some pointers on the bass in case he was called to double on a show. Sam gave me one basic tuba lesson, but before I had a chance to reciprocate, he moved to Boston to join the Empire Brass Quintet.

I bought several books of tuba études from Patelson's, a music store behind Carnegie Hall, and practiced until I could play all the exercises in them. The tuba sounded good in my kitchen, but I had no idea what would be required on a real job in terms of volume and stamina. My first gig was an outdoor job with a Dixieland band in Rockland County. Trying to sound as loud as I did in my kitchen, I blew my lip out on the second tune. With a little more experience, I found the right balance.

My first theater job doubling on bass and tuba was an Off-Broadway show called *Tickles by Tucholsky.* I had never heard of Kurt Tucholsky, but learned that he was considered by those who knew German cabaret music to be in a class with Bertolt Brecht. The music was interesting, but the show got poor reviews and closed at the end of the first week. Then John Lesko called to hire me for Yul Brynner's first revival of *The King and I* that John was to conduct on Broadway. He needed a bass-tuba doubler, and knew my work on both instruments from some industrial shows I'd been doing with him in Pennsylvania.

Yul Brynner gave a powerful performance as the King, and offstage he tended to stay in the role. He ruled the production with an iron hand. He made the theater install more steam radiators at stage level during the first winter. He got the conductor and assistant conductor changed. And he arranged to have his limousine drive into the freight elevator of the Uris Theater every evening and be taken up to the third floor so that he could step directly from the car to his dressing room.

When something was stolen from that room one night, he got the producers to hire a uniformed guard to sit in front of his door every show while he was on stage.

At the end of every performance, the King demanded and got a standing ovation. If one was not forthcoming spontaneously, he would frown imperiously at the applauding audience and command, "Up! Up!" until they stood.

The King and I ran for two years. It probably would have run longer if the producers hadn't refused to give Brynner the raise he wanted once the initial production costs were paid off. Brynner broke off negotiations and made his own deal with Richard Rodgers, the composer, who gave him the rights to the show for as long as he wanted to keep performing it.

Our Broadway production closed when Brynner's contract with the producers expired at the end of the second year, and then he took his own production of *The King and I* on the road for several years before bringing it back to Broadway on his own terms. I went on to do a string of unsuccessful musicals, including *The Grand Tour* with Joel Grey, *Carmelina* with Georgia Brown, and *Morrisey Hall* with Angela Lansbury.

A musicians' biggest problem in a long-run musical is staying alert after playing the same music a thousand times. After I made two or three slips during a performance of *The King and I,* I whispered to percussionist Rick Kivnick, "Did I come in today?"

"I don't know," he muttered. "You'd better ask someone who's here."

Outside work helped to keep the repetitiveness of the show from becoming oppressive. I happily took off to play a string of jobs with Al Cohn. He and Zoot hadn't co-led a group for some time, since Al had been earning his living as an arranger. He decided it was time to get back to his saxophone, and to build up his embouchure, he played without a microphone. He quickly recovered his old robust sound.

Al's musical ideas were always wonderful. He specialized in instant composition on his horn. When someone asked Stan Getz to give his recipe for a perfect jazz tenor player, he said, "My technique, Zoot's time and Al Cohn's ideas."

Al had begun wearing a bushy black moustache in those days. When I told him he looked like a cross between Groucho Marx and Emilio Zapata, he waggled his eyebrows, tapped the ash from an imaginary cigar and said, "Gaucho Marx!"

Al was always quick with a funny line. Bill Berry told me Al was once watching a football game on television when someone stuck their head in the door and asked, "What's the score?"

"Twenty to forty," said Al.

"Who's ahead?"

"Forty."

Warren Vache told me about walking down a street with Al one night somewhere in Europe. The new moon above them was lovely, just a pale slender crescent. Al said, "That reminds me. I have to cut my toenails."

chapter 51

42nd Street

Zoot Sims hired Jimmy Rowles for a few quartet jobs. I was glad that Jimmy had come to live in New York. Bob Brookmeyer had played with him in California, and had brought the word east about what a good piano player he was. Jimmy loved to invent musical surprises. He found unusual voicings and rhythmic patterns and imaginatively connected them to whatever tune he was playing. He knew a million songs, and played them in very original ways.

One day Jimmy complained, "Jesus, Zoot, you're still playing the same goddamn tunes you've been playing for twenty years. When are you going to learn some new ones?"

Jimmy taught Zoot tunes like "Dream Dancing" and "Shadow Waltz" and got him started looking for new material. Zoot's later recordings show what a good idea that was.

Zoot and Al Cohn got back together for a few jobs, with Jimmy on piano and Akira Tana on drums. I was delighted to be part of that rhythm section. One of our bookings was in Hershey, Pennsylvania. Since I lived near Zoot, I offered to drive him to the job. I packed his tenor and my bass in my car and we headed west. Zoot had stopped drinking. His doctor had warned him that he had seriously damaged his liver, and that any further use of alcohol would have mortal consequences.

Zoot was bright and talkative for a while, but after a couple of hours of driving, he began to shift uncomfortably in his seat. He looked out the window, consulted his watch and said, "Are you sure you know the way? We've been driving a long time!"

"Hershey is near Harrisburg, Zoot. You've made this trip before, haven't you?"

Zoot grinned sheepishly.

"That's the trouble with not drinking. Before, I always slept all the way."

Zoot had a collection of souvenirs of his life on the road. When I stopped by his house one afternoon, he showed me a bottle of whiskey he had found somewhere down in bourbon country. On a label that was shaded to look like old parchment was a drawing of an old fashioned rope-tension bass drum, battered and worn, with a large tattered hole in the center of the drumhead. Above this picture was the brand name in antique lettering:

"OLD DRUM"

Underneath, in smaller letters, was the motto,

"You can't beat it!"

That was one bottle Zoot never opened.

J oe Grimaldi, another saxophone player who lived near me in Rockland County, called one day:

"I've got the band at the Nanuet Dinner Theater, and my bass player just took another gig. Can you come to work on Monday?"

The theater was just five minutes from my house in New City. Zoot was back on the road, working with local rhythm sections, and no new Broadway shows were on the horizon, so I was glad to have the work. The salary didn't compare with the wages on Broadway, but Joe and the rhythm section made a little extra money after the show on weekends, playing jazz for dancing out by the bar in the lobby.

The shows were revivals of Broadway hits. There were two performances on Saturdays, and for a while they had also tried having two on Sundays. Business on Sunday evenings was rotten, so they dropped the second Sunday show for a while, but when Theo Bikel came in with *Fiddler on the Roof*, ticket sales improved, and the manager decided to go back to two shows on Sunday.

I usually went home between shows on matinee days, and I did so on the first two-show Sunday with Bikel, arriving back at the theater at what I thought was an hour before the evening performance. As I came in the stage door I saw the cast in costume waiting to go on stage and heard the orchestra playing the overture without me. I had completely forgotten that the Sunday evening shows had started at seven, not eight.

The theater was an arena with the stage down in the center and the orchestra pit beside it. Our usual route to the pit from the bandroom was around the upper circumference of the arena and down the far aisle. Since the house was dark and the orchestra was playing, I thought I could get there quicker by running down the near aisle that the actors used.

Unfortunately the light man, seeing movement in that aisle, thought Bikel was making his entrance. He hit the spotlight, and the first thing the audience saw was not Tevye and his cart, but an embarrassed bass player doing the hundred-yard dash to the pit. It got a big laugh, but I didn't repeat the performance.

Johnny Lesko hired me for both of my Broadway long runs: *The King and I* ran two years, and *42nd Street* ran eight years and four months. When Johnny called me for *42nd Street,* I nearly turned it down.

"I'm working a steady job in Nanuet, five minutes from my house," I told him. "Even though Broadway scale is higher, when you figure in the cost of commuting to New York, I'm doing just as well where I am."

"This show looks like it will run," said Johnny. "It will be a big band, full of old friends of yours. Morty Bullman is the contractor, and I've got Dick Perry, Bernie Glow, and Joe Wilder in the trumpet section, and Maurice Mark on drums. I'll have the arranger add some tuba parts for you, so you'll make a better salary."

That convinced me. I left the job in Nanuet and began rehearsing for *42nd Street,* which was going into the Winter Garden Theater. Since David Merrick was the producer and Gower Champion was directing, everyone predicted success, but no one knew it would be such a smash hit. Gower, who was obviously very ill during the rehearsal period, died on opening night, and the show was hailed by every critic as his masterpiece.

When the larger Majestic Theater became available, David Merrick moved *42nd Street* there, and we settled into our long run. Meanwhile, the Nanuet Dinner Theater went bankrupt and closed a few months after I left my job there. I can't say that my shrewd business sense caused me to make the right move. I'm afraid it was just dumb luck.

I had met Joe Wilder when he was with the Basie band, and we became good friends on the Russian tour with Benny Goodman. On his way to the Majestic one night, the handle on Joe's trumpet case broke. In the bandroom, I helped him rig a temporary substitute with a piece of rope and a strip of gaffer's tape. It was serviceable, but definitely shabby-looking. I said, "Joe, I'm afraid Barracuda is going to get this trumpet case."

Jerome Richardson had told me about Barracuda, the mythical guardian of the Lionel Hampton band's public image. No one ever saw Barracuda, but everyone knew that he would "get" any article of clothing or luggage that was loud, cheap, or worn-out enough to embarrass the band. The offending article would either disappear or would be torn to shreds.

Joe was surprised that I knew about Barracuda. He laughed and explained to the other musicians, telling about some raggedy old house slippers that Dinah Washington was wearing in a Pullman car when she was traveling with Hampton. Barracuda threw one of them out the window. A gaudy hat of Hampton's suffered the same fate.

While Joe was talking, I slipped a note into his trumpet case that said, "Barracuda is watching this case." Later I slipped another between the sheets of music on his stand: "Barracuda is watching this music." Joe laughed and waved to me across the pit when he found the notes.

There were a few minutes of dialogue late in the second act during which some of the reed doublers would leave the pit to put away the instruments that they didn't need for the finale. At that performance I slipped out at the same time and removed Joe's trumpet case from his locker, leaving a note pinned to the sleeve of his overcoat with a drawing of a many-toothed fish and the inscription: "Barracuda was here!" I hid Joe's case in my locker and went back to finish the show.

As I packed up my bass, I peeped out the pit door just in time to see Joe smiling as he read my note. Then he reached for his trumpet case. When he realized it was gone, he broke up completely.

"In all these years," he said, "that's the first time Barracuda ever got *me!*"

I kept a box of Kleenex in the pit at the Majestic for hay-fever emergencies, but someone swiped it one day, so I got a roll of toilet paper from the backstage men's room. I hung it on a convenient horizontal rod that projected from the drum set in front of me. At intermission one night a front-row theatergoer leaned over and asked me,

"What's the toilet paper for?"

"What else? A roll on the drums!"

The music on Broadway wasn't all inside the theaters. In good weather, on the sidewalks in front of every marquee, street musicians began to proliferate before showtime and at intermission; everything from violinists, to bagpipers, to Peruvian flute ensembles.

Earlier city administrations had taken a dim view of that sort of free enterprise. The blind percussionist who called himself "Moondog" was hassled so much during the 1950s that he gave up trying to play his subtle music on midtown sidewalks and became a beggar instead. It was all right for him to stand on the corner and beg, but not to play music.

During the 1980s, with a less repressive attitude prevailing at City Hall, street musicians began to appear everywhere. Midtown plazas and sidewalks attracted small bands complete with battery-powered amplifiers. Break dancers accompanied by a drummer or a cassette player did street-corner routines. Certain instrumentalists could be heard regularly in their favorite doorways, arcades, and subway platforms.

Not all the street musicians tried to please. One saxophonist walked through subway cars playing so horribly that people would make contributions in the hope that he would quickly move on. And a steely-eyed little mandolin player in the Village would stand beside sidewalk cafe tables while playing, fixing the diners with such a bone-chilling glare that they tipped him to get rid of him.

One of my favorite jazz players, George Braithe, worked the streets. He had developed an instrument that he called the Braithophone, made of two soprano saxophones with the mouthpieces fastened together side by side. He had rerouted the key mechanisms with rubber bands, so that with one hand on each instrument, he could play two-part harmony. He played the melody and a good harmony line on all kinds of fast bebop tunes. His two-part solos were inventive and swinging. He sometimes played on Forty-second Street on the broad sidewalk in front of Bryant Park, accompanied by a good rhythm section. I think they made more money on the street than they did in the jazz clubs.

A tenor saxophonist who used to work the sidewalk on Sixth Avenue near Forty-fourth Street was also a good musician, but didn't seem to attract many listeners. He improvised fluently as people on the sidewalk hurried by without stopping. I noticed him several times, always sounding good, usually ignored. Then one day I heard him playing but couldn't see him for the crowd of people standing around. I moved in to see what had caused the new interest. The man's music was the same, but on the sidewalk at his feet there were now a half-dozen battery operated toy bears, each clashing a tiny pair of cymbals. The onlookers were fascinated, and his tip jar was nearly full.

chapter 52

Jazz Anecdotes

Early in the run of *42nd Street* our orchestra chose me to be its representative on the Theater Committee of Local 802, and I was part of the union team that negotiated the musicians' new theater contract in 1982. I also joined a coalition of activist musicians who had long been dissatisfied with the policies of the old administration of Local 802. We formed the Members' Party and ran a slate in the union election. John Glasel, a good jazz trumpet player, ran for president, and I ran for a seat on the Executive Board. Our whole slate was elected, and John and I are now serving our fifth two-year terms.

Not long after we took office, John asked me, "How would you like to write a column for *Allegro?*" *Allegro* is Local 802's monthly newspaper.

"Sure," I answered, "and I know exactly the column I want to write."

For years, whenever musicians would begin to tell stories about each other, someone would always say, "Oh, man, somebody should write these down!" I thought that a monthly column in *Allegro* would be the perfect place to write the musicians' stories I had heard in bandrooms and buses, on bandstands and in recording studios. I named the column "The Band Room," and it has been running monthly since our first issue in February 1983. It's become sort of a literary Charlie's Tavern. I've never had any trouble finding material for it. Once the col-

umn got started, musicians all over the country began sending me stories. I've even received a few from as far away as England, Denmark
and Spain. Local 802's members are everywhere.

In late 1987, I got a call from Sheldon Meyer, senior editor at Oxford University Press. Oxford had published several collections of anecdotes from venues such as opera, literature, and the theater, and
Sheldon was looking for someone to put one together from the jazz
world. I'd been recommended to him by Gene Lees and a couple of
other writers. I sent Sheldon some of my "Band Room" columns, and
after reading them, he asked me to do a book called *Jazz Anecdotes*.
Assembling the material and writing the book took all my spare time
for the next two years.

When the book came out, Oxford sent me on a few publicity junkets.
During an interview on a Philadelphia jazz radio station, the reception-
ist came into the studio and asked me to write out the name of my
book for a telephone caller. I wrote "Jazz Anecdotes" on a slip of paper
and handed it to her. On the way out of the building I passed her desk
and heard her telling another caller, "Yes, the name of the book is *Jazz
Antidotes*."

Musicians love to retell the exploits of that famous prankster Joe
Venuti. I included a whole chapter of stories about him in *Jazz Anecdotes*. Later, I got two more from Ray Alonge. Ray was one of the busiest French hornists in the New York recording studios. Now retired,
he works in the recording department at Local 802. Ray's violinist father, Tommy, was an old buddy of Venuti's and often served as his
concertmaster.

On the bandstand, when Tommy needed to sort his music for the
next set, it was his habit to stand up and put his violin on his chair
behind him. He'd reach back and pick it up again as he sat down. One
night Venuti conspired with a musician in the second row, and when
Alonge stood up and laid down his violin, it was quickly removed from
his chair and replaced with a large wooden cigar box. Venuti then said
loudly, "Aw, siddown, Tommy!" and gave him a shove backward.

As Tommy fell back into his chair and heard the sickening sound of
fragile wood splintering under him, he nearly passed out, and Joe
chalked up another successful practical joke.

Ray also told of a church job Tommy worked with Venuti. Afterwards, he accompanied Joe to the minister's quarters to pick up their

money. The minister suggested that the musicians donate their services as a benefit to the church.

"Benefit!" roared Joe. "Hey, Tommy, he's talkin' about a benefit! That's a lotta crap! We gotta get paid!"

Venuti pushed a chair under a chandelier that hung from the ceiling.

"Here, Tommy," he said, "hold the chair."

Joe climbed up and began to disconnect the chandelier, fully intending to sell it to meet his payroll. The minister quickly changed his mind. Joe got paid.

Another Venuti story was sent to me from Vince Abbatiello in Las Vegas. It was told to him by his father, an orchestra leader:

Paul Whiteman often wore an all-white outfit that included a fifty-dollar white Barceloni fedora, imported from Italy. When Venuti was working with the Whiteman orchestra at the Paramount Theater, he noticed that Whiteman kept the hat on a shelf in his dressing room during performances. Venuti sent to Italy for six Barceloni hats of the exact same design, but he ordered them all in different sizes, larger and smaller than Whiteman's size.

Every night Joe would switch one of his hats for the one on Whiteman's shelf, so that from day to day Whiteman's hat got gradually larger, until it was resting on his ears, and then it gradually got smaller, until it perched on top of his head. Then the hat gradually returned to its original size. Whiteman never said a word about Venuti's expensive joke.

The one Venuti story that I left out of *Jazz Anecdotes,* about Roy Rogers's horse, seems to be the most famous one of all. I didn't use it because I found the same story in an old book, placing Joe's equine adventure at New York's old Hippodrome Theater, and said the horse in question was one of the Hippodrome ponies. I suspect the story is apocryphal, but I suppose it is possible that Venuti repeated this prank with other male horses that he encountered in show business. At any rate, the story seems to be permanently embedded in the mythos of the jazz world, and I'm sure Roy Rogers himself couldn't convince us that it didn't happen. Since so many readers and reviewers have lamented the omission of that story from my first book, here it is:

Venuti and his band were appearing at a vaudeville theater opposite Roy Rogers and his horse Trigger. Joe didn't mind that Rogers was the star, but he bristled when he saw the marquee.

"They got me billed lower than a horse!"

He got his revenge one night. While Rogers was entertaining the audience with a song, Joe reached into Trigger's offstage stall with his violin
bow and diddled him. (The assumption in this story is that horses find the
horsehair on violin bows exciting.)

When the time came in Rogers's act for Trigger's appearance, he would
whistle him onstage. Because of Joe's backstage ministrations during that
show, Trigger pranced out flaunting a spectacular erection. It can be assumed that the rest of Rogers's show that night was a considerable anticlimax.

Besides writing my column for the Local 802 paper, my work for the
union is interesting. But it has been disheartening to see so many musical jobs disappear. Musicians were some of the earliest victims of au-
tomation when sound movies pushed them out of theater jobs, and
they are still being replaced by music synthesizers, and by their own
recordings. The staff jobs in radio and television are gone, the club
date business is much smaller than it used to be, and the recording
industry uses far fewer musicians than it once did. Jazzman Arnie Lawrence finally got a record date, looked at his music and commented,
"This is the first time in a year that I've played with my eyes open!"

I enjoy the jazz gigs that still come my way. There are a lot of young
musicians coming up who are fun to play with, and there are still some
old friends on the scene. One, with whom I look forward to playing
any time, anywhere, is Carmen Leggio, a living legend around New
York. In his youth he played tenor with Terry Gibbs, Benny Goodman,
Maynard Ferguson, and Woody Herman, but the few records he has
made are hard to find. He's a world-class player, but he stays around
Westchester County, and not many people are aware of him. We often
play local gigs together, and sometimes just for fun at pianist Ben
Aronov's house.

Several years ago, Carmen fell on very hard times. He lost his apartment, and for a while he was reduced to living in his car. For a joke he
handed out business cards that had nothing printed on either side. When
he gave one to Leo Ball, Leo laughed and handed it back.

"Come on, Carmen, put your number on there, so I can get in touch
with you if a job comes up."

Carmen wrote a number on the card and handed it back. Later, Leo looked at it more carefully and realized that Carmen had written down his auto license plate number.

Long after Carmen had begun living indoors again, someone told his friend Steve Roane that he had passed away. Steve called Carmen immediately, and when he answered, Steve said, "I'm so relieved to hear your voice. I heard that you had died!"

Carmen was distressed to hear this. He said, "Steve, please do whatever you can to kill that rumor. Business is so bad, if people think I'm dead, they'll *never* call me."

J azz musicians don't seem to be a long lived breed. There are a few glorious exceptions like Doc Cheatham and Milt Hinton. My list of musical colleagues who have passed away is long, and keeps getting longer. I miss them all, but the one I miss the most is Zoot Sims. I enjoyed knowing him, playing with him, and hanging out with him at the house he bought not far from mine, in West Nyack, New York. We both enjoyed gardening. Some of the plants that now thrive in our garden came from cuttings I took from Zoot's backyard.

While visiting Zoot one day I told him about the airdrome up in Rhinebeck, New York, where antique airplanes are on display. Many of them are kept in flying condition, and on summer weekends, Rhinebeck air shows depict aerial warfare circa 1914. I had taken my son Daniel there, and I told Zoot that it was a great place to take a kid. Zoot immediately pointed to himself. He was the kid who wanted to go.

Later that summer Zoot organized a party of friends to visit the airdrome. He happened to pick the hottest day of the year, but we had a wonderful time anyway. Fortified with coolers of beer, soda, and Louise's fried chicken, we spent the afternoon watching the American Aces aerobatically pursue the Black Baron through the sky. I had enjoyed the show the first time I went, but it was even better with Zoot there.

Zoot and Louise liked to invite friends over for feasts of spareribs and Zoot's special chili. On their patio one summer evening, after everyone was thoroughly sated with food and wine, Zoot said, "I feel like playing some." Al Cohn and Turk Mauro had their saxophones in their cars and Bucky Pizzarelli had his guitar, but neither Milt Hinton nor I, the two bass players present, had brought a bass. Mine was the closest, but it still would have taken too long to drive home and bring it back. The music had already begun, so Milt and I just sat with our wives and listened. The sound of those three saxophones swinging happily in the dusk of a warm summer evening accompanied only by the soft chording of Bucky's unamplified guitar is something that Aileen and I still talk about. It was absolutely enchanting.

I made sure I wouldn't miss out on any more chances like that. When Zoot bought a good piano and fixed up a music room in his basement, I left a bass there. Jake Hanna, passing through from California, donated a set of drums. Zoot's friends could drop in and play any time.

Zoot was serious about playing, but it wasn't easy to get him to talk about jazz. Pianist Pete Brush, who now lives in the Canary Islands, has videotapes of a Canadian television show that Oscar Peterson used to host. When Zoot was a guest on the show, Oscar asked him, quite seriously, "What do you see for your instrument for the future? What would you like to see, maybe I should put it that way?"

Zoot glanced thoughtfully at his battle-scarred old Selmer and replied, "I can get a new lacquer job."

Zoot's good nature stayed with him to the very end. The liver cancer that eventually took his life had already begun to sap his strength on the last job we played together, with Al Cohn, at Struggle's in Edgewater, New Jersey. On the way out of the club he was almost too weak to push the door open. He looked around at Mary Schwartz, the owner, and said ruefully, "Heaviest door in jazz!"

About a week before he died, I took Zoot some old photographs from happier times. Barely able to sit up, he examined each picture carefully, slowly mumbling the names.

"Allen Eager. Jeru. Pres. Brew. Davey. Dizzy."

Once in a while he'd chuckle as if remembering something good, but he couldn't get his mouth around the words to describe it. After he'd gone through the whole box of photos, he handed it back to me and squeezed my hand. Then he slowly got up and began to totter across the room toward the kitchen.

"Where are you going, Zoot?"

"Glass of water."

"Let me get it for you."

"No. I'm the only one that knows the way I like it."

Al Cohn came by. Zoot said he'd like to play, so Al called Ben Aronov and arranged for us to meet at his house in Dobbs Ferry. I went home, got my bass and drove over to Ben's, but Zoot was too far gone to play. He spent five minutes trying to fit the reed and ligature onto his mouthpiece while we watched sorrowfully, trying to will him the strength he needed. When he finally got it adjusted and tried to blow, only feeble squawks came from the old Selmer that had been his beautiful voice for so many years. After a couple of tunes we called it a day. Zoot looked up sadly as he put away his horn.

"Well," he said, "it looks like I'm gonna have to start all over again."

As I was putting my bass back in my car, I heard Zoot feebly tell the friend who was driving him, "Stop by the music store in New City. I want to look for some reeds."

That night, Zoot went back to the hospital for the last time. When the doctor looked into his room in the morning, Zoot raised his head weakly and quipped, "You're looking better today, Doc."

The next day, he was gone.

The memorial service held at St. Peter's Church in Zoot's honor was just what he wanted—a party with lots of his friends playing good music. If everyone who came had played, the music would have gone on for days. The most touching moments came from two piano soloists: Tommy Flanagan offered a simple, lovely rendition of "All Too Soon," and Dave McKenna played one sweet chorus of "Thanks a Million." There really wasn't any more that needed to be said.

Index